HEARTWOMEN

HEARTWOMEN

An Urban Feminist's Odyssey Home

SANDY BOUCHER

Photographs by Sandy Boucher

1817

HARPER & ROW, PUBLISHERS, SAN FRANCISCO

Cambridge, Hagerstown, New York, Philadelphia
London, Mexico City, São Paulo, Sydney

"Amanda" is adapted from "Kansas in the Spring," which first appeared in *Conditions: Four,* 1979.

HEARTWOMEN: AN URBAN FEMINIST'S ODYSSEY HOME. Copyright © 1982 by Sandy Boucher. All rights reserved. Printed in the United States of America. No part of this book may be used or reproduced in any manner whatsoever without written permission except in the case of brief quotations embodied in critical articles and reviews. For information address Harper & Row, Publishers, Inc., 10 East 53rd Street, New York, NY 10022. Published simultaneously in Canada by Fitzhenry & Whiteside, Limited, Toronto.

FIRST EDITION

Designer: Jim Mennick

Library of Congress Cataloging in Publication Data

Boucher, Sandy.
    HEARTWOMEN, AN URBAN FEMINIST'S ODYSSEY HOME.

    Bibliography: p. 283
    1. Women—Middle West.   I. Title.
HQ1438.A14B68   305.4'2'0978   81-48204
ISBN 0-06-250095-3   AACR2

82 83 84 85 86 10 9 8 7 6 5 4 3 2 1

*To the feminists of the San Francisco Bay Area
who for twelve years now have been
my friends, teachers, and sisters in struggle,
I dedicate this book.*

Contents

Acknowledgments   *ix*

COMING BACK   *1*

AMANDA   6

ON THE LAND   *15*
The Earth's Stillness   *15*
Virginia   *29*
"A Man's World"   *39*
The Bunch from St. Joe's   *44*
Pushing Limits   *56*

IN THE TOWNS   *83*
A Mountain of Milo   *83*
The Troublemaker   *92*
"Everybody Dies Here Is Your Friend"   *97*
Survivor   *103*
Catherland   *117*

CULTURES SIDE BY SIDE   *144*
Standing Deep in Time   *144*
Proud Granddaughter   *148*

First People   *163*
They Came to Teach and Heal   *174*
Bessie Caldwell   *179*

CITY LIFE   *197*
Flight and Return   *197*
"The Earth Is Alive"   *198*
Clinging Vine   *212*
Black and Proud   *230*
Making Magic   *245*

TOWARD THE FUTURE   *264*

QUILTING   *275*

Bibliography   *283*

Acknowledgments

I send my warmest gratitude to all those women in Kansas and Nebraska who gave so generously of their time and insights, their hospitality, to help me gather material for this book. Many of them appear in the following pages. Some of those who do not I will mention here: on the Kickapoo reservation near Horton, Kansas, Vivian McKinney, Phyllis Johnson, Mrs. Rhoda Cadue, Malinda J. Mattwaoshshe; among the Potawatomis, Mary E. La-Clair; in Concordia, Kansas, Linda Newcomb, Shelley Swenson, who is the Home Extension Agent for Cloud County; in Clyde, Kansas, Lorene Charbonneau, Mary Mar Stolzenburg; in Lindsborg, Kansas, Pauline Glendening; in Lenexa, Kansas, Margaret L. Twin; in Riley, Kansas, Helen M. Oltman (and her husband Dr. T. V. Oltman); in Cuba, Kansas, Helen S. Makalous, Alice Fojt, Fontella Campbell, Irene F. Dulin; in Omaha, Nebraska, Mary Williamson; in Lincoln, Nebraska, Harriet Desmoines, Catherine Nicholson; in Lawrence, Kansas, Marty Dunn, Bonnie Boswell; in Medicine Lodge, Kansas, Alice M. MacGregor, Frances Heath.

Some California women and one man sent me to visit their Kansas relatives and friends. I thank Terry Lyons, Jane Ciabattari, Kathie Bailey, Frances Reid, Sherry Thomas, Mary Hackney, Vicky Southern, and Ronald Feldman for trusting me with those introductions.

Four women whose contribution was crucial to the writing of this book are Ann Hershey, who first took me to visit Clyde, Kansas; Susan Griffin, who encouraged me from the time of my first idea for *Heartwomen* and gave valuable criticism during the later stages of the writing; Treelight Green, whose love and unflagging support took me through the difficult times; Tillie Olsen, who brought me materials from her own Nebraska heritage to start me on my way.

The photographs that appear in this book were printed by Cathy Cade, who gave me much valuable advice about the photographing itself and the selection of the prints. Debbie Hoffmann contributed her technical knowledge to the taking of the pictures.

There are more women I wish to thank both for reading parts or all of the manuscript in its various stages and for giving me encouragement toward its completion. They are Karla Boyd, Jill Lessing, Gina Covina, Bella Debrida (Zweig), Liz Krainer, Mary Wayne, Maggie Borell, Marie Scott. Especially I am grateful to Lucy Phenix, whose sharp film-editor's eye helped me to see this book at critical junctures in its coming together.

Lastly I wish to acknowledge the support of the National Endowment for the Arts, whose Literature Fellowship awarded me during the writing of this book allowed me to devote my best energies toward its completion.

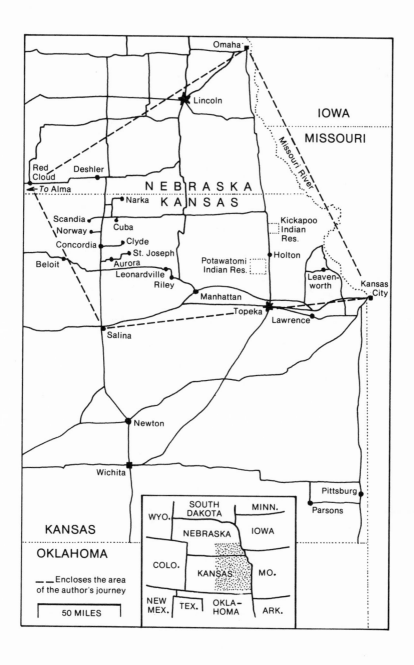

Omaha

Lincoln

IOWA

MISSOURI

Missouri River

Red Cloud   Deshler

←To Alma   N E B R A S K A

Narka   K A N S A S

Scandia   Kickapoo
                          Cuba   Indian
Norway   Res.
                          Clyde
Concordia   St. Joseph   Holton
                  Aurora   Potawatomi
Beloit   Leonardville   Indian Res.
                      Riley
                                                     Leaven-
                            Manhattan   worth
                                                              Kansas
                                       Topeka   City
                                          Lawrence
                Salina

                    Newton

                    Wichita

                                                  Pittsburg
KANSAS   Parsons

OKLAHOMA

___ Encloses the area
of the author's journey

┌──────────┐
│ 50 MILES │
└──────────┘

                    SOUTH
        WYO.   DAKOTA   MINN.

                  NEBRASKA   IOWA

        COLO.   MO.
                   KANSAS

        NEW   OKLA-
        MEX.   TEX.   HOMA   ARK.

Coming Back

It was early spring in Cloud County, Kansas. My friend Ann and I, on our way across the country, had stopped in the town of Clyde to visit her old Uncle Earl. From the house in town where we stayed, we drove with Earl out to the farm that had been his home for most of his life. There we explored the abandoned farmhouse, and I climbed partway up the frame of the windmill to look out across the new wheat flowing in the fields, a tide of short, bright-green blades whipped into ripples and torrents by the wind.

Back in town, we ate in the cafes and stood on corners talking to neighbors, and in the midst of this homely activity I was surprised to find the experience of my own midwestern past arising in me. At moments I was caught in wondering sadness, then lifted by joy that had nothing to do with the circumstances, or held in a listening that sharpened my senses almost to the point of pain. This awakening I had not anticipated, for my native Ohio is situated in a different kind of Midwest than this prairie state of Kansas. But the people of Clyde were known to me; the land, the smells, the thousand details of ordinary life were familiar. For the first time in twenty years I felt drawn to the region of my growing up.

That powerful pull aroused my memory of leaving the Midwest so long ago. I recalled how, by the age of sixteen, I had longed to escape to New York City. It was the "navel of the world," I thought, where I would learn life's secrets and become a writer. I suffocated in my parents' house on the outskirts of a sprawling city. Stoically, I endured the boredom of our occasional weekend visits to small towns on the river, the long drives through rolling farmland. When I was twenty-one I finally arrived in New York, armed only with the fragile sword of defiance, and toughened by the working class awareness that everything depended on me alone. Each night I came home from the magazine where I worked to struggle with the material of my life, which seemed a heavy, shapeless mass resting on my heart. That same midwestern experience I had rejected now became the raw material I used in my attempt to make what I hoped would be "literature." But soon I left it behind to pursue adventure in the "real world."

From New York I went to Europe, where I married, and then to California, where I have lived ever since. In those years I had many jobs, wrote a great deal, became politically active, left my ten-year marriage to join with women in the raising of children and the publishing of a newspaper, and continued to live in large metropolitan areas. Eventually, I realized that the qualities that had given me the strength to leave the Midwest and begin a different kind of life had become in themselves a trap. The sword of defiance had as often turned against me as toward the world, so that I defeated myself again and again. Now I wanted to know more of what was around and inside me, to arrive at a larger freedom than defiance allows. When I had achieved a little of this, I—who had rejected the provincialism of the Midwest—began to notice a provincialism in the life of coastal city dwellers. Many of my neighbors and friends today are ignorant of the basic elements of their existence: they do not know how their food is produced or brought to them, they measure the seasons by athletic events or theater programs, they never see the living animals whose flesh they eat. Urban life, so emphasized by the media, comes to seem the only reality, or the only important one.

I began to wonder about the knowledge I had grown up with. It seemed that in rejecting it I, and all of us who fled the Midwest with such alacrity when we reached a certain young age, had sealed off a crucial part of ourselves. This early knowledge had to do not only with ideas and attitudes but with our bodies as well, which had their beginning in the heartland and are even now nourished by food grown in that great center of the country. However vigorously we may have denied it, there is a connection to the earth itself in many of us, a response to the look and feel and odor of it, an imprint on our spirits too deep to be worn away by decades of city living.

Two years passed before I could honor the feelings so powerfully aroused in that first visit to Clyde, Kansas. When I was finally able to come back to the Midwest, I brought with me a huge curiosity about the women there. Each woman I met awakened some knowledge that had been mine before, or pointed to an awareness I could never have had alone. I saw that while I had turned away from the lifestyle available to me in the heartland, the solid midwestern virtues of hard work, persistence and independence had sustained me through the most difficult periods of my life. I wanted to clarify for myself what is wholesome in this lifestyle and what is constrictive and limiting, how life in the Midwest nurtures development and in what ways it prevents full growth. I was curious to know how the values of those who first hunted or broke sod on the prairie operate in the lives of farm women and the women of small towns, how those values translate into the experience of women living in the cities.

Midwestern women are the Native American women whose ancestors were brought to the plains in the mid-nineteenth century to be settled on reservations, the black women whose forebears emigrated by the thousands from the South after Reconstruction. They are the descendants of the waves of Spanish, French, Norwegian, Danish, Swedish, Bohemian, Scottish, Welsh, British, Irish, German, and Russian immigrants who settled the plains, and the few Dutch, Italians, Poles, and Yugoslavs who came with them. This ethnic and racial diversity intrigued me, for it challenged society's stereotype of midwesterners as blond, blue-eyed Swedish farmers.

I went back to Cloud County not only to see the women I had met there in my visit with Uncle Earl, but because quite near it is

the exact geographic center of the United States, the point from
which all American, Canadian, and Mexican mapping originates.
This area is literally the heart of the nation. The women here are
insulated from the social upheavals and accelerated changes of the
East and West coasts; their lives reflect a particular steadiness.
From Cloud County I ventured out in an irregular rectangle,
roughly a hundred and fifty miles to a side, its corners marked by
Red Cloud, Nebraska, and Salina, Kansas, to the west; by Omaha,
Nebraska, and Kansas City, Missouri, to the east.

I began among the farm women, whose lives and livelihood
depend upon the earth, who are closely identified with their particular locale. They took me into their lives and into their concerns. Next I entered the small towns, drawn by my recollection of
those Sunday visits when I was a child, to talk with the women
who live there. In cafe and funeral parlor and historical society,
the women told me of their role in the community, their relationship to self and family. The third stage of my journey led into the
past. When I met white women of various ethnic origins, black
women, Native Americans, it seemed important to know something of the events that had brought their forebears to the plains
and shaped their lives. Finally, it was inevitable that I would want
to meet some midwestern city women, although I was not primarily interested in an investigation of urban women. In a number of
different cities I spoke with women whose occupations or view-
points seemed to cast new light on the midwestern experience.

While circumscribed geographically, my journey ranged wide
in the women I met and chose to present. I discovered, not surprisingly, that women's struggle for equality, autonomy, and dignity goes on as vigorously in the Midwest as it does on either coast.
The concern about chemical use in farming and possible contamination from nuclear sources is strong among many women, farm
women especially being in a position to recognize the dangers to
the environment. With farm women and small town women, with
urban teachers and activists, I learned about the several aspects of
the movement of women in the Midwest to change the conditions
of their lives.

When I returned to the San Francisco Bay Area to sift through the material I had gathered, I saw how I had met myself again in the Midwest, my own association with the heartland growing out of the experience of my childhood and the years since of alternate avoidance of and fascination with the area, so that my relationship to it is not simple. I found the questions recurring, the answers slowly emerging. I experienced my journey as a coming home and settling into place of much that had floated uneasily in my psyche for years.

Many of the women who helped me to these insights appear in the following pages. Some of them the reader may find familiar: they are so like our own sisters and cousins, mothers and grandmothers and aunts in whatever heartland gave us life. Others are people we may be surprised to find in the Midwest. In their particularity they challenge us to adopt a larger and more accurate view of women—women who have often been overlooked or misrepresented, whose stories are rarely told.

Amanda

In that first visit to Clyde, Ann and I went in search of Uncle Earl. He would be in his eighties; could he still be alive? Ann remembered his kindness to her when she was a child. He had let her ride his horse alone about the farm, in long, summer days of freedom. He had laughed when she drank from the horse trough, had shown her how to care for the animals she loved. He was the one grownup from her childhood whom she remembered treating her with respect.

We inquired at the storefront funeral parlor, where an old man lay in a coffin. The funeral director, a woman with a deep, vibrant voice, told us Earl was not only alive but had been there that day to pay his respects. On the register was a big, shaky signature—Earl Erickson—proof of his existence. The woman sent us the few blocks down and over to where Earl's house stood, saying he would be there if he had not gone out to his farm.

That afternoon we found him. He was a short, round old man in overalls and a filthy yellow shirt fastened at the collar with a large safety pin. On his feet he wore black, high-top tennis shoes; on his head a brown, billed cap that he always removed when he came inside, revealing a head covered with white stubble, just like his chin.

In the next few days he took us to a stock auction, to a barn sale, where we met and talked with, or sometimes just glimpsed, the women. Listening to Earl's stories, I began to know the memory of Ann's Aunt Amanda, Earl's wife, and Ann's mother, Marie. These two sisters had grown up in Clyde, children of the

L'Ecuyers, a big, joyful, prosperous French family in a house on Main Street. The townspeople remembered the sisters as carefree girls, showed us photographs of them clowning on a stepladder, wearing bloomers in the line-up for the high school girls' basketball team. To the townsfolk, Ann, now in her thirties, was still "Marie's little girl," remembered for her visits here when she was a child.

But there was a somber edge to these memories, for both Amanda and Marie had suffered long, painful illnesses and died early deaths. Ann showed me a letter in which her father, Amanda's brother-in-law, had written, "I do believe if Amanda had been blessed with good health to go with her natural drive she could have given Earl leadership and direction and they could have had a really good life." Instead, Amanda and Earl lived a hard, discouraging time together, plagued by poverty and illness. I wondered about Amanda. I sought the feeling of her living, the texture of her days.

One afternoon I went to Earl's farm and sat on a rusted refrigerator in the yard outside the abandoned house, waiting for Earl to arrive. The sun was falling; a bitter wind clawed at my jacket. Cows mooed hungrily. It was depressing out here, the land strewn with rusting broken machinery, carcasses of dead animals, objects from the past. The ancient siding of the house, warped away from its nails, all color and sap and life drained from it by the decades of weather, tapped randomly, gently against itself in the wind. Inside the house a closet door creaked, a rag of dress squeaked on a hanger. There was almost no inside to this house now, all apertures torn or smashed or simply left open. The piano stood foot-deep in cow manure on the living room floor, the ivory of its keys curling up like the fingernails of a Chinese empress. All the small noises of the house were quietly indifferent—sounds of a ship becalmed and abandoned in this great flat land stretching out to a smear of color where the sky lifted up from beneath it.

In this house Earl had lived with Amanda. I wandered through, seeing the old flat metal bedpans, an ordinary wooden straight chair with small wheels attached to its legs to make a wheelchair for Amanda. The bedframe was piled over with rags, boxes, rusted objects, jars, photographs, papers flapping in the wind. The broken mattress spilled brittle yellow corn shucks. It was the beds that shocked me most, their desolation arousing thoughts of the woman who lay suffering year after year with rheumatoid arthritis, her body curling inward, in that house without electricity or running water.

Ann realized that in her happy childhood visits to this farm she had understood little of what went on in the house. Even then, apparently, it had been full of trash and falling apart, once with a big hole in the floor. And Earl had not bothered to fix it. Amanda was crippled by then, sitting in a wheelchair. She was Catholic, saintly; on her face was a smile of sweetness and resignation.

"He who has seen the sufferings of men has seen nothing," wrote Victor Hugo. "Let him look upon the sufferings of women."

That evening Ruth Chaplin, proprietor of the South Side Cafe, had invited Ann and me to supper at the cafe. Her two sisters and her niece joined us.

We sat in a booth, eating Ruth's excellent pancakes, and Ann began to question the women about Amanda. "When Amanda came back from California," said one of the sisters, "when she had just married Earl, why she was real good-lookin'. She was tall and I remember she wore a white coat. She had real nice clothes and she looked nice."

"Yes, I remember that," Ruth said. "Then I went off to Oregon to live for some years, and when I came back, why, it was a shame. I couldn't believe it was her. She was all bent over sideways and so crippled she could hardly walk—and the clothes she had on, well, I don't want to say anything about them. But it was a terrible sight."

The sister nodded. "But over the years, for all she went through out there on that farm—and I never went out there to see for myself—but for all she had to suffer out there, I'll say one thing for her: she stuck with him!"

The second sister remembered, "When she came to town, no matter how bad off she was, she always had that smile."

When Ann suggested extending our visit for a couple of weeks, I was glad to agree, for I felt at home here in this town of a thousand people. Clyde reminded me of the towns in which my father's sisters had lived. I had married a man whose mother came from a Kansas farm town very near this one. The people I met on the streets of Clyde seemed much like my aunts and my former mother-in-law.

The house where Ann and I stayed dated from the 1890s. Conspicuous for its dormers and deep, wraparound porch, its tiny observatory room at the peak of the roof, it was set by itself on a lot a little out from the center of town. From the bedroom window I could see across the open field to the grain elevator, a great, high, rounded building filling the space within the windowframe. Just beyond it was the railroad track, some scraggly trees. Now and then a train came clacking along to screech to a stop on a side track near the elevator; a chute was moved over the track, and one by one the boxcars of the train clanged into position to receive their cargo. All across the great flat central plains, the freight trains snake their way, picking up the crops from grain elevators in each tiny town and taking them to the cities. Who in New York or San Francisco ever thinks about this vast, flat land where the wheat for their daily bread is grown? I sat gazing out the window, a book open on my knees. The grain elevator, usually so monumentally silent, today emitted the low roar of machinery. Not a soothing sound like the ocean or even the flow of traffic on a highway—this was a factory noise, whine of metal on metal, loud thumps and groans of weight being moved. It invaded our house. I thought of how it would be to live here as a wife and mother, caught in the house, surrounded by that noise.

Although the bedroom smelled of mildew, the little gas heater in the corner made it a warm private place in which to read the book I had brought with me from San Francisco. Titled *Women-friends: A Soap Opera,* it was a dual journal over a period of years kept by two women who had been friends since college.* Now in the quiet afternoon here under the din of the grain elevator, with the little town spaced out in yards and houses around me, I found the communications of these two articulate New York women exotic. That women should be self-identified and intensely questioning, seeking full intellectual lives and professional fulfillment: is this heresy in Clyde? Perhaps these ideas would not be so foreign after all, I thought, on pondering further, for Kansas has a strong feminist history, and there were independent women on the frontier, the entrepreneurs and adventurers, the scratchy, cantankerous, separate women whose history is not always readily apparent. Their counterparts must exist here right now.

Certainly the idea of options for women was alive on the prairie, a fact we discovered in our evening at Ruth's cafe. Jolene, Ruth's niece, who was in her twenties and the mother of two children, asked of her mother and aunts: "Did it ever cross any of your minds, though, that you would ever be anything other than a wife and mother? Did you believe that was your role? Your destination?"

They answered in a jumble, all talking at once: "There never was anything else. . . ." "No, see, we all got married." "You have to take what comes in life." "Who had the time to sit around making decisions?"

Jolene: "Take girls today just coming out of high school—they can go to college and they have a choice. They can at least *think* about it. They may end up that way too, but you guys didn't really have a choice."

"We did what we had to do," said her mother.

Jolene (determinedly): "My daughter is real small now, but as she grows up I'm going to let her know that she can be anything she wants."

As our visit continued, I felt myself drawing close to Amanda,

* Esther Newton and Shirley Walton, *Womenfriends: A Soap Opera* (New York: Friends Press, Inc., 1976).

as surely my forebear as if I, like Ann, had been "Marie's little girl." I gazed at a photograph of that big-featured face, long and skull-like with jutting nose, the dark eyes, the black hair hanging straight to just below the ears. Amanda in her wheelchair was placed at center-front of the group at the family reunion, her wasted face gently smiling. Her body, boney and contorted, leaned sideways in the chair.

The women in the cafe spoke of her suffering. She had sixteen operations, first for arthritis, then later for cancer. During one early surgery something was left inside her body when the incision was sewn up. They didn't remember what exactly—a pair of scissors? Some packing? Its presence inside her caused terrible complications. Later, the surgeon opened her up again and found it. Earl did not sue the doctors or try to get any restitution from them. Amanda simply endured.

On the days when we went out to visit the farm, the wind whipping through the broken windows of the house murmured to us of Amanda. What had it been like to come back from each surgery to this house without lights, without a bathroom?

And the summers! Earl never planted a tree. The house had no shutter, awning, porch, and never did. There would have been no shade, no relief from the heat.

Yet the past was slippery. What could I *know* of Amanda, dead since 1952, except that she was a wound in me by now, torn open. Inside was found the object, the perception, the anguish I thought I had buried or never knew was there. Perhaps it was some deep childhood yearning, the loneliness of growing up here, shut away from the life I sought, a life that must be more passionate than the one I lived, more full of meaning. Or the leaving. I remembered those first months in New York City when I longed for the smell of grass, the unobstructed view of a sunset raging over open land, the sense of being surrounded by growing things. I had covered over the hurt, pushed it deep enough to be forgotten. Now with Amanda, who did not leave, whose suffering was so obvious and so intense, it rose in me again: I felt her being, and my loss.

Earl told a story set in the Depression, a cruel time for him and Amanda: "Amanda and I, during the hard times ... we had her dad to take care of and work was scarce then. We had to do something! We'd go make these trash piles and pick out stuff to wear, shoes and whatnot. Now Mandy, was, you might say, raised in wealth ... and that was an awful comedown for her. As a girl she had about everything she wanted ... she wasn't forced to work and go off and make these trash piles, that was quite a comedown for her. Well, one day Mandy and I were in the trash pile looking for things. The bus and preacher come by and they stopped to see who it was, and he saw it was us. Well, he just stuck his head up and drove on, like he didn't even recognize us. And Amanda says ..."—Earl lifted up his head and laughed in admiration—"she says, 'Well, go ahead, it doesn't matter to me, if that's the way ...' She didn't care who saw us."

Ah, she must've been a feisty one, Ann and I told each other. She must've given that Earl a hard time. But we had begun to perceive the breadth and depth of Earl's stubbornness, his obduracy slyly masked by the appearance of yielding. ("How come you never brought that piano into town when you left the farm?" I asked. Earl glanced at the ruined piano standing in its layer of cow shit, and said serenely, "Oh yeah, you bet, one day I'm gonna do that.") Amanda, isolated out here with only Earl for company, had to live *around* that immovability, had to make the best of what little comfort, companionship, there was in that stark, barnlike house.

Ann's father wrote in a letter, "Earl came of old, basic Swedish farm stock. Stolid, unimaginative and rather insensitive. Never vicious, mean or cruel. ... I suppose to Earl and the men of his family women simply endured the frailties of their lives. It was Amanda's misfortune to have more than most to endure."

Ann proposed a theory. "Think of the illness as resistance," she suggested. "If she was sick she couldn't breed; if she was crippled she couldn't work." To resist by destroying oneself, to sacrifice one's body. A gruesome idea, but better than the thought of Amanda as passive victim with *no* control over her destiny—or "destination," as Jolene put it.

Our stay in Clyde was drawing to a close. On our last day, Earl took us to a barn sale. Although it was springtime, the weather that had been balmy two days before had turned so cold overnight that snow powdered the red roof of the barn. Earl explained that the owner was giving up his farm to move elsewhere. He wanted to sell all of his equipment and farm vehicles, everything he had used to work with over the years. In the barnyard a sharp wind whipped our clothes; the two auctioneers at work up on the flatbed trucks among the piles of junk were bundled up to the ears. Mud was everywhere, and scattered snow. The farmers wore bright, billed caps—orange and yellow and red and green—bearing the insignia of farm machinery companies and feed companies.

I retreated to the barn. Inside, a dozen women were busily at work. Before them were board tables loaded with homemade pies and sweetrolls, urns of coffee. Behind them were the makings for ham sandwiches, barbecued beef, hotdogs.

The farmers stamped about the doorway, huddling half in, half out, drinking coffee. A raw wind entered among them.

There was something in this shadowy barn of great urgency for me. I stood in a corner eating a piece of warm apple pie, watching the women busily setting out the food. There was not one woman here under the age of fifty. Their eyeglasses, their headscarves, their thick wool coats drew my gaze; their mouths were tight with all the years of doing what was necessary, their eyes shy and curious behind the glasses, noticing me as a stranger. I was so relieved to be here among them. They couldn't know that. Possibly they would not have wanted it. Nor would they have understood my affection for them, how much I wanted to talk with them, let them speak their lives. The cowgirls at the auction hall, the waitresses in the cafes, the wives on the farms: they gave me inklings of a society of women only glimpsed this

time around. I knew I would return, for they brought me back to
myself—to the child, the adolescent, the young woman I was before I went away. In their lives I saw my own, lived differently.

Earl and Ann waited for me outside, among the crowd of
farmers around the truck. But I was not yet ready to relinquish
the good feeling I had there inside that dim barn. I wanted somehow to take it with me, and I thought of the camera I was carrying in my pocket. Yes, a picture.

When there was a lull in business, I approached the table. I
told the women that I was from California, I'd never been to an
event like this barn sale and I really wanted to have a picture of
them, if they wouldn't mind. They looked embarrassed. There
were some moments of hesitation, in which I felt ridiculous, aware
of how conspicuous I had suddenly become. But the women clus-
tered together for the portrait, and the viewfinder of the camera
framed the faces of these stolid survivors.

As I left the barn, I saw the women return to work again,
arranging food on the table, stirring the barbecued beef in the
steamer, slicing the pies.

That day we drove back to town for the last time, knowing we
would leave the next morning. I wondered when I would come
again to this land that had roused so much in me.

*At the barn sale: Margaret Lesovsky, Helen M. Leshosky, Cora Branum,
Olive Huncovsky, Elizabeth Piroutek, Pauline Trecek, Lillian Pihl, Nellie
Taylor*

On the Land

The Earth's Stillness

Little has changed in Cloud County since my visit two years ago. This barnyard in which I stand looks much like that yard where the barn sale took place. The woman who talks with me here might even have attended that sale. But I am more deliberately attentive, for this time I have come with the purpose of learning all I can about this woman's life, and the others who will lead me on my journey. Jane Snavely has agreed to show me something of how she spends her days. She took me first inside her small frame house, one like the many I had seen on my drives through the countryside. Then she brought me out into the wind.

"I've got four horses now," she tells me. "Like I said, at my dad's place we'd have up to thirty head sometimes, but we never raised 'em. It's just an expensive, long-term proposition. My dad thought it was cheaper to *buy* one than it was to raise one."

We are walking from her house toward the corral, where two of the horses stand. Jane is a tall, long-legged woman who strides easily in her cowboy boots, reminding me of my first glimpse of her as she was herding the animals at the stock auction barn in Concordia. Out among the corrals in back, where the air rang with the squeals and snorts and lowing of the penned animals, I first met and talked with her, and accepted her invitation to come visit her at home. She is thirty-four years old, she told me today, and her name before marriage was Hay, her family principally Scottish. She grew up in the Swedish-Norwegian town of Scandia, some twenty miles north of Concordia. For the last seventeen years she has been married to Armand Snavely, whose family comes from the Concordia area, and has lived with him on this four-hundred acre farm some miles outside Concordia.

"When I first got married, for a while I broke a few horses for other people, but now my time is kinda packed, it seems. I'm breaking one of my own now. I just started riding him and I hardly have time to do *him,* let alone any others."

A few minutes before, in her living room, Jane had shown me the riding trophies won by her teenage daughter. Jane has reason to be especially proud of Peggy's accomplishments, because Peggy was born with a heart defect and has had open heart surgery twice, the last time just four years ago. Peggy works now and then at the auction barn, as does Jane's eleven-year-old son, Mike.

"Those trophies in the middle she got from the fair," Jane explained. "The tallest one, Grand Champion of the pleasure class, she got the first year she was in 4-H, and the one just south of it, there, is the one she got this year. There was a boy in there with a horse that his grandpa shows professionally, in registered shows, and Peggy beat him. All the kids was real tickled because they thought it was real good that one of the just regular kids was able to beat a professional horse."

Jane and I stop at the fence of the corral. I feel how she herself must have been one of the "regular kids." We are comfortable here together on this sunny afternoon. She reminds me of my best friend when I was growing up, whose parents came from the mountains of West Virginia. She had the same gentleness and dignity I feel in Jane. As we talked in the house earlier, I sensed Jane's watchfulness, her reserve, and then her gradual acceptance of me. I wonder if this came about because I am as tall and sometimes as still as she, not in a hurry; because I listen intently.

Now we lean our weight on the wire fence of the corral, and for a few moments are silent, looking at the animals, at the pale, hoof-marked dirt, at the water trough with two yellow spears of hay trembling on its surface.

"These horses that we have now," Jane says, nodding at them, "three of them ... are the first registered ones we've had. But with horses, it's a big 'if.' There's so many things can happen. You know, with cattle, as long as they grow and put on weight and get big, they're worth the going rate, but with horses you've got to be a lot more particular. If they've got a leg that's a little crooked, or if their conformation is not as good as it can be, it detracts from their value a whole lot."

Jane opens the gate and goes inside the fence to show me her two-year-old, the horse she is currently training.

"He's not turning out quite as good as we had hoped," she explains, stroking his spotted back. "He's not as big as he should be, and, see here, he hasn't got enough muscle across the front, and here ..." touching him to show me his flaws, while his eyes roll freakishly.

"What about that big horse over there?"

Jane turns to look at the palomino standing by the opposite fence. "Oh, she's so big because she eats too much." She smiles. "Now, that's a strong horse, real good at herding cattle. If a calf is running and you can't turn it, she'll run into it and knock it down.

"But she's hard to ride because she's got so much strength. She'll stop all of a sudden and change direction, and there you are just tryin' to hold on. Had a neighbor borrow her to work cattle with, and when he brought her back he says, you know, she'd stop so sudden he'd be shot out there over her nose, and then she'd be takin' off in the other direction. He didn't actually fall off, but he had a hard time." We both laugh at this picture, and I look at the palomino's muscular haunches. She turns to eye us, the powerful golden curve of her neck shining in the sunlight.

It is a bright, cold day, the wind blowing briskly, whipping Jane's long dark hair about her face. She wears big-lensed spectacles with a tiny gold monogrammed JS on the glass. She does not flinch from the wind's sharp pressure, but only tosses her head to shake the hair out of her face, shoving her hands more deeply into the pockets of her hooded sweater. It is obvious how at home she is in this farmyard with its corrals and barn, storage bins, and outbuildings. Like many farm women, she spends much of her time outside, working here or in the fields.

We go on for a walk about the farm, looking out across the land where tractors and combines move in slow procession. The fields stand thick with ripened grain. It is harvest time in Cloud County. A good proportion of its inhabitants are out on the land bringing in the corn and alfalfa, and especially the red-topped milo packed close and shuddering in the fields, or plowing the ground to sow the winter wheat that will sleep under the snow until spring.

Jane explains that she and Armand grow wheat, milo, and alfalfa. "We're waiting for the milo to get dry so we can harvest it. A lot of guys are doing theirs now, but ours isn't getting ripe for some reason. We plant ours with a drill and a lot of people plant with top planters, which puts it in the ground a little deeper, and this spring, at the time we planted, it was a little dry, so ours wasn't down in the moisture as good and it didn't come up as early. That makes it later getting ripe, too." Patiently she explains things like this to me, treating me like a city cousin come to visit.

When I arrived at her house today, she had been embroidering designs on a western-style shirt she had made for her son, and she told me that she does most of the sewing for her family. She makes her husband's shirts, her son's shirts, her daughter's clothes, and her own clothes. In her time free from house and field work, she leads a youth group and plays the organ at the United Methodist Church, to which she and her husband belong. She also goes into town to act as a judge for 4-H clubs' record books.

I admire the focused energy it must take to perform all these tasks. But Jane points out to me that farm life is seasonal, allowing for months in which there is less work to do.

"Right now I don't have too many chores," she says, " 'cause the cows are all big, but I do raise a lot of bucket cows. You buy a baby . . . a lot of dairy farmers sell their bull calves as soon as they're born, when they're three or four days old, and then you get 'em and you feed 'em artificial milk, milk replacer, it's powdered stuff . . . unless you have enough cows to feed them. I take care of them in the morning and my daughter takes care of them at night. For doing the chores at night, she gets a calf. That's her money for the year. She pays for the calf now, with her labor, and we furnish the feed and the milk replacer and stuff for it, then when she sells it she gets the money for it.

"We raise a few chickens, just enough for us, you know. My son decided he'd like to raise some pigs and Armand's been wanting to get some so they've got six sows up there now. They'll have some small pigs in about a month, I guess. We have quite a few cattle that we have out in pasture. In the wintertime that's chores too, 'cause they have to be fed every day."

We are approaching the shed, now, where the new tractor sits in shadow. It is an enormous machine, topped by a cab with greentinted windshields. Jane has been telling me about its cost, and now she describes it more fully as we climb up to sit in its cab.

"There's an air conditioner in here. They all come that way. They have air conditioners and heaters and everything anymore, the new ones. The only way you could get one *without* a cab on it would be to special-order it. It's going to help a lot of people's hearing with these cabs like this, because it's real quiet in here, it's not much noisier than a car. But there again, if something breaks in the machinery, you don't know it until it's plumb apart and you *see* it."

We mull this over in silence for a time, and I feel from Jane that calm presence, that seeming core of stillness I have noticed before. I wonder if it is developed in years of working with animals: a certain steady alertness, simply being present without the necessity for expression. No doubt, while this life of labor on the land can plant the earth's stillness deep inside one, surely it is Jane's particular personality that leads her to be measured, thoughtful. When we talk later about farm politics, she flashes out in righteous anger; when we speak of economics she is restless in frustration. But even beneath her emotions, I feel a certain deep steadiness.

Having climbed down from the tractor, we head toward a

wire pen in which ducks waddle importantly about. A chained
dog jumps on us, and Jane explains that he was out running loose
and getting into trouble or she would never have tied him up. In
the shadows of an equipment shed, Armand Snavely, a stocky,
crewcut man, glances up from his work to wave at us.

Finally we arrive at a tornado cellar out behind the house, a
wide door set slanting in the ground between concrete supports.
Jane pulls the door up and we go down the steps into a small, cold
room with jars of canned fruit and vegetables standing on shelves
against the back wall. Here in this stark enclosure, this shelter
against the worst eventuality of prairie life, is evidence of women's
industry. For more than a hundred years women on this Kansas
grassland have been gathering, preserving, providing. We talk
about the differences between women's labor, now, on the farm,
and the tasks our mothers and grandmothers used to perform.
Jane points out that economic conditions as well as ethnic background often dictated the breakdown of labor.

"Between me and *my* mother I don't think there's quite the
difference as a lot of them, because my mother was out in the field
and everything and she had a part in saying what would happen
on our farm. My dad would consult her as far as when they went
to buy livestock. She knew stuff like that more than a lot of people
did. We never had too much, so we couldn't hire help; it was all
just up to us to do everything. But when I came down here to
around Concordia, there again it's a difference. That's a different
ethnic group up in Scandia—up there it's Swedish and Norwegian, down here it's French. That makes a difference. I was really
surprised by my mother-in-law. When they would hire kids to
help with the hay work, you know, and stuff like that, even if
there was only one or two extra people at mealtime, she would
serve them but she would not eat until everybody else was ate and
out of the house and then she eats her meal. She wouldn't sit
down and eat while the hired help was in the house. I always
figured if I was good enough to cook it for them, I was good
enough to eat it with them.

"There were some of the old women here that were that way.
These communities are only twenty miles apart, both rural com-

munities. In fact, Scandia's a lot smaller than here. But there's a lot of difference between them in how people do stuff. Like I say, when you had hired men, the women cooked and fixed stuff for them and the men ate what they wanted and the women took what was left. I'm not saying that was wrong, you know; when they had harvest crews and stuff there might be thirty people there, and I think that's probably where it started because cooking for them was a full-time job. You didn't have time to sit down. I think a lot of that is just carried over. It was just a habit. It hasn't been very long ago that my mother-in-law wouldn't go to the bank. She might now, but I doubt it. I know when we got married, she wouldn't have thought it her *place* to do something like that."

Now we come out of the tornado cellar and start toward the house, and Jane shakes her head.

"This house, now, my inlaws lived in it, and then when we got married they moved it over here and remodeled it and we worked on it. I still feel fenced in 'cause this house is so small."

In this she echoes the complaint of other farm women. Their homes are modest frame houses with battered porches on which litters of halfgrown kittens play. Some are set right on the ground without foundations. Rather than build onto the house to accommodate new additions to the family, they will remodel an attic or basement room. The idea of constructing a new house does not occur to them, for these are small farmers whose earnings must go to buy feed or machinery, make the payments on the land. The overriding reality for Jane Snavely and her neighbors, the motivating force like a great dream figure—menacing, chasing, never quite escaped, though heroic efforts are made—is the high cost of farming.

"Like parts and stuff has gone up so much," Jane says. "We had to get that new tractor, and I say *had to*—the other one was just shot—and it's a medium-sized one, and the price of it was $37,000! That's just one piece of machinery. With just that tractor, you do nothing. If you don't have all the other equipment.... Combines, now, are from that price on up."

Jane turns to glance back at the shed where Armand is at

work, and tells how they are able to stay ahead of this problem.
"We started farming with Armand's dad, and he and his dad buy
the machinery half and half and both use it. The land here belongs to my father-in-law. We own a quarter section* a mile west
and a mile south of here. And we rent two other quarters. We're
pretty small farmers actually. For the first time in our life we were
almost out of debt, until we had to get this tractor, then we had to
jump back in with both feet. Last year we paid off our place over
there but it took us fifteen years to do it. But that's only a quarter
section. If we had to make a living on that, it's impossible. In all
we have about four hundred acres and part of that's pasture so it's
not all farmland. But if we didn't have these extra calves like I
raise most years ... and since I've started working up at the sale
barn in the winter, that's about what we live on is what we make
up there. That's what we buy groceries and stuff with."

She scrapes her boot in the dirt, takes her hand from the
pocket of her sweater to gesture at the shed where the combine is
parked.

"I drive tractor, drive truck, whatever. The combine too, yeah.
I work outside with my husband. You have to. My mother
worked outside a lot, though many of the older women didn't
because they had larger families and it took longer to do the
cooking and stuff. They had to carry the water, and the things at
the house took longer. That makes a difference." Her daughter is
old enough now to do much of the housework, she says, allowing
her and Armand to stay out very late at harvest time. "The last
couple, three years, Peggy does most of the washing; when we're
out in the field, she fixes the meals for us. When the kids were
really small and somebody had to stay with them, they was usually
over with my mother-in-law while I was out in the field.

"This year we've been so busy that I've either had to do my
canning on Sunday or at night, one or the other. One night I
stayed up till three o'clock in the morning canning corn and took
off and went to the field at eight o'clock the next morning. It's a

---

* A quarter section is 160 acres.

whole different kind of life than people have in town. If you've got dinner in the oven and a cow decides to have a calf, and needs help, why, too bad, your dinner goes to heck. You know, she can't wait. That happens pretty often."

Jane meets my gaze, her eyes earnest and proud. I see that she, like many of the farm women here, is satisfied with her life. Again and again these women say they wouldn't have married anyone but a farmer. They are comfortable in their families, in their communities, and in the labor and rewards of life on the land. They speak of the benefits of farm life, among them having space in which to let off steam when they need to. "When I can't take it any more," Jane says, "I just go out back and *yell!*"

There is a great relief to be known in the spaciousness of the land. Now and then I stand in a field with nothing around me for miles, the distances so great that it seems I can see, though perhaps I only feel, the curve of the earth. To see so far feels like power; to be unobserved, distant from other human beings, is a particular freedom.

But there is community, too, in Jane Snavely's life, and regular meetings with other women. We lean against the worn siding of her house, our faces turned to the sun, while she tells me about the Extension Homemakers program that is operated out of Kansas State University at Manhattan. The purpose of the program is to bring university learning to women living out in the counties. At the monthly meetings of the local Extension Homemakers units, lessons are given in subjects such as the drying of foods, tailoring, and effective discipline for children. Selected women who are instructed each month by the extension agent, take the lessons back to teach to their groups.

"Our unit's one of the bigger ones," Jane says. "At one time there was twenty-one members. Must be seventeen or so in it now. You have a meeting every month and everybody just takes turns being hostess and giving a lesson. And you usually have a service project of some type; we've helped the retarded children's center up here quite a bit. We had a meeting yesterday and was picking lessons. There's gonna be one on automobile maintenance and dietary stuff for when people get older, and different things on health. I think there's one on exercises coming.

"It's a way to get together and also to accomplish or learn something, like our lesson yesterday was on Swedish heritage. The lady that give the lesson, her parents both came from the old country. She's one of the older members of our group, and her and another lady gave the lesson. It consisted of a background of the Swedish people, how they happened to come here. And then we had a traditional Swedish meal ... so you get a lot of goodies to eat. There's usually one or two lessons a year like that."

One of the meetings that was most useful to her, Jane says, was a presentation on estate planning, given by a lawyer. The issue of estate taxes is a vital one for farm women. In the early 1970s, with land values rising and farm size increasing, the women discovered that their labor did not give them legal standing as property owners. "If my husband died," Jane tells me, "the inheritance tax I'd have to pay would be terrible, because as far as the tax people is concerned I have had nothing to do with making a farm go or paying for it. Now they say the more times the woman can get her name on pieces of paper with money coming and going the better chance she's got. They'll still fight you, but at least you got something to stand up. Now if the *wife* dies, the husband owns everything, unless she has some of it in her name. At one time they said the best way to get farm property was with Tenants in Common with Rights of Survivorship, I believe is the way it's worded. And that's the way ours is set up. And now they say that's not always the best way to do it, but in order to change it, the wife has to either buy part of it or the husband makes her a present of part of it. In that case, she has to pay gift taxes. So they get you coming or going. I don't know, it gets kind of confusing. Like in our case, if something happened to my husband, I'm sure I'd stay here and try to keep farming, but if you get up to where you had to pay too much taxes, you'd almost have to sell in order to pay them."

This has been the fate of many farm widows. The situation remains problematical, with women in several states applying pressure to change the inheritance laws, so that homemakers will have equal rights to assets accumulated during a marriage. Despite resistance from traditionally sexist legislators and organizations such as insurance companies, who in one way or another benefit from the widows' plight, some progress has been made. Farm women are becoming stronger in this struggle to establish and protect their rights.

They have come together in recently created organizations. As the male-dominated, established farm interest groups did not view estate tax as a priority for action, the women developed their own programs.* In the mid-seventies, two major organizations were formed: WIFE (Women Involved in Farm Economics) and AAW (American Agri-Women). Both their memberships soon found that they were concerned with many issues besides their original focus on the estate tax, and they expanded to become general farm organizations.

WIFE is centered in the wheat and feedgrain areas of the Great Plains, the same area that saw the flourishing of the Populist movement. Much of the selling of commodities, even in the 1890s, took place in large-scale markets over which the farmers had no control; it was the disadvantages of this system that prompted the Populist revolt. WIFE is concerned with the same issues, except that the markets now are worldwide rather than national. From its beginning in 1976, the organization has grown to include some 116 chapters in eighteen states.**

American Agri-Women, founded in 1974, has a more diverse membership; its three thousand members are scattered from coast to coast, in thirty-four states, and are dairy farmers, fruit growers, truck farmers, as well as producers of grain.**

Both these groups take stands on issues, mostly economic.

---

* In a recent letter to me, Jane Snavely wrote, "The work of these [farm women's organizations] and some individual farm widows who fought their cases through the courts, as well as some sympathetic legislators, has changed things since we talked. Due to some recently passed bills, a husband's farm estate can pass to his widow nearly tax free except in the cases of very, very large ones. The amount that we can give or leave our children tax free has greatly increased."

** These figures are for 1979.

They organize in their home states and work to build their influence in Washington. The Nebraska WIFE chapter was the first organization to demand briefings on the MX missile sites proposed for western Nebraska. Current important issues are production of gasohol and conservation of water resources.*

Jane Snavely believes that farmers must organize themselves, and like many of the women here she feels defensive and misunderstood by the general population on this issue. She especially harbors resentment at the public response to the farmers' massive 1979 march to Washington to press demands for higher farm price supports. Then Secretary of Agriculture Bob Berglund called the demonstration "an unmitigated disaster," and legislators were unsympathetic. The farmers, members of the American Agricultural Movement, snarled traffic with their tractors, clashed with police, tore up the smooth grass of the mall between the Washington Monument and the Capitol, broke the bottom of the Reflecting Pool, and were in general a disruptive presence.

The roots of this agricultural movement might be traced to the Populist movement of the late nineteenth century, in which hundreds of thousands of farmers worked within the National Farmers Alliance (NFA) to improve conditions throughout the country. On July 4, 1890, in Winfield, Kansas, NFA leader L. L. Polk told a crowd of six thousand people, "From New York to the Golden Gate, farmers have risen up and have inaugurated a movement such as the world has never seen. It is a revolution of thought. . . ." It was a Kansas *woman,* Mary Elizabeth Lease, who exhorted the farmers to "raise less corn and more hell."**

Jane, who worked in the office of the organizing group for the march to Washington, passionately defends their right to organize and their reasons for doing so.

---

* Nebraska's *New Land Review,* Summer 1979 issue, gives excellent information on farm women's politics. See especially the penetrating analysis by Francis Hill of the origin and political implications of this movement.

** Both quotes are from Lawrence Goodwyn, *The Populist Moment: A Short History of the Agrarian Revolt in America* (Oxford, London, New York: Oxford University Press, 1978), pp. 133, 339.

"It's getting so bad that something had to be done," she says, her angry eyes bright behind her glasses. "People don't think much about it if a labor union goes on strike. Oh, they're entitled to more pay and that's it. It's inconvenient till they go back to work. But when the *farmers* did that, that was terrible. Supposedly the farmers were starving people and I don't know what all. I had a cousin in Oregon that works for a farmwomen's organization, a national organization, and she went to a convention of world hunger people that works through the churches and she said that out of five or six hundred people there she was the only one from a farm. She said when she tried to explain why the farmers had to have more, that they just couldn't make a living, why, she said some of these people just nearly blew a fuse. They told her she was trying to make money off of people's hunger! And she asked them didn't *they* get paid for their work? 'Well, yeah, but that's different, you know, we're not feeding people!' At that convention, she said, they really thought that the farmers should just give them a share of what they raise and not expect to be paid for it. She said they actually had lobbyists in Washington at one time trying to swing the Congressmen into passing laws that the farmers were supposed to just *give up* part of their crops to people. So I don't know, it gets real strange."

She looks out across the land, her face thoughtful, and I follow her gaze to a plowed field, a great striated sweep in which the lines stretch almost perfectly straight, far out there bending just a little to accommodate an almost imperceptible rise in the ground, soon lost again in the flatness that extends to the horizon. This land is known by Jane with particular intimacy, for she has plowed and harvested, ridden and walked across every yard of it. She exists in as vital a relationship to it as she does to the horses in the corral, to the people with whom she shares her life.

I turn to look at her, feeling how trustfully she has accepted me here, how candidly she gives me her opinions. She continues.

"Well, farming anymore, it's like going to Las Vegas and playing a slot machine, I guess, because the grain dealers like in Kansas City and Chicago, they buy and sell more grain than there actually is. I mean they're making money on grain that's not even there. It's only on paper. They'll buy it on one market and sell it on another one just to control the price, and a lot of that's what the farmers went to Washington for, you know, to try to get some controls so the *farmers* can control their prices. You know, the labor union or the manufacturers if they're not getting as much profit as they think they should have, they set their prices higher. But the farmer can't do that, you have to take more or less what you get."

She tells about one action of the agricultural movement, a parade of women driving tractors on the main street of Concordia. "I was gonna be in it but then I don't know what we were doing that I didn't think I'd make it, and so I got up there just in time to watch them. And you'd hear people say, 'Well, they can't be in too bad shape with those big tractors, and they got cabs and they got air conditioning.' There's this one lady, I said, 'You got air conditioning in your house?' She said yeah. I said, 'Your husband got it for his office?' She said yeah. I said, 'Why can't we have one where *we* work?' "

Jane walks with me now across the yard behind her house, the wind lifting her long hair and tangling it, one hand raising to gesture in annoyance as she talks. I glance at the shed where the tractor stands, remembering its cab with the dashboard bristling dials and knobs.

"They spend eight hours in their office and we spend fourteen hours in that tractor in the summertime when it's hotter than heck," Jane says. "Sometimes more than that. When we're plowing, it's not unusual to go out at six o'clock in the morning, stay till midnight. So what's the difference, if the businessman sits in a chair all day with an air conditioner, why can't someone that's out working in the dirt have an air conditioner too? What's the big deal?

"You'd think the people in a town like Concordia would know about the farmers' lives, but the women that live in town—especially the ones that their husbands has good jobs—you'll be in a grocery store, you know, and they'll say, 'These dumb farmers, there's no reason for this meat to be that high!' And you try to tell them that bread went up when wheat went up, but when we went down, bread didn't do down. And this last couple of times bread went up and *we* didn't go up. Out of a loaf of bread, the farmer gets about three cents; the wrapper costs more than the wheat that's in the bread does. And the price of everything you have to have, the equipment to take care of stuff, gasoline: when we go to cutting milo, it's going to cost us about eighty dollars a day for fuel. If we're lucky.

"But people don't take that into consideration, I guess."

Jane turns to look at me, and then she shrugs, her shoulders lifting, her hands returning to her pockets.

"I don't like to argue with people," she says apologetically, "but sometimes they get me a little aggravated."

Virginia

Now that the South Side Cafe I visited two years ago has closed, Sandy's Cafe is the one eatery in Clyde. In its long, well-lighted front room is a steam table providing breakfast, dinner, and supper at specified hours (there is no such thing as lunch in rural Kansas). Beer is sold in a dark, wood-panelled back room, where booths line the walls and a waitress serves from a corner bar. It is here the farmers come in the late afternoon to drink and exchange accounts of their day.

Shine Racette has had a few beers already when Virginia Racette and I arrive through the back door to join him. With him are his youngest son, Sean, an intelligent thirteen-year-old, and the Lambert family. All are settled at the long table in the middle of the room, where Virginia and I now take seats across from each other. Shine sees to it we each get a beer.

Virginia is a bright, spirited woman in her late forties. I remembered her from my previous visit as nervous, the tension showing in the tight lines of her face, the way she pulled her lip down over her long teeth, the occasional loud bursts of laughter that overtook her. This time I found her, while no less forthright or outspoken, a little more calm.

Shine I recalled as a quiet man in worn cowboy boots. Drinking my beer now, I listen to him telling about how he had to deal with a runaway cow today while he was running cattle.

"What happened?" Virginia asks. "Did your horse give out?"

"Oh, I couldn't turn her," Shine says. "She run over the horse and everything else."

Across the table from me, next to Virginia, sits Pat Lambert, a beefy, dark-haired young man in a cowboy shirt, who chuckles now, enjoying Shine's predicament.

Shine turns to me to explain. "A cow gets crazy like that, they got their mind goin' north that's where they're goin' to go. If they want to go east they're goin' east, and you can't turn 'em. Come to a four-wire fence, they go right through it."

He is a short man with graying hair cut close around the sides of a balding head. His eyebrows are very dark above eyes filled with a particular gentleness.

While the grownups go on talking, I make the acquaintance of Christie and Lana, the two Lambert children. Christie, who looks to be nine or ten, chews away at a hamburger, telling Virginia about her day at school. Lana, a demure six-year-old, picks languidly at a huge plate of french fries.

Leaning over to me, her mother, Madeline, explains, "Lana is a vegetarian!"

Her voice fully communicates the outrage of this.

Lana gazes serenely at her fries.

I don't know *where* she got the idea for *that!*" Madeline states, eyebrows severely disapproving. "Sometimes I *make* her eat meat."

Shyly, Lana glances up at me to see what I think of this, and I smile at her, appreciating the character strength it must take for the daughter of a cattle farmer to refuse meat.

Madeline shakes her head, exasperated, and I see how fond she is of this unusual little girl.

Madeline Lambert is a slim young woman with light hair up

in curlers under a gauzy scarf. We begin a conversation now as I tell her about my talk with Jane Snavely concerning estate taxes. Madeline describes the steps she and Harold are taking to protect her if something should happen to him.

"Everything we own we've got both our names on. Oh yes, we do not buy *anything*—a piece of land, piece of equipment—that both our names aren't on it. And it's that way with our banker. If the note comes up, we both sign it. But still I wouldn't be considered a partner in the farm. I'd have to go to court and fight it.

"So far now there are some women fighting it and saying they *are* partners with their husbands. There's been one in Minnesota, one in Wisconsin, and another one in either South or North Dakota, that have *went* to court and fought this inheritance tax. They had to prove that they had put as much into that farm as he had, and then that wasn't considering that they also had to run the house, raise the kids, do his washing and ironing, and fix the meals and stuff besides."

Like Jane Snavely, Madeline works outside on the land; but just now, she tells me, her activities are restricted. "Since Lana had an asthma attack, I haven't been able to go out as much because she's not allowed outside of an air-conditioned vehicle or a house." Lana does not look up at us, but I can tell she's listening. "It kind of put a stop to a lot of things I used to do. I used to just pick up the kids, throw them in the pickup and take off for the field. Lana always went with me when we'd go with trucks, you know, to haul milo, everything ... "

So it is Madeline, not her husband Harold, who stays in with Lana, I note, just as it was Jane who did the canning; in this and other ways preserving the conventional demarcations between male and female roles. Still, the fact that wife and husband labor side by side, that these farm women take responsibility for and have a comprehensive knowledge of the endeavor that supports the family, leads to a greater equality between husband and wife than is found in most city couples. "I don't really consider myself a housewife," Madeline says. "On my income tax anymore I put farmer's wife, or sometimes I just put farmer. Because that's what

I consider myself. If I'm going to go out and work with him, I think I'm a *farmer!*"

She lowers and lifts her head in a defiant nod, her face determined.

At the head of the table, Shine is flirting broadly with the waitress. I listen, hearing once again something unusual in his way of speaking, an extra effort, a blurriness now and then. I remember Virginia's telling me about the mysterious illness that struck him only a few years after they were married. He collapsed in the barn and she dragged him to the pickup and took him to the hospital, where they kept him for a week. Although no doctor has confirmed it, she is sure the disease was polio, for ever since his recovery "he has no muscle on the one side of his jaw."

Shine joshes the waitress, a heavy, cheerful young woman.

"Now you wait till I take care of my honey here," she tells someone who has asked for another beer, and glances wickedly at Virginia, with whom she is obviously excellent friends.

Harold Lambert sits in silence, drinking his beer and eating a large plate of beef stew, mashed potatoes, and corn. The talk turns to cattle again, and then Pat Lambert, Harold's younger brother, is telling about a visit to a doctor.

"He told me to come down there and make me an appointment at the hospital and get it cut off."

Virginia is incredulous. "You sure that's what he told you?"

"Yeah!" Pat's face is flushed, his dark hair catching the colored lights of the beer signs. He turns to Virginia and fixes her with a challenging stare. "He sure did! Said there's no use having any more trouble with it. Just get it took off and that's the end of it."

Virginia shakes her head, pursing her mouth. "You better go to another doctor, Pat, and see what *he* says."

"Well, this is a pretty good one. Why, after I seen what he done for that fellow's face . . . had the whole side of his face took off, and he sewed it back on and you could hardly tell. After I seen that I figured he knows what he's doin'. Besides, he has to be all right: he wears cowboy boots," Pat concludes, grinning.

"I don't know, Pat," Madeline puts in. "They say if you take off a toe it throws off your balance."

"That's *two* toes!" he states emphatically. "One and you're still okay."

"What's wrong with your toe?" I ask, fascinated.

"Well, they tell me I've got the black arthritis," looking to Madeline for confirmation.

"That's what they call it," Madeline says. "And it travels. They say it'll go up into the foot pretty soon."

"I seen it on an X-ray," Pat explains. "All the other bones was white, and this here one the bone was black."

"Get another opinion!" Virginia looks worried.

"Isn't there some way you could treat it?" I ask.

"I wouldn't know what. That toe's had everything done to it. It's been broke and stepped on and run over so many times there's nothing you can do for it now. And *hurt!* Sometimes I grit my teeth and wish it was *off* of there."

"We's talking the other night how we could save him some money," Madeline says gleefully. "We could get him real drunk and then take them wire cutters and snip it off, he wouldn't know the difference."

Everyone launches enthusiastically into the possible modes of amputation for Pat's toe, mentioning various farm tools, while he sits looking slightly drunk and troubled.

Virginia follows the conversation for a time in silence, her concern for Pat apparent in the expression of her eyes, and then she breaks in, "No, seriously, Pat, you get yourself another opinion before you do something like that!"

She has told me about all the "doctoring" she had to do for her own children when they were little. Besides Sean and a grown daughter, Tina, Virginia is mother to two grown sons. When the two older boys were very young, the family lived on a farm where she had neither telephone nor vehicle of her own, so that when Shine was out in the fields with the pickup, she was left to fend for herself. Rick fell in the cornfield once, a cornstalk piercing the roof of his mouth. "I had to pull that out and doctor that." Terry

split his ear on a piece of barbed wire, and Virginia put the ear
back together. "I must've done a pretty good job because you can't
tell it now." Then there was a well full of rattlesnakes on their
farm. "I caught the two boys, they weren't very old, they had one
cornered in the garage and was teasin' it with a broom. Heart
attack time! 'Cause I'm scared to death of snakes. Any kind. If I
go up against a bullhead, it might as well be a rattlesnake, 'cause
if it bit me I'd die!"

Virginia married when she was nineteen years old, Shine
twenty. She had been working in restaurants in town since she
was in the seventh or eighth grade, through the school year and in
the summers, right up until the day she married. Then she went
to live on a farm where she had to heat water for washing, where
she scrubbed her baby's diapers in the kitchen sink on a wash-
board. There one of her most deeply felt hardships was the lack of
companions, women like herself to consult with, to share her
experience. Isolation is the other side of the spaciousness the
women value so much. It was one of the trials of pioneer life, and
up until the time of Virginia's mother, farm wives still did not
often come together to share their lives.

Maybe it is this history that makes Virginia so very enthusiastic about the group of women who meet each morning in the
front room of Sandy's Cafe. She lives close enough to town now
that she can join them, and I see that her participation in the
group is a significant element in her life.

"When I was raising my little ones, my mother was still alive,
so I had support. I had her to tell me if she thought I was doin the
right thing or the wrong thing. We never had a communication
problem. But even in that day when my mother was alive, the
women didn't meet uptown to talk like this, and I think it
would've done her a lot of good if she had had that chance. If a
woman had walked into the restaurant back then without her
husband, they would have figured she was a little loose. And that's
not been that many years ago.

"My mother didn't have too much contact with other women.
She had a lot of hobbies. That's where I learned to embroider, I
learned to crochet . . . quilting . . . things that the women did then

to keep themselves busy if they took any time off. But to go up and have a cup of coffee in town was unheard of then. I know we used to get together every week and play cards of an afternoon. But then you was busy playing cards. You didn't have time to talk about any kind of a problem, and if you did have a problem you wasn't lettin' anybody else know about it anyhow.

"These days, the women are far more frank than they used to be even just a few years ago. There isn't much that we don't talk about. They're very frank about the way they feel, which I think is marvelous! Of course there are things that are personal and private. They may come out in general talk, a little at a time, but they're coming out, they're not stayin' in the way they were before, and I think that's great, I think that leaves a lot of room."

Virginia describes how the daily coming together at Sandy's Cafe happens. "Most of the women, when the kids are old enough that they can get away for a few hours, or if the kids are in school, we meet uptown. We have our own little seminar at the restaurant over coffee in the morning. We generally go about nine o'-clock and sometimes, if the seminar is really good, we don't get home until eleven or eleven-thirty." She laughs delightedly.

"It's all kinds of people. Like my friend, she and her husband are going to have their fiftieth wedding anniversary. She's a generation older than I am. There's a couple of generations older than I am, and a lot of kids younger than I am, and we get together and talk like this. You bet your booties a lot of stuff gets hashed over. It's a chance to release a little tension and find out how everybody else copes with a problem. You get maybe six different opinions on how to take care of something. You don't know how much it relieves the mind to find out there are other solutions, especially when you're dealin' with a kid's life."

Generational differences do not count for as much here as they do in urban settings. Farm women share common hardships and problems. Although the women may differ widely in age, they tend to voice the same preoccupations, hold similar opinions, adhere to a common morality. Of course there are always exceptions, but in a very small community, to diverge too far from accepted practice is to risk the disapproval of one's neighbors.

Virginia, who in most respects is an outspoken, aggressive woman, expresses her acquiescence to the social norm in talking about the bicycle she had hoped to ride for exercise. "I sent it home with my daughter Tina. I said, 'Enough of that, take it home.' If I rode that thing to town they'd think I'd lost my marbles. And if you get out and *walk* here they think that too. You can walk up the road and people look at you" (she raises her eyebrows and peers down over her nose) " 'Hmmmm ... I wonder when *she's* gonna go.' "

Here is the constriction, the narrowness that afflicts these farming communities. I wonder about the young women here in Clyde and Concordia who do not wish to marry early, who are drawn to study or work or adventure. What do they do? Laura Vytlacil, one of the women who lives in Clyde, told me of her nineteen-year-old daughter who joined the air force and is now stationed in Guam. "She wanted to get away and she wanted to travel. We are so unlucky here to have girls who lose themselves and are pregnant before they graduate so there's nothing for them to look forward to except marriage and motherhood. Susan was determined that she was going to do something else. And she had to leave here to do it." They are still leaving, the different ones, the adventurous ones. But what of those who don't leave?

I think of Yvonne Hauck, a young farm woman of sophisticated views who stayed in the area, but who admits that her early pregnancy was a gesture of defiance. I think about all the other young women, who may live their whole lives within a few miles of their birthplaces. Social life for teenagers in Clyde consists mostly of driving up and down the main street in pickup trucks, sitting at the bank lot or the corner filling station to drink beer. Many of the boys are heavy drinkers while still in high school, and it is because of the drinking, says Virginia Racette, that some of the girls get "knocked off balance." One of her own sons was a prodigious drinker.

"When my kid was in high school he could drink the town dry. It was a drinkin' class. They'd have a keg party—what else is there for the kids to do? A lot of times they were out in my front yard or out in my pasture: that way I knew where my kids were at, and how long they'd been there, and how much they drank. I knew what they were doing. The kids just are not physical like they used to be. They spend too much time in cars now and they figure they have to go farther away from home to get the entertainment. We'd go out in the country and ride horses all after-noon. We kind of made our own excitement. These kids get in their cars and try to see who's gonna do the most U-turns uptown, I guess."

The young women who ride in the cars and "have a beer now and then" have no official access to birth control. Virginia's own daughter became pregnant when she was in high school. While abortion was not considered a possible solution, neither did Virginia pressure her daughter to get married. Tina finished high school, very noticeably pregnant. Her fellow students understood her position and were supportive of her, but some of the teachers, according to Virginia, assumed a self-righteously critical attitude. After graduation, when Tina wanted to marry, the priest at the Catholic Church refused to perform the ceremony. Tina, born and raised a Catholic, left the church.

The young women I talked with use or have used the pill, but they worry about the side effects. As Jane Snavely put it, "I always figured that something like the pill, that controls what nature intended for you to do, by that method, couldn't help but mess things up somewhere." After giving birth to her two children, she underwent a tubal ligation.

Virginia Racette, who points to the possible medical dangers of the pill, has yet another reason for disapproving of birth control for young women. Older than Jane Snavely and a staunch Catholic, she says of her own daughter, "When Tina was a teenager, she knew the facts of life. We had talked about it from the time she was menstruation age and up." But Virginia did not help Tina get birth control. She speaks firmly. "No. That's like saying, 'You have my permission to do anything you're big enough to get away with.' And I don't like that. I hope mothers these days talk to their daughters, but at the same time I hope they don't hand 'em birth control, because it's dangerous. It's like handin' a kid a gun and saying, Go out and have a ball. There's too many of these teenagers that are takin the pill as their right. I'd just as soon they'd use their own common sense. If they know the facts of life, and hygienic cleanliness, and know how to take care of themselves, you shouldn't have too many problems. Mine just got knocked off balance, that's all."

At the table in the back room of Sandy's, Pat Lambert has left, and Madeline and Harold Lambert are urging their two daughters into their sweaters. Almost everyone has gone home to supper now; the room is quieter and somewhat forlorn with its colored blurs of signs, its odors of beer and deep fried food.

When the Lamberts have disappeared out the back door, Virginia and I join Shine and Sean at the head of the table. Why, I ask them, when farming is such a loved occupation for them, have none of their children become farmers?

Shine waits, letting Virginia answer sadly. "After they get married and start having their families, they have to go where the jobs are. I've got two kids right now who would love to go into farming but they can't afford it and we can't afford to help them. Land is the big expense, yes. You can always rent, maybe, if you can find land to rent, but then most of the land 'round here is already rented. And if you wanted to buy, there's no way, unless you put your whole family in jeopardy for the rest of your life, there's no way you can borrow that much money and pay it off. And on top of that you've got your machinery, your livestock, your crops. There's no way those kids could get into farming." And as Shine nods in agreement, she says that she and Shine do not own the land they farm. "We've been here for twenty-nine years and we've never owned any land. Shine's always talking about not owning any land, he'll never own anything when he dies. His father and mother both are still alive. We've never had enough money left over to try to buy the land from them. I've been after a new barn since nineteen sixty some, and I'd like to have a new room on the house. I don't have that either.

"Farming used to be a family thing," Virginia adds wistfully.

"But when Shine and I are gone, I haven't the foggiest idea what will happen to our farm."

"I'll take it!" announces Sean, and we all jump, for he has been so unaccustomedly quiet that we have forgotten his presence. "I'll get rid of the cows and keep horses."

"Lotsa luck, George!" Virginia says, and we laugh, relieved at a thirteen-year-old's optimism in the face of the facts.

"A Man's World"

Virginia has invited me to go with her and Shine to a Saturday night celebration at the VFW hall in Clyde, the fiftieth wedding anniversary party of a friend of theirs. I accept, and later I am grateful for this invitation, for it gives me a chance to see Virginia differently than I have known her before.

When darkness falls, we gather in the yard of the Racette house to get in the big, heavy car to drive to town. This car, Virginia tells me, was bought for her by Shine, after her compact car was wrecked by a joyriding nephew. Shine considers compacts unsafe for driving on country roads. Having sat in my own small car on a narrow gravel road watching a giant tractor pull out of a field and grind toward me in a cloud of dust, looming above me as it rumbled slowly past with earsplitting engine noise, I can understand that belief, for I have rarely felt so vulnerable.

We arrive in town at the VFW hall, a big, square, plain building across the street and down a block from Sandy's Cafe. Inside, we find ourselves in a long room with tables against the walls and a bandstand. We walk through it to a back room where couples stand three deep around a bar. Everyone turns to greet Virginia and Shine and take a long, curious look at me.

Virginia takes a pint bottle of liquor out of her purse, and Shine elbows his way in to the bar to buy set-ups for himself and Virginia, a beer for me.

"Come on, I'll introduce you to Darlene Tate," Virginia says.

We move around the bar to find a sturdy young woman with tight-curled hair. She turns to greet us, her face opening in a brilliant smile. When Virginia tells her I want to talk with her, Darlene laughs, lifting her hand to indicate the noise and confusion, and says amiably, "This sure isn't a good time to do it!"

Next to her stands a tall, sandy-haired man. This is Thad Tate, Darlene's husband.

Ever since I arrived in Clyde, people have been telling me I should meet Darlene Tate from St. Joseph. In many ways, she is typical of farm women in this area. A good Catholic and mother of four, she worked with Thad on their farm and, until recently, held a job as an aid in a nursing home. Then she changed her employment. She holds down a "man's job," people tell me, at Northern Natural Gas; and it is apparent that by so doing she has become a woman who is watched and talked about.

Sample opinions: "She's a good worker. She does her job and she doesn't take no guff from the men either. They respect her."

"Yeah, I talked to one man works out there, said she did her job real good."

"Well, they tell me I shouldn't say this, but I heard why they hired Darlene was so they could fill their minority quota and they wouldn't have to hire a black man." (This response puzzled me when I heard it, for there are no black people in Cloud County, and I wondered if the neighboring county, which houses Northern Natural Gas, is different. I suspected that this opinion smacked more of racism than actual conditions.)

Darlene turns back into the crush at the bar as Shine brings us our drinks. We leave the noisy back room to go out into the larger room, where I am reminded that this is a fiftieth wedding anniversary by the age of many of the dancers. They circle sedately about the floor as a three-piece band desecrates the old favorites. I am home, returned to those drafty meeting halls, those square dance barns where my parents brought my sister and me. The music used to swirl and sometimes a voice sang "To spend one night with you, in our old rendezvous ... " I would thrill at the intimations of sensuality, the bodies moving together in the dimness, the crepe paper swaying.

Now, on the bandstand, they are playing the same songs. I sip my beer, feeling like that child I was, watching Darlene Tate and another woman arrive to sit across from us at our table. In a few minutes her husband joins us also. I try to come back fully into my adult self who should now start a conversation, make some friendly gesture. There is strained silence as I search for a way to begin. Darlene and her friend eye me discreetly for a time while Thad stares at me. We exchange a few tentative remarks, hampered by my sudden shyness, and then they fall back into an apparently familiar way of relating to each other: I am treated to a performance of the merciless ribbing that the "bunch from St. Joe's" specializes in.

"Oh, that bunch from St. Joe's," Virginia whispers to me reassuringly, "that's just how they talk, they don't mean anything by it."

The wit is precisely honed and at times brilliant. I find myself retreating out of its range, to concentrate on my beer and wait for an opportunity to ask Darlene about her unusual occupation. But her remark at the bar had accurately summed up the situation: there is no opening for serious conversation.

Soon Virginia and Shine have left the table, and I am invited to dance by a man who comes from across the hall. When I return, Darlene and Thad and their friend have gone. I sit for a time watching the couples on the floor, and I realize that back in those dance halls on the outskirts of my city, some of the women I watched must have been doing "men's jobs." For those were the years of World War II, when the women went to the factories to become welders and machinists and munitions experts, to hold those jobs until the war was over and they were sent home to bear children; or, in the case of working class white and minority women, were shunted into lowpaid "service" jobs or less skilled factory work.

Now once again, for different reasons, the percentage of women in the work force is high (though most women still do the so-called menial jobs); and here in the Clyde-Concordia area, which I had thought of as insular and protected, more and more women are out looking for work. The ones who find it in jobs

like Darlene Tate's often run up against male resentment of
women's new roles. This evening at the VFW hall in Clyde,
where by now some of the men are very drunk, one man acts out
this frustration, using Darlene Tate as a target.

We have greeted the fiftieth wedding celebrants, a couple in
their seventies, the woman beautiful in a long dress, both she and
her husband looking vigorous and radiantly happy. As it nears
time to leave, Virginia, Shine, and I go into the back room where
the crowd has thinned enough to allow us to find stools at the bar.
Several men come over to find out who I am, intrigued by the
presence of a stranger who is not somebody's relative. Outsiders
come to Clyde, apparently, only to see their kin. To my explanation that I have come to talk to women, their responses range
from interest to amusement to incredulity to belligerence. Why
don't I want to talk to *them,* they wonder.

A man approaches to lean half on the bar and half on me,
peering at me close up from bloodshot eyes. His voice is thickened
with whisky as he talks earnestly about the situation at Northern
Natural Gas. He seems to know a great deal about the operation
of that firm, and regales me with a long-winded account of its
history and present fortunes.

Virginia tells him I am going to speak with Darlene Tate
about her job, and he gives his opinion.

"Why, they only hired her because they got one girl out there
already don't do nothin' but throw her tits around. They hired
Darlene so they could get rid of the other one."

His certainty, his arrogance, irritate me. While Virginia and I
defend Darlene, I move so that his weight slips off my shoulder.
Glancing around the back room I am relieved to discover that
Thad and Darlene have gone home.

The man straightens up to confront Virginia and me. "Don't
tell *me* you can do the same work as a man. When you've got an
eighty-five pound wrench and a sixteen-pound mallet, you're not
gonna be able to do the job!"

At this I watch Virginia transform, her eyes going hard, her face tightening, her upper lip again pulling down tight over her teeth.

"Why, I could too. I'd have to learn how. No man goes in there the first day and knows how to use those tools. You *teach* him how!"

He shakes his head bullishly.

"No we don't either. He picks 'em up and uses 'em the first day."

Virginia sputters in disbelief. "Oh, now you tellin' me there's no training necessary to do those jobs?"

He thrusts his face toward her. "I'm tellin' you you couldn't do it no matter what."

Virginia gets off her bar stool, straightening to her full height.

"I could be as strong as any man if I put my mind to it."

She stares the man in the eye, meeting him head to head. Then suddenly she turns away in disgust, hissing, "Let's get out of here," and walks quickly toward the front room, Shine and I following.

A few minutes later, when we have come through the hall and out the front door, we stand on the main street of Clyde, where the scent of manure hangs in the warm night air.

"He sure was obnoxious," I comment.

Virginia, still highly annoyed, shrugs into her sweater.

"I've known him all my life!" she mutters, and with this ambiguous remark she leads us to the car.

Now I glance at Shine to see what he may be feeling. His face is impassive as we get in the car. Probably he himself would not challenge someone publically, I imagine, as his style is so much more easygoing; but he stayed near her during the conflict, watched to see how it would go. People living together over time sometimes find a way to accept their differences and stand behind each other when the heat is on.

As Shine backs up the car to drive out of town, Virginia growls, "If we'd stayed one more minute I would've shoved that whiskey bottle right down his throat."

I have seen Virginia Racette as farmer, as mother, as friend and confidante of her neighbors. Now I have watched her stand up in defense of herself and other women, act from an awareness of her own dignity and the understanding that women's condition is a shared one. I remember, during that first visit to Clyde, wondering where the scratchy, cantankerous women were. Now I see that they are all around me, hidden behind placid exteriors until a situation calls forth that particular mettle.

Shine drives in silence, and I sit in the back seat looking out at the sky enormous above us, dusted with stars, velvety black and unreachable. Virginia falls silent now, too, and it is with a sense of relief that we pull into the yard of their farm, where the tree throws a skirt of deep shadow on the grass before the house and the high old barn stands like a crooked ghost.

The Bunch from St. Joe's

As I drive toward Northern Natural Gas to visit Darlene Tate, I can see for miles in all directions, to a horizon on which a stark tall farmhouse stands silhouetted. Perhaps it is one of the houses abandoned by people who retired and moved to town, standing against the weather, its windows shattered by teenagers, its contents overturned and sorted through, its doors hanging open.

A few days ago I had visited Uncle Earl's farm, much like this one. While he dozed in the car I entered the house alone and sat on the stairway, listening to the noise of the loose metal side of an outbuilding as it was lifted by the wind and slammed back against its frame. Behind the house, the windmill clacked swiftly. I sat for a long time in the silence, thinking of Amanda. This silence, these thoughts, drew me back inside myself, as the separate things in the rooms had sunk back into the debris on the floor: a thick layer of paper, cloth, manure, stuck through with objects, transformed into a soft loamy substance by years of weather. Amanda. There was the vestige here of her body's ceaseless aching, of her long nights when she looked at the flat black rectangle of window and waited for Earl to adjust the pillows propping up her legs. I saw her fingers with their swollen joints, closed on a black-beaded rosary. Soon her presence with me was so real that it was shocking to come back to the rotting sideboard, the open mouth of window, a rag flapping against its frame.

When I stepped down out of the house, Earl's head had fallen forward, his chin coming to rest on his chest, his stubbly white hair shining in the sunlight.

Now as I drive to Northern Natural Gas, the memory of Amanda seems incongruous, for Darlene Tate has carved a place for herself in this community that could not have been imagined by the women who lived in those tall, plain farmhouses. My visit with her is about to convince me, however, that her life is firmly built upon the same foundation as theirs. I am especially drawn to Darlene Tate because she *is* so traditional; she is so like those pioneer women who learned to survive in situations completely unfamiliar to them, who rose to the challenge of necessity. Born and raised on a farm, married to a farmer, she had children, learned to till the soil. Yet now she wears a hardhat and repairs giant machines. She is a salaried worker who must arrange the care of her four daughters around her work hours; she contributes a substantial paycheck to the support of her family. She is learning, excited by the machinery, by the possibilities for her own acquisition of skills.

Darlene stands at an intersection of cultural expectations, and is fully aware of the delicacy, the tenuousness of her position. Because of her solid participation in the farming community, her credibility here, she has managed to move into the realm of work with little friction. Because of her determination to succeed, she has been able to overcome the reputation of the only other woman in her position. She represents, at the same time, the most accepted and respected values of her community, and the innovative courage of women who work in fields dominated by men.

Northern Natural Gas sits on the prairie to the east of Clifton. Arriving at its gate, I pull in past a cluster of tanks, giant pipes and fittings, all painted white and sparkling in the sun, backed by a long, warehouse-like building. In the office, a man in a glass cubicle leans back with his feet propped on his desk. Another stares at a stack of papers. The secretary says she'll be happy to call Darlene Tate.

Waiting, I am once again for a few moments in Earl's ruined house, gazing at the piano. Amanda had played it, before her hands became twisted and filled with pain. Now it stands like a great, sad animal crumbling into decrepitude. I touch a key, and hear the dulled answer of hammer hitting string. How different Amanda's life might have been, I think, if there had been a job to go to, children to care for, something of her own to fill her days.

Now, in this business office, I watch the secretary at work at her desk, and wait for Darlene to arrive.

A few minutes later she comes in, and she seems to me to look exactly as she had at the VFW hall, even though she is dressed in jeans and plaid shirt, a hardhat crushing her short dark curls. Perhaps it is the grin that makes her look the same, that vibrant greeting that made me like her that first evening and reminds me today how much energy radiates from her.

Darlene takes me out into the yard to talk. She is twenty-seven years old, a solid woman with sturdy shoulders and an air of vitality and endurance.

"So what does all this equipment do?" I ask.

She ponders for a moment, looking at the brilliant white tanks and pipes. "Well, the natural gas that comes out of the ground in Texas has to be piped up north. So in order for it to go along the gas lines, it has to be pumped by these engines. I think Beatrice, Nebraska, is about the next plant that shoves it on farther."

We stand on the patch of grass before the office, ignore a group of men in the back of a pickup jolting past us on the company drive. But when one of them hoots, I turn to see Virginia's adversary from the VFW hall leaning over the side of the truck to gawk at us. Darlene's only acknowledgment of him is an annoyed tightening of the eyelids. I wonder if she is regretting my visit here, for my presence makes her even more conspicuous than she is normally. But her smile, her patient answers to my questions, betray no such feelings.

I ask her how she came to take this job, and she tells me that when the opportunity to work at Northern came up, she was working at a job she liked as a geriatric aide, but it paid only $3.00 an hour. So when a friend told her Northern was hiring summer help, preferably female, she came out here to apply. A month later, when the job came through, she had been accepted into a school to become a licensed practical nurse.

It was hard to choose between the two opportunities but, urged by a friend whose husband works at Northern, she went for an interview. They asked her if she had ever driven a tractor, and she said yes; if she knew how to drive big trucks, and she said she did. And then they told her she could start as soon as she had a physical. That day, Darlene gave up the idea of nursing school.

"When I first came to work out here," she says, "the guys really shut me off, because they thought, you know, 'We're going to get another one.' " She looks around uneasily, but there is no chance of our being overheard, standing as we are in the middle of the yard before the office. "The lady that works out here, who was here when I came, she relies on—oh, I don't know how you say it—ways to get out of work. Like, oh, it's her period time. . . . So I really had a lot to do to overcome that. The first job they put me on was overhaul. They were tearing down these machines. They have to be all completely overhauled every five years at least. These are great big huge machines. The inside of one of them, the intermediates they call them, the opening is as big as a kitchen table. I'd climb right down in there with the grease and every-thing and I'd be doing things and they'd say, 'Take off these bolts.' I'd take off the bolts, you know. I figured that's what I'm here for. Well, after I was there three days, one guy told me that I'd done more in three days than this girl that'd been out here three years had done in three years. Well, that really made me feel good. So far, luckily, they've never given me anything I couldn't handle. There's never been a job that they've said, go do, that I couldn't go do."

At her farm outside St. Joseph the next Saturday, the barnyard is well kept, the modest house neat. A child's swing set stands in the yard, one seat drifting slightly back and forth in the wind.

Darlene meets me at the door and leads me into her kitchen where we can sit and talk. Soon she is telling me that it was not her father who taught her to plow and use heavy machinery, but her husband Thad, after they were married and had started to farm.

"I had four older brothers, and my father was passing this down, that women stayed in the house and did the housework while the boys went to the field. When the boys came home they were tired. You were to have supper on the table for them. They were to eat first, then they went to bed, and if they dropped their clothes where they stood, you picked them up after them, and that was life. Boy, that used to make me mad! If I wouldn't of had a really spunky mother! My father is 6′1″, my mother is 5′2″ or something like that. He didn't push her around, you know. She stood her ground! But still, he expected everything clean and everything cooked and there was never hamburgers for supper, there was a full meal. ... I think he's come quite a ways." She laughs, her eyes meeting mine in annoyed amusement. "I *hope* he has.

"But when I got married, my husband came from kinda the opposite family. It was mostly girls. Most of his sisters were older and they were the ones that had to help on the farm. So when we got married, he really taught me what I knew about farming.... Whenever we started in on the farming, he put me on a tractor and he showed me how. It took a long time, it seemed like, for everything to fall into place, but it did. And so we were really virtually partners, because I'd be out there when he couldn't. The farming, if you've been around it, you know it's not a very profitable business. So as soon as the real heavy season, harvest, was over he'd go to work nights as a welder in a factory around here. He would sleep during most of the day. I would go out and do what he couldn't be doing. So I learned quite a bit about machinery, because if the tractor broke down and I was out there, I had to *do* something about it, you know. Or else I was going to just sit out there." She laughs at the idea of this. "So I had a head jump on any of the girls that worked at Northern."

Darlene's three daughters become noisy presences in the room. (Her fourth is sleeping off a bout of flu in the bedroom.) I feel a little guilty for taking their mother's time when she has so little to spend with them. Cathy, a dark-eyed eight-year-old with brown bangs, would sit quietly listening, I imagine, if she did not have to care for her younger sisters. Cindy, blond, with long hair, smiles sweetly at me. The baby, Carla, is alternately cooperative and fussy. "It's her nap time," Darlene confides. But when I ask if she wants to put Carla to bed, she says no.

To Cathy she says, "Dress her in her boots and go outside and play."

The girls obey, but drag out their leaving to get maximum contact with us. When they have gone out the screen door, Darlene goes on about her job.

"I was called in the superintendent's office and he wanted to know if I would ever accept an operator's job, which is shift work. It's twelve to eight, eight to four, four to twelve. And I said, 'Well, I'm not crazy about it at this time, my kids are a little young. But in another couple of years, you know, and besides that, I don't think I'm ready for anything like that.' I could tell they were down on women for the one they had, so whatever I do out there I gotta do the best I can. Because I'm already gonna get a knock because I'm a woman. And that's life. I'm just not gonna be as good. And if I can be the best I can out there, that's all they can expect of me. Then I'll feel like if I'm called down for something, it isn't going to be because I didn't try hard enough and that's kinda the way I's brought up, 'cause I couldn't ever measure up to what my brothers could be, in my father's eyes, I mean.

"So anywhere ever I started to work, I always wanted to be the best I *could be*."

There is a knocking at the kitchen door, and Cathy, Cindy, and Carla come into the room, bringing the smell of fresh cold air with them, their eyes eager and curious. Carla goes to her mother, who holds her close against her. Cathy and Cindy wander around the table, looking at me.

"Don't you girls want to swing some more?" Darlene asks.

They shake their heads.

"Well, you can stay in here if you'll be quiet."

Darlene looks back up at me, her eyes blank for a moment as she tries to pick up again the story she is telling. Then she finds her train of thought.

"The guys out there—I joke with them, I kid around with them. They never insult me. This woman, they'll come up and they'll undo her overalls. None of them has ever tried that with me. They know better. They can just tell, I guess, or maybe it's because, like this girlfriend's husband out there, I think he told them one time there'd be no pinching *me,* because I'd knock 'em on their butts! And I would. I'd hit 'em, you know, because I'm just not there for that."

I believe she would, watching her square her shoulders, and remembering those four brothers, with whom she must have learned to hold her own.

"Right now they have me working with an evaluation technician," Darlene goes on, "and I kind of have an idea they need another one of those. I'm hoping they have plans for me to go into this. I hope so. It's evaluating the engines themselves, and it's a lot of relief valve work. If anything ever blocks up in the line, the relief valves are supposed to shoot off before the line blows. We get this . . . os-kil-i-o-scope, if I'm saying it right, and we go to the machine and put this technical machine on the unit itself and try . . . well, I think I got some pictures. . . ."

Darlene separates herself from Carla to go in the livingroom to find the pictures, and brings them back. I look at the graphs, the line rising and falling in deeper or shallower curves.

"This machine will read out in different ways what's wrong with the engine. I haven't learned it all but it's really interesting. You can tell whether the rings are worn, just from the vibrations. . . ."

Cathy interrupts her. "Where are the clothes?"

"They're in the washer," Darlene replies.

"I'll put them on the line."

"No, you leave 'em there. Mommy'll get 'em later."

Carla has been whimpering tiredly, and now Darlene takes her up to cradle in her lap.

"It's awful challenging. The evaluation tech can't go in and say, hey, you better tear apart this machine and then be wrong! Which happens. He's wrong at times, who isn't? So this is one thing that does scare me, that there's quite a percentage that I'll be wrong for awhile, if I do go into this."

I am curious how much her taking this job has affected her working here on the farm, where she and Thad have about four hundred acres.

"Well, that's the bad thing," she admits. "There's been several times he's said, 'Now if I had somebody to go get the truck, I wouldn't have to walk today!' You know, stuff like that, and I say, 'Well, if there's a way I could go get your truck, I'd of gone and got your truck, but there was no way.' He's been real good about it. He really has. And the money is a big help.

"This summer when I could I'd come home, load up the kids, and go out there and do what I could, you know, but there's a very short span of time from about five to dark, and there's not much you can do that doesn't have to be done during the day anyway, so.... I've gone out on the tractor in the summer but it hasn't been like it was. We did a lot of custom plowing. Like I said before, farming doesn't pay for itself. So we did custom plowing. You go out and plow for people that want help and you charge them so much an acre.

"We'd go out and plow twenty-four hours a day. He'd plow eight hours, I'd plow eight hours, he'd plow eight hours, and boy, we got the job done! We had to do it to keep our landlords happy. We have three of them, you know, for the land we don't own."

Darlene and Thad have been married nine years now. She grew up north of Clyde, went to school in Clyde, and married the summer after she graduated from high school. At first Thad worked at the grain elevator in Clyde. Then they decided to go into the farming business. Being in Darlene's house with her I feel how strongly she is identified with the land, how much she resembles Jane Snavely and the other farm women in this area. This house and land near St. Joseph was "in the family" and, when an uncle died, Thad and Darlene bought the farm.

St. Joseph is a community of about forty-five families, so small that it does not even support a grocery store. Darlene and her good friend Shirley ran the store in St. Joe's for a short while and then gave it up. The little cluster of houses that is the town is dominated by a majestic Catholic church. Red brick, trimmed with white granite, its twin towers rise four stories high against the sky. A round stained glass window dominates its facade; behind it stretches a cemetery where the gravestones carry some of the oldest names in the area, many of them French. Darlene herself comes of French and German stock. Inside the church, the tabernacle is lofty, ornate, cathedral-like. Darlene and her family are Catholics who come regularly to church; Cathy has already taken her first communion.

The summer after she married, Darlene had her first child.

"I did not believe in birth control," she says. "That was all right for other people but not for me. When I had my first child I was tickled to death, and then we were going to wait about a year and we tried the rhythm method, which did not work. Carrie was totally unexpected! Cathy was born in June of '71 and Carrie was born June of '72, and I told Thad, 'Boy there's gotta be a better way!' I love kids, and it wasn't that I didn't want her or anything, but it was so soon afterwards. I hadn't forgotten labor. I thought, I can't go *through* this right away. I developed an ulcer, in fact, while I was pregnant. I worried that much about it. It was really silly to worry that much. It was on my mind all the time, thinking, Oh, to go through all that again! Can I *stand* it again?"

Carla is squirming on Darlene's lap. Darlene feels her bottom, and calls to Cathy who has gone into the living room. "Cathy, bring some panties and slacks for Carla."

She tells me she uses birth control pills now, that the births of Cindy and Carla were planned.

Cathy brings the clothes, and Darlene tends to Carla, talking to me as she pulls off the child's wet pants. "I wouldn't want to use pills for a long time. I don't know what exactly is the right thing to do on that. We've been thinking about something more permanent but we haven't decided yet, so I don't know."

Cathy and Cindy disappear up the stairway to the second floor.

"A lot of people say, 'Oh, are you going to try for a boy?' " Darlene pulls the clean pants up over Carla's smooth bottom. "No, why should I? I got four healthy kids, nothing wrong with them. Thad was really disappointed with the third one, 'cause everybody said, 'Oh, third one's the charm, you know.' He really knew it was going to be a boy. I was really disappointed in *him* 'cause he was disappointed. He wasn't, at the hospital. But when he started calling my family, my brothers, and they'd say, 'Oh, another girl, another girl' . . . I know that's what did it. . . . Then he got to feeling sorry for himself. But I really got upset with him one day and he snapped out of it. Because, you know, he was moping around. I said, 'There's nothing wrong with her! She's not retarded, she's not sick. You know, count your blessings!' And I really laid into him, and after that he just kind of snapped out of it. Then she grew up to be a Daddy's girl and just wrapped him around her finger and that was the end of that."

From upstairs comes the rhythmic clumping of small bodies bouncing recklessly on a bed. Darlene glances at the ceiling.

"Sometimes I think I'll get rid of a few of them."

She laughs, and then yells at the upstairs. "You girls quit that jumping!"

The noise stops.

"They're practicing cheerleading," Darlene tells me.

"But it's not important to me whether they're girls or boys. I don't care if they don't carry on the name or whatever. Don't make me any difference." Her expression changes abruptly. "If I don't shoot 'em first!"

She peers with mock fury at the stairway where the giggles of Cathy and Cindy can be heard from behind the door.

"You get back upstairs!" Darlene says loudly. There is a burst of delighted laughter and the sound of quick scrambling up the steps.

We speak of her father's domination of the family in which she grew up, and Darlene tells me again that he has changed. "What really woke him up was that his sons grew up with his attitude about women. My oldest brother *really* did. Maybe he could see how ridiculous it was after my brother took it over.

"The attitudes around here generally have changed a lot. But I think there was a lot of guys shocked when I went out to Northern, shocked that they hired me in the first place. In fact, so was I—kind of overwhelmed. You're not usually lucky enough to fall into one of those jobs! There was a lot of guys jealous. I've run into that. Thad and I were in the club one night and one guy said, 'I wish *my* wife worked out at gas city!' You know that's total jealousy. I said, 'Tell her to go up there and fill out an application. I'll put in a good word for her.'" Darlene's voice becomes jovial, reproducing the encounter at the bar. "And then that didn't work, so he goes on, 'Well, I wouldn't let my wife work out there among all them guys; boy I wouldn't let her.' And Thad, he was prepared for it already. He had thought it out before, you know, when I first started working there. He said, 'Well, I can trust my wife out there, can't you trust yours?' Well, then, that stopped the guy dead in his tracks. He didn't know what to say!" She explodes into triumphant laughter.

We talk about her sense of partnership with Thad. But she admits that if he were to die the landlords would not allow her to keep on renting and working the land. She is certain these particular landlords, one of them Thad's aunt, would not hear of a wife taking over her husband's land.

Carla has quieted down now, lying back drowzily against Darlene's arm. A little girl in a rumpled nightgown comes from somewhere beyond the living room, headed for the bathroom door. Her face is pale, puckered in discontent. Darlene watches her. "Are you feeling any better, Carrie?" The child gives a miserable "no" and disappears into the bathroom.

Darlene is distracted for a few minutes with concern for her child, but when Carrie has gone back to the bedroom, we talk about the St. Joseph community, to which Darlene is strongly loyal.

"Yeah, there's people around here that are great, really great. If Thad broke his leg, whatever, couldn't put the wheat in, he'd have no worries because the next day or two days after there'd be fifteen tractors in our field putting our wheat in. They might not have theirs in but they'd do it. And I'll tell you, the people in St. Joe will break their backs to help each other. They'll do it just because they want to. Our neighbors, Larry and Shirley, the ones you met at the club, he got really really sick, almost died, about three years ago or so. When he was in the hospital, people came over, I still got the pictures, it must have been forty tractors, and did all his farm work. He never had to worry. It was a touching thing."

Darlene and I speak of the impact of the Vietnam war on the families in the area. There was a lot of fear, she says, among the older people, that their sons would have to go.

"One of my brothers went. I got an attitude that the ones that were in it, you'll never ever know what they were through. My brother wrote letters back to me that just didn't make any sense at all and just was really. . . . I know he was either drunker than a skunk when he wrote them or something. Big deal, he was going to go out to the war and he was going to fight and everything, and they got into a situation where they were killing women and children and things like that. . . . I don't know what he did up in a plane, but they'd fly night raids, and he didn't know who he was bombing. It was that kinda deal. He's a kindhearted person, and he will not talk about it to this day. He's just really bitter, bitter, bitter. A lot of people come back like that. They got no respect for the flag or anything because of it."

There comes the rumble of a vehicle turning into the yard, and Cindy races downstairs to announce, "Daddy's home!" In the ensuing bustle Darlene and I acknowledge that we have finished our talk for now, and I thank her for taking the time. She grins, telling me it was fine, it didn't matter.

Soon Thaddeus Tate enters the kitchen, come from the field where he has been planting winter wheat. Cindy and Cathy go to stand on either side of him as he sits down at the kitchen table.

"Did you make it through the dance okay the other night?" he asks me.

I assure him I had a good time.

Then I am leaving, saying goodbye to Darlene and each of the girls, going out into the brisk autumn day again, waving as I get into my car.

On my way back toward Route 9, past that towering church building, I remember my first visit to St. Joseph two years ago. Ann and I had driven out from Clyde to look at the church and graveyard. The sky hung heavy and threatening; the air was damp. Inside the church, elaborate statues tinged by the glow from the stained glass windows gazed benignly down at us. Racks of candles stood ready for the flame. The silence filled the room up to the lofty ceiling. Outside, snow had begun to fall. I stood on the porch looking out across mile after mile of farmland, and it seemed I was in the Midi. French names on the plaques on the windows, French names on the gravestones, the church building rising weighty and dignified up out of rich farmland, the snow slanting across the open fields. I might have been in the country-side near Aix-en-Provence.

Now I drive past in the glorious sunset colors of October evening. A third of the sky is aflame. Swirls of deep apricot unfurl across the horizon like bolts of silk and billow upward. Distant trees are etched black against that vivid tint. I think of Darlene Tate, her enthusiasm, her caring. As she talked to me, I had been struck by the goodness of these women, their willingness to be so fully and generously in the center of their lives, demanding the best of themselves.

Pushing Limits

The land lies bare and stubbly now, awaiting the snow, and the countryside around Aurora looks unfamiliar. I drive out

among the stripped fields, make a few turns, and come down a
narrow gravel road, raising a huge cloud of dust behind me. As I
turn in the long driveway, I remember my visit here two weeks
ago, a short getting-acquainted time, in which Yvonne Hauck
strode about the kitchen of the small, white frame house I am
approaching. She wore a T-shirt, bluejeans, and hiking boots, and
paced with a certain dangerous energy about the room, her motions quick and tight. In her pointed face with its high forehead
sat wide, blue, imperious eyes; her blond hair was tied at the neck
and falling down her back. She was a woman of strong opinions,
I discovered quickly, as she spoke to me of the nuclear plant in
Burlington, of the use of pesticides on the surrounding farms, as
she spoke of how difficult it is for the community to accept her as
a farmer in her own right.

She and Bob Hauck are organic farmers. For three years they
have worked this 160 acres of land. It is the realization of a dream
not only for them but for a wide-flung net of friends who planned
in the early seventies to live together on a farm and who support
Bob and Yvonne and their friend Dan Davis (who lives with
them) with, in Yvonne's words, "enthusiasm, money, advice, good
will, and visits."

Yvonne is a self-conscious innovator. Whereas Darlene Tate
acted out of necessity, taking an opportunity when it arose,
Yvonne has tried to create a place for herself where there was
none. Born on a farm only thirty-five miles from this one, and
steeped in the same rural values as Darlene, Yvonne has chosen a
different path, deliberately challenging the prevailing mores in
every situation in which she has found herself in the last ten years.
She is thirty-one years old now, mother of a teenage daughter.
Not only because of her explicit feminist views but because of the
manner in which she and her husband farm their land and raise
their child, Yvonne Hauck is set apart from the women in her
area. They would judge her a "radical," probably, and find it hard
to hear her ideas. But as is sometimes true with radicals, her
words and actions express many of the dilemmas lived out or
dimly perceived in their own lives.

Now as I enter her house again, she greets me in a much more relaxed manner than last time. There is less tension in her body; her blond hair is untied and falls loose down her back. This morning we are not to speak of politics and nuclear dangers but of Yvonne herself, the family she comes from, the life she has lived.

Her husband Bob leans into the kitchen to greet me. He is an angelic looking man with blond soft curly hair, blond beard, and blue eyes in a round face. His shoulders are enormous, and a substantial beer belly pushes out his faded blue overalls. Dan, the third partner in this farm, is gone for the weekend, I am told. I notice that this room and the living room are orderly today, though the lath showing on the unfinished walls still gives a raw, transient quality to the rooms. When I came last time the kitchen and living room were scattered with dishes, clothes, papers, tools, items left because there was no time to pick them up. Bob Hauck had just pulled a piece of machinery from the broken combine, and Yvonne measured it on the kitchen floor as he talked by phone with the dealer, asking about replacement parts. Everything had happened in a great sweaty hurry, and I felt the pressure of that milo heavy in the fields.

Today there is time for Yvonne to tell about her German heritage, and about her father's ambivalent attitude to farming. "He didn't want any of his girls to marry farmers. My younger sister lives in the city. But my older sister and I married farmers. He doesn't understand that he instilled that in us. One of my oldest sister's and my clearest memories is watching tears run down my Dad's face when it's two days till harvest and it's hailing his crop out. My folks have a south sun porch and it's wheat from there to the river ... and that, that is what we learned from him. It wasn't what he *said*. He can't understand that. So on the one hand he feels like we've failed him because we didn't go on and be successful city people, and on the other hand he's really very proud of us because we're doing what he's doing. In a different way."

Yvonne's daughter Michele comes in now. She is a bright, energetic fourteen-year-old who, the last time I saw her, was wearing a cheerleader's sweater and short skirt, spilling over with news of the game at the junior high school. Now she smiles at me and stops to peer into the sack of donuts I have brought. "Take some," I offer. She extracts two and wanders back out into the bright day.

I realize Yvonne and I have been talking only of her father. "What about your mother?"

Yvonne shakes her head. "My mom's been browbeaten for forty-five years. Really, she needed to leave him, and she never could, because of the times, I think. If she were my age now and were living under those circumstances I think she probably would leave, but forty years ago, in the middle of Kansas...! In the first place, it just wasn't thought of, and in the second place, it wasn't that unusual for my Dad to feel the way he did. I mean he felt it to an extreme and he really hates women and that isn't a generalized thing you know, but his attitudes weren't that unusual. He never beat her or anything like that; it was all verbal and mental. Like his making her sign over her social security check to him, because he says she hasn't done anything in the last forty-five years! Well, when I was a kid we had twenty hired hands that worked 'round the clock and my Mom had a meal on the table every four hours through the whole twenty-four hour thing. And then whenever Dad needed help, she did that too!"

As she makes her point, Yvonne turns sideways and looks at me over her shoulder, her eyes wide in a blazing blue, outraged stare. She is a warrior, focused, intent, full of righteous anger.

"Growing up in that situation, seeing what happened to my mother, is what has made both my big sister and me make sure, whether it be fifty cents or ten thousand dollars, that we can say, 'This is *mine.*'"

She tells of how, in her last year in high school, she became pregnant, largely as a way to escape her father's home. "I didn't see any way out from under their control other than getting pregnant and getting married," she says. That was something they couldn't take away from me. It was my statement: I am who I am and there's nothing you can do about it."

Bob was not quite so enthusiastic about marriage, because he wanted to continue his schooling, Yvonne says. "So I convinced him that it was possible to do everything that he wanted to do and everything *I* wanted to do, all at the same time. Which of course it wasn't."

She explodes in a laugh that is both genuinely amused and somewhat bitter.

Once married, with that first rebellion in the past, she put all her effort toward becoming the perfect wife. She worked while Bob went to college, and she made sure Bob had no responsibilities for baby Michele. He himself was working nights. But even during the summer when he wasn't going to school, Yvonne still hired a babysitter rather than ask Bob to care for their child. I wonder if perhaps she did all this out of guilt, but she assures me it was simply what she had been trained to expect of herself.

"That's still the trip my older sister is on. The perfect wife, breadwinner, and childbearer. She can do it all. And somehow or other she *does* manage to do it all, and doesn't seem to resent it. But one day *I* woke up and said, 'Hey, this is a bunch of foolishness!'

"Bob was going to Washburn University in Topeka, working toward a psychology degree. Michele was three or four. It was funny because our next-door neighbor who was, by that time, a very good friend of ours, one day told me that Bob was the envy of every married man on campus because of how I treated him! You know, he actually said in words all the things I was doing. That woke me up to say, Now listen, I'm not living my life so that Bob can be admired! It just kind of came down to me, how far I was stringing myself out, and I think I also started acknowledging my feelings of resentment."

"So what did you do with all that?" I ask.

"Well, I just stopped, and it was real hard on everybody. I said, 'Okay, if you aren't working, I can't afford to pay a babysitter: here's your kid.' And for more than a month I cooked only my own meals, I washed only my own clothes."

I remember that during my first visit to the house, I had seen Bob come in, stand at the sink in his overalls covered with field dust, and wash the leftover dishes. Then he cooked the vegetables for supper while Yvonne tended the meat. Since that night, I had seen no other man in this farm country lift a hand to help with housework, and no woman had told me that her husband shared the household chores with her. I admire Yvonne's resolve as I recall the trauma caused, ten years before, by my own insistence that my husband prepare half the meals.

Yvonne and I note that her domestic rebellion occurred in 1969 or 1970, a time in which the protests of the antiwar and Third World movements had reached their crest, when the first spokeswomen of the new women's liberation movement had begun to speak out. As Yvonne remembers, student activism had erupted at the universities in Manhattan and Lawrence, but at Washburn University in Topeka, there were no ripples as yet. Of her own life, she recalls, "I really pulled the rug out from under all of us, but it was a good thing I did. If I'd have waited two or three more years, Bob and Michele would never have really gotten to know each other. It would have been too late by that time."

The next seven years, she tells me, were a chaotic, difficult time, a checkerboard of starts and stops. She and Bob were sometimes together, sometimes living separate lives. Yvonne fought discrimination at the insurance company where she worked, and after she quit, fought a legal battle to receive unemployment compensation. At her job building trusses for rafters, she suffered the harrassment of male coworkers. She went to carpentry school, then decided to become an electrician, but could not win acceptance into an apprenticeship program. With their daughter, Yvonne and Bob lived in several rural communal situations. They and their friends dreamed of an ideal communal farm, a utopia.

Bob comes into the kitchen to get a sixpack of beer from the refrigerator. "Guess I'll go see what Clint has to say for himself," he says to no one in particular, and goes out the door, his blond curls shining in the sun, Yvonne looking after him absently.

I think about their different characters, as she has described them: she a methodical planner who charts every step before beginning a project, he who trusts to his ingenuity in the moment, picks up a tool, and plunges in. He is volatile, she says, and sometimes vents his frustration by yelling at her, while she never shows anger unless she is dead serious and has thought it out beforehand. These differences make it hard for them to live together sometimes, isolated out here on the farm, so far from friends. Always before, one of them had been working at an outside job, so there was some diversity of interest. Here, they are having to learn to live together twenty-four hours a day, and in the summers when school is out, Michele is always present.

"When I started living with Bob again," Yvonne continues, "it was obvious we both wanted to find a farm. We spent three years working jobs, doing big gardens and that kind of thing, hunting for a place, until we found this place. That was three years ago. I was still trying to become an electrician, and I had to make the choice whether that or being a farmer was more important. Bob and I chose farming because we didn't want to deal with the eight to five and the total lack of control over your life, and neither of us liked to have to do the same things day after day after day. I don't know that we do any less of it here, but we can at least fool ourselves into believing that it's our own choice."

She gets up to put some water on the stove to boil, takes a teapot from the cupboard, and searches for the alfalfa tea. Even in these simple acts, her motions are quick, efficient, and I sense the determination behind this choice she has made. I appreciate the stubborn independence of these farm women, their willingness to tolerate the pressures and uncertainties of their chosen lives. It is a privileged position, in our society, to pursue a business of one's own such as farming, but it carries with it tremendous responsibilities and risks. Yvonne began with more advantage than the other farm women I talked to. Her father had given her a piece of land, and when she found this farm she sold that land back to him, took the money, and applied it to this property. So it was her money, and largely her energy, that established this farm. But it was meant to be a place for many more people than herself and Bob.

"I assumed that everybody was behind me," she says. "It was like there was eight to ten of us that all had this dream. And we had lived with a lot of people around us, in our home, in mutual homes, to the point where we all—or at least everybody *thought* that everybody understood that we wanted a communal farm, but that everybody would have their own piece of it or part of it, especially separate living quarters. And it ended up not working out that way. For a long time, everybody lived in this house. This past year, there was four of us. My friend Betsy was here and she and Dan were living together and they weren't getting along and it ended up with a fairly large confrontation with me and Bob and Dan, as I made it very clear to both Bob and Dan that I felt that, okay, Betsy and Dan were needing to separate, but that did not automatically mean that Betsy was leaving." She sits up very straight and turns sideways again to stare at me, her blue eyes wide and fierce. "They were to know that I was not going to allow them to push her off this farm. She had as much right to remain here as a single person as anybody else. I don't know whether Dan's ever gotten over that or not."

"What did Betsy finally do?" I ask.

"She did end up leaving, but it was her choice to go," Yvonne says. "What it's finally worked out to is just in this last week, Dan's picked out his own sixteen acres. But it's been a real hard struggle . . . and there will be legal papers drawn up. Like Bob and my idea was: okay, start with everybody saying you own this and you own this, and it will evolve into whatever kind of communal situation it evolves into. And if we draw the lines, then we can fuzz the lines however we want to. And Dan's idea was he didn't want to draw any lines to begin with."

I remember Dan from my former visit. During supper, he had discoursed on politics, the gold standard, world events, local news, their friends, the ferocity of badgers, and a number of other subjects. Yvonne now and then threw a remark into the steady stream of talk, as one throws a line and bobber into a rushing creek. Dan had wandered restlessly about the kitchen after supper. He was a young man with beard and thick brown hair, dressed in ragged jeans. He reminded me of some of my husband's friends, back in the mid-sixties, who hung around our place, sometimes lived with us—young men caught in protracted hesitation toward life.

"So there was always this unknown thing," Yvonne goes on, "of when one person decides to do something, never knowing how much slack to give everybody else. It's never been a question of the physical work getting done. Dan's helped us make the land payments and he's put a lot of work into this place. It was just a lot of noncommunication. What has evolved—and this is my own interpretation—was that he was satisfied that we would have the responsibility of the place and he would be involved in it but not really have the final responsibility. And that just became not acceptable to Bob and I. It was like he wanted his hand in every pie but he didn't want to have to deal with the pie when he didn't want to."

Michele comes into the kitchen, her face flushed, her hands full of eggs. "Mom, is it okay if I candle some eggs?" she asks, and Yvonne tells her to go ahead. She disappears into the little back room next to the glassed-in porch.

"Bob never did want to live in a communal situation," Yvonne continues. "That always has made him uncomfortable. Me, I can or not, whatever. I've always got to have my own space and I will kick everybody out of it if that's what needs to happen. And as far as I am concerned, the three of us are still living in a communal situation, because it's definitely not a typical family situation."

Yvonne toys with her cup. I can tell from her strained face, her lowered eyes, that it has been difficult for her to talk about the struggle with Dan. How much disillusionment they must all have felt at the flaws in their bright collective dream. But I sense that Yvonne has not given up or become embittered by her experience, that given the proper conditions she would do it again.

We leave this topic behind, finding it easier to talk about the concrete details of running a farm. In this, Bob and Yvonne are different from their neighbors. They farm many less acres and own none of the giant expensive machines described by Jane Snavely and Madeline Lambert.

"I don't think Bob and I have five thousand dollars in all in machinery because we go pick up what everybody else throws away," Yvonne explains. "We go to farm sales, you know, and come home with other people's junk. We've got a neighbor over here who welds for practically nothing. Our neighbor came over last summer and with a bunch of Coors beer cans, rebuilt the clutch on the tractor. He was over here all afternoon, charged us five dollars. He'll do that for us because we like him and we understand the importance of what he does and will listen to what he has to say. I mean he's incredible, what he knows.

"The only money we owe is the contract on this farm and we try real hard to keep it at that. Sometimes we borrow among our friends. We borrowed a thousand to buy and fix up the combine and we pay it back in beef, milo, you know, what have you, and some cash, and they do that with us. I mean, it's a collective bank in very loose form, I guess.

"We started out hunting for forty to eighty acres, ended up with 160. Our neighbors can't understand what we do with that little ground, but it doesn't matter.... If you have a garden this big," she holds out her arms to indicate a small patch of ground, "you're going to pay more attention to each small square inch, and the bigger you get the less attention you pay to any one particular part. Even 160 acres is too big in that we can't pay attention to all of it at once. My dad's got a thousand acres and he's considered a small farmer, small to middle, I'd say: nobody's a big farmer until they have six or seven thousand acres."

But the most distinguishing aspect of Yvonne's and Bob's farming operation is their avoidance of chemical products. They are organic farmers and belong to Kansas Organic Producers, an organization of likeminded people. I ask Yvonne why they have chosen this method of farming in a region where the overwhelming trend is to chemical fertilizers to produce high yield and insecticides to control pests.

She reaches up to brush back her hair, pauses a moment to think, and then says, "We don't use chemical fertilizers on our farm, I suppose basically because that would make me dependent on somebody else. I mean I believe that the chemicals are bad for you, but I don't like the organic salesmen that come around either. I don't think that you have to put something on the soil to make it healthy. I mean you may need those products to do it faster if you can afford it or if something's wrong with the soil, but nature did not intend to have to bring rock phosphates from Florida to put on Kansas soil to make it healthy. I'd say ninety percent of the people that belong to Kansas Organic Producers can't deal with not putting anything on their soil. They want to buy products because that's the way they have grown up farming, is buying fertilizer.

"The best milo we had this year was on ground that we just let go to weeds for three years. And that's probably the best way to let soil recoup, is to let it do it itself. But on the other hand, we couldn't let the whole farm do that because we had to make something off of it. So we walk this fine line between having to have something out of it and trying to put something back into it."

Yvonne laughs. "Crop rotation is becoming a new discovery of the U.S. Department of Agriculture. It's hilarious to watch them try to deal with the fact that they're going back to the forties type of farming, and calling it their new invention. But they're having to. People have grown corn on soil with chemical fertilizers for so many years that in Missouri this year, they had corn come up that doesn't have any roots, period! It gets up to about six inches and falls over. And they have sprayed pesticides to the point where most of the pests are immune. If you got root worms and you just keep growing corn on it, year after year, you know, you're breeding root worms. When you do the crop rotation you eliminate a lot of weed problems, you eliminate a lot of pesticide problems, a lot of plant diseases."

Their heretical views and lifestyle cause the Haucks to stand out in the surrounding community, but because of the double standard the attitudes encountered by Yvonne are different from those met by Bob. They have not yet paid off their farm, so they are always, as Yvonne puts it, "working on the brink of disaster." But the pressure falls more heavily on Bob.

"Nobody will blame *me* if we don't make a go of this farm," Yvonne explains, "everybody will blame Bob. As far as the community and the world at large, my parents included, are concerned, you know, it will be Bob's failure. It's real hard for him not to put those pressures on himself. Everybody assumes that I do as much manual labor as I do because Bob is too lazy to do it himself, which isn't the case, but it's real hard for him to live with that. It's real hard for him to live with me out here when I demand that I do my share, when I demand that I have my share in the decisions. And I demand that I have my own income separate from his. And he is incredibly supportive, but it's real hard for him to deal with the outside world."

As for herself, she is continually coming up against the established practices of the agencies she and Bob deal with. "The pigs are my project," she tells me, "and the field crops are Bob's projects, that's what he likes to do. But when I go over and buy pig feed and stuff, the manager writes down Bob Hauck, and I have to say 'No,' and we go through this little game of how was it you spell your first name again? and all this little garbage. I do almost all of the business that we do at the Miltonvale elevator. And they keep all the time wanting to know when *Bob's* going to become a member, and all the tickets they write out to Bob Hauck. He almost *never* goes down there."

Yvonne stares at me, her eyes unblinking, her shoulders tight in frustration; and I wonder if the men at the grain elevators enjoy baiting her or if they behave as they do simply out of habit.

"Most of the time, though, it's the women I have the most trouble dealing with," she admits. "It's very easy for me to intimidate the men. I mean they're so unused to it that they really back off. But I have a really hard time dealing with the women. Well, it's like my neighbor down here. For the first time in the three years I've known her, this year she said, 'I don't know if my wheat's gonna come up,' and it's like she didn't mean to say it and she was embarrassed by having said it, and I'm sure felt that she stabbed her husband in the back by saying it. But what she was acknowledging to herself, when she wasn't putting up the front, was that it was her that had gone out and planted all the wheat. Because everyone was so hurried this year, they were doing things on top of each other. It just happened to be her job that she drilled the wheat. And she had done it day after day after day, unstopping, so that just in the course of the conversation, she called it 'my' wheat. But she puts in as many hours over the year as he does and it's always 'his' cattle."

Yvonne participated in a women's consciousness raising group when she lived near the University in Manhattan. Now she misses the company of women who are actively questioning their lifestyles. The isolation of farm life is sometimes hard for her to bear. She is not interested in the Homemakers Extension units to which Jane Snavely and many other women belong; she would like to join the Young Farmers Organization, but only its wives auxiliary is open to women.

She is continually chaffing under such inequities, and yet she recognizes the ambivalence in her character. In a letter to a friend in California she had written, " . . . my ego is too abrasive to fit into accepted practice and my self-confidence not high enough to ignore it," a self-assessment inevitably laced with pain.

She gets up to pour me some tea, and her body seems to crackle with outraged energy as she tells me about a friend of hers down the road. "She's incredible in what she does. She works all week at a job in town; she does all the cooking, all the cleaning, all the taking care of the household; she does more than half the chores; she is a mechanic, a carpenter, a farmer . . . and she lives with this idiot who thinks that everything she does, if she does it well, wasn't worth doing in the first place. Who's raising his son to treat his mother exactly the way he treats her. And it's just . . . that's the accepted way of life for her. She doesn't understand that she doesn't have to take that!

"Bob can hardly stand to be around the man. He comes home and says, 'To have to build up your ego by making believe that what your wife does is totally worthless is just . . . what a way to live!' And I can't believe that deep down she doesn't hate him."

Bob himself appears, as if summoned, at the door, and comes in to put some meat in the oven to bake. Yvonne turns away from me to ask him about their two friends, Mike and Micki, who are to arrive later in the afternoon. They talk, Bob working at the stove, Yvonne getting up to stand near him. Seeing the two of them this way, I remember what she has told me about his need for security, his desire to relax into the routine of daily life, while she is always pressing to right some imbalance between them, to open some new dimension of their relationship. He is steady foundation for her.

But I am being observed. I turn to meet the gaze of dark-lashed eyes below definite brows. Michele, who finished her candling some time ago, has been sitting at the table observing me.

Now that her mother has left the table, we regard each other with equal interest for a time.

"Will you take me out and show me the farm?"

She shrugs. "Sure."

We get up and say goodbye to Yvonne and Bob, and then are out in the sunshine, ambling down a grassy slope past the parked combine. A striped cat follows us for a few yards, and Michele tells me this is her favorite of all the farm cats.

She is a young woman with lightly freckled skin and curly brown hair in a short halo around her head. She responds to me with more than usual composure for a fourteen-year-old, product perhaps of her contact with many adults in various communal living situations.

"Do you like living on a farm?" I ask.

She kicks at the lumpy ground. "It's all right at times. I like the city a lot." Glancing up at me with a half-defiant, half-embarrassed smile: "I don't like to work hard."

Her chores include feeding the chickens and gathering the eggs, cooking one meal during the weekend and washing dishes every third day. Sometimes the daily chores are neglected in favor of her activities at Miltonvale Junior High, where she is a cheerleader, plays on the volleyball team, and is president of Y-Teens. When she graduates, she will go to college, she says, to become a psychologist, as her dad almost did. Her admiration for Bob is obvious.

As we talk, the phrase "if we lose the farm ... " comes up more than once. "The farm is Mom and Dad's dream," Michele says, "and if we lose it I don't know what would happen. I don't know if there'd be a chance to start all over again." I feel her worry.

She counts herself lucky to have Yvonne and Bob as her parents, she says, because she can tell them almost anything that's going on, and they will try to understand. Her dad finds it hard to comprehend, however, why she gives her time and energy to activities at school rather than staying home to work on the farm. She tells me it's simply because she likes being with people. Out here, especially as she has no brothers or sisters, she feels isolated; she spends her time watching TV and indulging the fantasy that life mirrors television, which she knows not to be true.

"Mom and I have talked about sex," she says. We sit now in the long dry grass with its heady odor. Michele tells me Yvonne has explained pills and the diaphragm to her and told her that, if she should ever feel she wants to begin a sexual relationship, Yvonne will take her to a doctor to get birth control. I note how extraordinary this attitude would seem to most of the women I have talked with, remembering Virginia Racette's hope that mothers will talk with their daughters but they won't "hand 'em the pill."

Michele tells me she is scared of sex right now. Sometimes she necks with boys but when the possibility of "going ahead with sex" comes up she gets "very nervous." It is the unknown she fears.

"It's another change of life that I really don't know what it's gonna be like." This she says, head down, playing with the grass between her feet. That phrase, "another change of life," sounds oddly stilted and grownup, yet I am touched by the vulnerability she admits to as she uses it, and I experience an instant's remembrance of what it had been like *not to know*.

Michele seems as apprehensive as my friends and I were when we were fourteen, even though she has been given some information, while we had exchanged misinformation in fields such as this, on the banks of creeks, behind our families' garages.

We speak of her friends at school. Soberly she explains to me that friendships and flirtations are stormy, unpredictable, "because we're changing so much." And I wonder how soon they will act on their sexual desires. Surely it will be much earlier than the young women of my generation did, for this is a much different time in which Michele is coming to awareness of sexuality.

Because her mother is a feminist, Michele has a well-developed view of women's strength and potential. She says she wants to get an education, does not want to get married as young as her mother did; and she believes the world is a more accepting place for women now than when her mother was fighting the sexist policies at the insurance company or trying to become an electrician's apprentice. "But there's always gonna be the nerds that are male chauvinist," she adds. At school the discussions on women's liberation invariably become arguments between the boys and the girls. Michele talks about a recent conflict around the Pep Club, in which the girls are required to participate. The newest president of the club felt this was discriminatory and insisted that boys also participate in Pep Club. There followed a battle in which the football coach lined up against the president, a fairly elaborate quarrel, as Michele describes it, which ended with the integration of the boys into Pep Club. A victory. But I am made uneasy by Michele's belief that her life as a woman will be less difficult than her mother's, and even more uneasy by her remark that the boys at school "are pretty good at lettin' us try to be equal to them."

We sit in the grass together, hearing the wind sigh.

"I wish I wasn't feeling so left out." Michele prods the earth with her toe, something stubborn and bruised in her expression. "A lot of times I feel left out of everything else. I wish I could be more a part of the farm. It's going to be an important thing in my life, I can tell already. And I feel left out at school, because my point of view seems a lot different from most of the kids. I feel that people have a free choice about how they live. A lot of people feel like they need to tell everyone what to do.

"Here, I'm an outsider, really, to the farm. I'm not really into going out and plowing the field, other things like that. I mean, I help my Dad drill the wheat, but that's all I do in the field. Some of the girls, by now, are already out there on the tractor."

While I feel Michele's alienation, still I have to point out the contradiction in her stating she does not like farm work and yet saying she wants to be more a part of the farm.

Looking wistful, she admits her confusion.

"Sometimes I want to be more in on things here, and sometimes I just want to run away."

She will most probably live in a city when she grows up, she says. As for now, she would never try to get her parents to move into town.

"I want them to have their dream. I wouldn't want them, just because I don't want to live on a farm, to just close their dream and move into town or something like that, 'cause that wouldn't make them happy. I want for them whatever they want for themselves."

I believe this. I sense that Michele takes care of Bob and Yvonne in some ways, almost as if in this instance they were her children, she the old woman one step outside of life, spreading a canopy of concern over these two people so engaged in their struggle.

We sit in silence for a time, Michele staring at her feet, and then she turns to look full at me, and she smiles, her eyes serious, her mouth very young.

When we hike back up the hill to the house, Michele picks up the cat, talks to it, cradles it, coquettish, almost but not quite certain of her beauty, poised precariously amid the changes in her body, her awareness, her possibilities. She brings her furry, reassuring friend with us around the house, where we find Yvonne stretched out on the hood of a car, her back resting on the windshield, reading her copy of *Mother Earth News* and smoking cigarettes.

When I come out of the house later, alone, I stop in the doorway and see the family posed together in the fading light: Michele perched beside Yvonne on the car hood, Bob standing next to them, his back bent, his head resting on Yvonne's shoulder.

Yvonne is at the center, Bob's great muscular body wholly focused upon her, Michele sitting close aginst her on the other side. Yvonne's eyes are hidden by dark glasses; I cannot tell what she feels. We have spoken of conflict, of striving, of uncertainty, never of love.

I step back inside the house. All noises cease, and I feel for the first time here a sense of peace.

Evening grows full and vibrant with the arrival of friends, Mike and Micki and their baby, Katie. Micki has long red hair pulled up into a bun. Katie is a contented baby with carrot-hued wisps brightening her head, who smiles at all of us and responds happily to Michele's ministrations. Mike is a quiet, friendly young man. We play "pitch" at the kitchen table while Bob gets up frequently to tend to the dinner. I play this new card game timidly, and Yvonne at one point advises me, "Your first time you might as well just be bold!" Then we clear the cards off the table to make way for dinner. Bob dishes up the pork roast, baked sweet potatoes, fresh kernel corn, and rice that he has cooked. This roast comes from the pig whose pen I saw on my walk with Michele. The talk turns to butchering, and Yvonne tells me she has a piece of writing she has been working on for a long time. It is an article on how to butcher small animals, a step-by-step guide including all the details left out of most descriptions. She keeps revising it because each time they butcher a hog she realizes she could have described some step better or could have said something a little differently, and she goes back and changes the piece again. I ask to see a copy, and once she realizes I am genuinely interested, she goes to get one for me.

When I prepare to leave, Michele looks up from playing with baby Katie on the living room floor, to protest my going so early. Bob and Yvonne give me precise instructions on how to get back to town in the darkness. Mike and Micki wish me luck on my project and luck getting back to Concordia, Mike admitting he gets lost almost every time he comes out here. Finally I tell them goodbye.

Somehow I know I will encounter no problems finding my

way. I have learned to navigate, now, as the farmers do, by the
points of the compass and distance—one mile north, six miles east.
Once back in Concordia, I sit down to look at "Butchering Small
Animals." The idea of killing and cutting up a pig creates reac-
tions in me ranging from distaste to horror. But soon the text
draws me in. Early on, Yvonne states:

> My belief has always been that if you aren't willing, given the right
> circumstances and opportunity, to kill and butcher your own meat then
> you should be a vegetarian or be resigned to being a hypocrite. But then
> that's a rather puritanical attitude, I realize. When butchering, however,
> you do take on a responsibility to do your best to see that it is done as
> cleanly and swiftly as possible. It's one thing to be willing to butcher your
> own meat and quite another to mess around and let the animal suffer.

There follows a painstakingly detailed account of the preparations for the act of butchering, and then a step-by-step description
of the actions that transform a living pig into pieces of meat in a
freezer.

In the list of equipment, Yvonne includes "people."

> At times we've had 7 or 8 people around at butchering time, watching,
> participating in one phase or another or just hanging around to help
> clean up or to help cook the liver and onions that always comes at the
> end of butchering day at our place. I should mention, however, that too
> many people with knives not only slows the process, but also increases
> the band-aid consumption.

From killing the animal through hanging, bleeding, scalding
and scraping, cutting off the head, skinning, gutting, and sawing
in half, each smallest consideration is meticulously attended to in
Yvonne's article. Her intent is that the process be performed with
the utmost accuracy and economy of motion. The account is so
readable that I am led through it to the end with surprisingly little
revulsion at the subject matter. The piece rings with her intelligence. I wonder where will she find herself three, five, ten years
from now.

I remember when I stayed overnight in her house after my
first visit, one of the few times I slept at the home of someone I

interviewed. I came downstairs to the living room to find Yvonne wrapped loosely in a robe, her blond hair down over her shoulders. She looked at once rested and tense, blue eyes challenging even in this early morning. She sat with her legs curled under her, drinking coffee, smoking cigarettes, watching the news on the color TV with one eye while she talked with me. Our conversation was about drug use, and she told me why she had never taken LSD.

"Huh-uh, I can't imagine it! Like, I do that to myself all the time anyway. I view life from the edge. Why push it!"

Yes, why push it, and yet her whole endeavor is to attack the boundaries, push out the limits that define her possibilities. She would be satisfied nowhere but living on the edge.

I sat with Jane Snavely in the cab of the tractor, she with the worn pointed toe of her cowboy boot propped against its side, and she was quiet for a time, letting me imagine what it would be like to drive this monster out over the land, air conditioner purring, motor roaring, enormous tires revolving under me. The wind blew against the greentinted windshield; through it I could see the Snavely's house and the corral near it where the horses walked and flicked their tails. The sky was bright and wide, with a few small clouds racing far out near the horizon. Jane's quietness seemed drawn from the flat earth extending for miles around us. I remembered having carried this same stillness inside me, in my life, and thought back to when that might have been, remembering a tractor, earth being turned over in long rows, the smell and feel of it. I recalled my family's yearly ritual of providing for ourselves.

Each spring we hired a man to come with his tractor and plow the lot behind our house. Then with hoes and rakes we broke up the clods and sifted and spread the earth. This labor continued for long hours into the spring twilight and then into darkness, the smell of lilac sweet in our nostrils as we straightened to rest, the warm air soft as water on our skins. On those evenings my father did not change his clothes when he came home from work. He only took off his white carpenter's overalls under which he wore workpants, leaving on his big clumsy shoes. After dinner we went out back, and he told us that tonight we would plant tomatoes and corn, or potatoes that he would cut in chunks, each with a little pale protruding eye; or green beans; or we would set out the delicate strawberry plants. He turned on the faucet behind the garage, and I carried bucket after bucket of water out to the rows, treading carefully on the earth in my bare feet, stopping to pour, to inhale the fresh musky odor of earth, to admire the infant plants that even now had risen in some rows, fragile and pale green. We hardly spoke to each other as we worked, my father haloed in the odor of his perspiration, moving at the steady quick pace of one who has known all his life how to labor.

When the plants had matured, my father and I hoed the weeds, moving down the rows under a sun that lay with insistent weight on our shoulders. It was hard and sweaty, dirty work, my ankles and hands and knees caked soon with earth, but I loved the exertion, loved being near the plants.

Throughout the summer months we ate food from this back lot, and my mother canned the excess. Here, in the stifling hot kitchen, I too worked amid the great pots of boiling water, the pan in which the chunks of wax melted into clear liquid, the pots of tomatoes bubbling, or corn, or green beans, or rhubarb, or grapes from the vines on our garage. My mother, I remember, wore a housedress with cap sleeves and buttons down the front. Her freckled arms were bare, her forehead below red wavy hair shone with sweat; tracks of moisture snaked down over her temples. In a quiet voice she directed my sister and me, making sure we understood what we were doing, that we would not hurt ourselves.

But I liked the outside work better. Often I watered or hoed alone, feeling good in my body, accepting with all my senses the dirt and plants, happy to be solitary. I became very still inside myself. Sometimes, when there was no work to do, I simply came and sat where the grass gave way to bare earth, to think my thoughts. Here among these farm women I recognized a similar need. With Jane Snavely especially I felt the steady, slow pace of this life tied to the seasons. I found I understood these women's existence, centered around work, consciously chosen no matter the risks.

Here in the heartland there is also the dark underside to women's lives. I think of a woman, still quite young, mother of several children, who lives in a certain small prairie town. She is known by all in the surrounding countryside because ten years ago, when she lived on a farm far from town, she pointed a shotgun at her husband's stomach and pulled the trigger. He drank, he beat her regularly. Now she works to support her children, living under the shadow of his lingering painful death. The women at the County Clerk's office, where I went to read the record of the trial, said "he deserved it" and they wanted to protect her, now, in her new life. "You won't use her name, will you?" they said. "She's suffered enough."

Now and then there are the news items, cryptic, flat, that arouse a hundred speculations like a flock of birds taking flight. Out of what frustration, what despair and isolation was this deed done? What particular details of kitchen, bedroom, barnyard intersected to push this woman to where she was found " . . . hanging by the neck from a bridge northeast of here." The Undersheriff ruled it an apparent suicide. She was a "twenty-year-old housewife." Her body was found by her husband and mother after her husband realized she was missing. "M. notified his mother-in-law, who drove to _____. The two began a search and spotted Mrs. M.'s car on a county road two miles northeast of _____. They walked to a nearby bridge and discovered her body."

So the soil is sometimes moistened with blood, the sacrifice not always restricted to the bodies of animals. The wind roaring across the prairie sings of a bitter side to life, where sometimes a woman must act to protect herself, or she falls out of harmony with her existence, finds that she cannot continue, and chooses a swift end. These are the few, the women whom the others read about and mourn and wish there had been a way, some way, to help. Their tragedies are like holes poked in the surface of this life, opening momentarily into a starker realm, then covered over again in the endless repetition of farm existence.

The life itself is tightly woven, rich in the interrelations of human and animal and vegetable existence, close to the slow throb of the earth's pulse.

Jane Snavely, Madeline Lambert, and Virginia Racette share common concerns and preoccupations, live in the manner usual for this area. Probably only Virginia would have stood up to the man in the VFW hall, summoning all her power and the authority of her years in Clyde to meet his attack. Darlene Tate also ventured out of her role, yet I remember her as vividly in her farmhouse kitchen with her daughters as at Northern Natural Gas wearing hard hat and jeans. Yvonne Hauck lives in some ways a unique existence, finds herself isolated and is sometimes at odds with her environment.

These farm women together create the standard by which the other lives in this book will be measured, for in their closeness to the soil they are the women who live the most essentially midwestern lives. They are "conservative" in the best sense. They live in houses handed down through the generations; they own machinery in common with family members. Yvonne goes to barn sales to find used equipment instead of buying new, sales at which even the smallest items are bought to be recycled back into use on a neighboring farm. Human energy is conserved too, as neighbors sometimes work together on big jobs, help each other when someone is sick or injured. For the most part, the women fully accept their place in this scheme; yet there are the limiting expectations still: that they will marry early, that their education stops with high school. Some of them struggle to change, and to keep their equilibrium amid the changes going on around them. They want to be recognized for their labor and to reap its rewards, and they are becoming more sophisticated and more active in their own behalf.

But the dominant reality in the lives of these women, no matter their particular circumstances, is the turning of the great wheel of the seasons. Here among these farm women, I remembered with gratitude that even in my family's small measure, we lived by the earth's rhythms, understood the subtle movements of nature in which a seed opens in the earth, a plant breaks its surface, roots reach down. I felt again the peace at the center of such a life, the silence that surrounds it. I remembered in the winter the rows of stubble poking up through the snow in the back lot. We glanced wistfully, speculatively, at the ground, seeing a brown rabbit statue-still near the fence, noting the tiny tracks of fieldmice in the white covering. Then my father would plan the garden once again, each time a new design. And with the first wafting of lilac scent on the spring air, he called the man with the tractor and went to buy the seed.

Bed in Earl and Amanda Erickson's farmhouse

Jane Snavely with her two-year-old

Darlene Tate at work at Northern Natural Gas

Darlene Tate at home, with daughters Cindy, Carla, and Cathy

Yvonne Hauck

Michele Hauck

In the Towns

A Mountain of Milo

One of my aunts lived with her husband in a tiny town on the
Ohio River, where he ran an automobile dealership. Above his
showroom was their large, dark apartment, in which everything
was ponderous and stuffed: the furniture, the heavy glassware, my
aunt herself, who actually wore a corset laced tight under her
beige or rose Sunday dresses. The corset prevented her from bending, so that she sat as straight and taut as a sausage; and when she
napped in her chair after dinner, the upper part of her body
seemed to spill over the top of the rigid tube that was her corset-
ted midsection. I would stare at her and breathe carefully, testing
the expansion of my own ribcage, imagining what it must be like
to be strapped in so tightly, and terribly glad I wasn't. The im-
pression I formed of her life was one of idleness interrupted only
by trips to the beauty parlor to have her hair waved and the
preparation of the heavy meals that caused everyone to doze off
soon after eating.

In Clyde I sometimes remembered this aunt and the apparent
leisure she enjoyed. As I grew to know the town women more, I
realized how partial my child's vision of her had been, restricted
as it was to weekends and holidays. But it became clear to me that
town women do live very differently from women on the farms.
They may labor as steadily, but their fates are not tied directly to
the land, are less controlled by crops and weather. Jane Snavely
said it: "These guys in town got a regular paycheck coming in, the
wife knows just how much she's got to spend every month, you

know, and you can set up a budget. It don't make any difference whether it rains or whether it doesn't, whether it hails or the wind blows or whatever." Certainly this allows for more security. Here, because people engage in different occupations, there is some variety of lifestyles. Clyde has a library and a historical society, a grade school and a high school, and a retirement home. On the main street are the remodeled Clyde Hotel, Sandy's Cafe, the pool hall, a Ford service center, a hardware store, a filling station.

I walked here in the early morning, before the dawn burst in the sky, on streets where bricks gleam in the circles of light from the streetlamps. In the yards, the trees stand generous, old, their trunks hidden in pools of dense shadow. This town is much quieter than Concordia. I remember that, when we were here before, with each day another layer of city-induced tension dropped from me and I relaxed to a deeper level in myself. Here on the main street, I stand before the house where the L'Ecuyers lived and raised their children, where Amanda and Marie grew up. Looking at its strict red brick facade, its porch set almost on the ground, I imagine the elder L'Ecuyer leaning back in a rocker on this porch, playing his violin. Inside, the sisters and brothers gather about the piano in the parlor, their faces flushed with the pleasure of their singing. Amanda and Marie lived carefree lives during those early years. Daughters of a prosperous merchant, they were free to give themselves to amusements and sports and the music that all members of the family played and enjoyed. Sometimes the children sang in French, simple children's ditties taught them by their mother.

When this town was founded, the French language was heard often on its streets. Giroux and Lavalle opened the first hardware store here. Juneau sold butter, eggs, and poultry. The Reverend Mollier arrived on his way to St. Joseph, where he earned a reputation as the "pioneer priest of Northwestern Kansas." But in Clyde, as in the majority of new towns on the prairie, men with Anglo-Saxon names were the city fathers. The Swedish farmers, among the first homesteaders in the area, are not named or even mentioned in histories of the founding of the town. The contribution of women is generally overlooked also, though there is brief notice given to the first delegated body of women ever assembled in Cloud County. This was the Convention of the Women's Christian Temperance Union, which met in 1885 to establish a county organization. Temperance has always been a matter of great concern in Kansas. Even now one cannot buy a mixed drink in a bar, and liquor stores are strictly regulated, allowed to advertise only with one small sign of prescribed dimensions.

Some of the families in and around Clyde have been here for generations, the great-grandparents having claimed the land, fenced and developed it, or having begun the businesses in the town. Newcomers in such communities often remain outsiders no matter how long they may stay. I met Laura Vytlacil at the funeral home, where she is the assistant funeral director. In Clyde, a name like Vytlacil is recognized as Czech, and its owner assumed to have come from the area up around the tiny town of Cuba, some twenty miles north, as did Laura and her husband. Even though she is a relative newcomer to Clyde, her job involves her in a particularly poignant way with her neighbors. She is on call day and night, and spends many hours at the mortuary when a body is being viewed.

Today we are sitting in the living room of Laura's house a few blocks away from the funeral parlor, a room in which the walls are lined with shelves of glassware. I can see into the dining room where there are many painted figurines of chickens, one tall proud rooster in bright colors. Photographs of Laura's three sons and one daughter stand on the sideboard. She herself is a woman of impressive dimensions, a large, solid, straightforward person who seems to dwarf any chair she sits in. Now, leaning back in her chair, she points to the glistening contents of the shelves of the cabinet behind us, where stand rows of ornamental pitchers, fluted and delicate, oldfashioned painted cream pitchers, large water pitchers, tiny pitchers of ceramic and glass.

"That's my hobby," she explains. "Now I bought only one or two of those, the rest have all been given to me. The green glass there on the third shelf—no, I take that back—this handpainted pitcher here, this was the starting. I received that blue frosted white set there for a wedding present. The sugar, creamer, and butter dish are Bohemian ribbon glass. They were my son Norman's most expensive purchase. And that pitcher with the four tumblers, that was given to me by my landlady. She was an interesting lady. She was Czech, but she went to Chicago and taught French and music. When she was still a young lady, she had her tonsils removed and she lost her singing voice. So when she was seventy-two she was determined that she was going to sing again, and she did! She took lessons and cultivated her voice back by the time she was seventy-five, and she gave a concert in Chicago then, in one of the community halls. She was quite remarkable about that!"

"You're Czech too," I say. "And you were born somewhere up around Cuba?"

"I was born and raised in Narka, that's about twelve miles farther north. And Wesley, my husband, was born and raised northwest of Belleville. My maiden name was Chaloupka. Now I didn't learn the language, but Wesley did. You see, my father farmed a lot of land so of course he had to have outside help. . . . When you hired outside help, you had them for dinner and supper too, and so there is that mingling with the family and you had to speak American so they'd understand you weren't talking about them."

After she and Wesley were married, she tells me, they moved to Norway, Kansas, a little town southwest of Cuba.

"Now I'm Czech and in Norway they're Swedish and Norwegian. I lived with them there for four years and basically we do things alike—except, of course, Czechs use garlic and caraway seeds and the Norwegians and Swedes use onions and raisins and cardomon seed, you know, just little incidentals like that."

I tell Laura about my recent visit to the town of Cuba. I had gone to get permission to use the photograph I had taken at the barn sale two years ago. When I showed it to Uncle Earl he said the women in it were all from Cuba, and offered to go with me up there to find them. Cuba is about as far from Clyde as Clyde is from Concordia. It is a town of approximately three hundred people, a dusty main street with a row of storefronts: grocery, feed store, beauty parlor, cafe, meeting hall. On the plate glass of the grocery window Czech words are lettered. The meeting hall bears the legend VITAME VAS ("You Are Welcome") above its door. But there was one rather astounding feature of the town. At the turning of the main street stood a mountian of milo. Earl told me the grain elevator was full, so they had had to pile the excess here in the street. This red-gray mountain rose higher than the buildings and fell on every side in a soft uniform curve down to the ground. In its twilight indistinctness, with its subtle coloring, it looked like a mountain in a Georgia O'Keefe painting of New Mexico. Here, next to the battered one-story buildings, the parked pickups and big old cars, this red hill rose mysterious and pure, elegant, monumental.

Earl had not seemed to see anything extraordinary about it, pausing only to give his brief explanation of its presence before he led me into the feed store to inquire about the women in the photo. The feed store owner knew them all, and reeled off names: Huncovsky, Pihl, Lesovsky, Piroutek, and several Anglo names. He gave us directions to two homes a few blocks away, and Earl waited in the car while I talked with the women in their neat living rooms decorated here and there with a wooden figurine, a bright doll, or miniature chair painted with stylized flowers and vines that spoke of the old country. The women in the photograph comprised a chapter of the Eastern Star, one woman told me, and had been serving at the farm sale to make money for their group. I looked up from the square, thin-mouthed face in the photograph to this flesh and blood original, her eyes guarded behind her glasses. She agreed to show the photograph to the other members of the Eastern Star to get their approval.

Earl and I were conspicuous, then, eating our ice cream in the cafe. The town doctor, who had spent fifty years ministering to Cuba residents, came over to talk to us, and ushered us outside into the twilight again where I looked up to discover, yes, I had *not* imagined that giant presence at the end of the block. There it rose, looming over us, still and seemingly ancient as a pyramid.

Now, in Laura's home here in Clyde, we talk about the mortuary where she works. Does she like her job? I ask.

"Yes I do, really. To me it's not morbid. It's a clean, quiet job."

She tells me how she began this work. When she and her husband moved to town some years ago, she was restless, for she was used to holding a job and did not like staying home. "I don't belong to any clubs or organizations and I don't go visit people unless they call me, you know, and I was about to crawl the walls here. Then some friends of ours were killed in an airplane crash and their children asked me to be in their home to greet people. When I went to the funeral, our funeral director from Belleville was there and I've known him for years and years—it just seemed so good to see somebody I knew! And so I told him that I was footloose, I was looking for a job, and he told me they were trying to buy the business here and ... I thought it would just be a phone sitter job, but when it all came down to the nitty gritty, why he asked me to be what they call assistant funeral director."

Soon she grew accustomed to the job, and has liked doing it ever since. "It's not depressing either, unless.... There's been times when we've had three bodies in there at the same time and when you're in there for a week and you don't see anything but just sadness, why then it does kind of get to you. But we average probably one funeral a week, and so it gives us time to revive from one funeral until we have the next."

We have been talking about her job long enough, it seems, for now we change the subject and I ask Laura how she made her way from Narka down to Clyde. "I was a farmer's wife for several years before we moved to Norway, because Wesley farmed and taught school before he finished getting his degree. So we were farmers and we hated to leave the farm so badly because our two younger boys enjoyed animals so much. But we didn't own the land, and at that time owners were hunting renters who had big, big machinery, you know, and of course our machinery was just common. We couldn't get together enough money to buy a farm either. We just couldn't find another piece of land to farm so we just moved to town, and everything we have done in our lifetime has worked out for the better."

She shifts in her chair, resting her forearms on her plump middle, nodding slightly in confirmation.

"Yes, because when we lived on the farm, out by Narka, there wasn't anything for the boys to do except haul bales, and the farmers out there made their bales so heavy that the boys couldn't hardly handle them. So then when we went to Norway, of course the boys did go help the farmers there, and they still had their lawnmowing jobs too. And then when we moved down here to Clyde, they had just all kinds of work to do. If I'd have had eight boys, I could have kept them all busy."

Only one of these sons lives still in Cloud County. The oldest is a captain in the air force; the second, who served eight years in the army, now attends college. The third son, who shares his mother's interest in antiques, lives in Concordia. Speaking of her children, Laura tells me she and Wesley encouraged them to learn and seek new experience.

"We have never had enough money to have a vacation, but any rainy day that Wesley couldn't work in the field, we would take off and go someplace that was within a drive of a couple, three hours, and visit there and then be home by bedtime. When we lived in Narka, we usually went to Lincoln, Nebraska, and there's so many things up there for kids to see, at the college. They always wanted to go to the museum there, and Wesley took them. I never went 'cause I wasn't interested in that sort of thing, so they left me to roam around the stores. But Wesley would take the kids and show them all these things and we would go to Salina, and we would do that just as a day trip rather than one long vacation. And so they were acquainted with these extra things that a lot of kids don't get to see. We'd leave early in the morning and be home by bedtime and they'd still see things that interested them."

When the children were small, her husband helped care for them and loved to be with them, Laura says. It is clear as she speaks of him that their own caring about each other has been enriched by this nurturing they did together. I can feel her affection for him as she tells me about his years of teaching school.

"He enjoyed especially the first four grades. That was his preference to teach. He had a couple of years of eighth grade and he just about tore his hair out. But the first four grades are so eager to work and please the teacher.

"We were real strict with our own kids," she comments. "We always told them that was their penalty of being born to old parents because Wesley and I was 28 and 29 years old before we got our first one. We just kind of more or less raised our kids like we were raised. In the days of the short skirts for the girls, you know, I didn't let Susan go with her skirts more than two maybe three inches above her knee. Because she was longlegged, she didn't look good in short skirts. And the girls down at school told her that she really must've had an old-fashioned Mama!"

This daughter, who is now nineteen years old, is a corporal in the air force, stationed in Guam. When she was younger, Laura had wanted to ensure that Susan be more informed than she had been about the life changes she would experience as a young woman. Laura's own grandmother and mother had never told her about such things. But when Susan came near to puberty, Laura found it difficult to know how to talk about these matters with her.

"She was getting twelve years old and was filling out physically, and she was having backaches and I knew that her time was coming pretty quick, but I couldn't quite figure out how I was going to explain it to her. She was in the sixth grade then, and the county health nurse came down and talked to all the girls. She took all the sixth grade girls into one room and she talked to them and showed them pictures, you know, and it was very, very good. I was real pleased because Susan got it the straight way. Not like I got it. I didn't have any idea of anything to happen to me. And now with television and all, the girls can't get by it. Susan knew beforehand what was happening, and she was all prepared. We got all of her things that she was going to need and she was all prepared, and then it was another year and a half or so before she really needed it. She just was so impatient!"

"How did she decide to join the air force?" I ask.

"She had talked about it for two years before she graduated from high school—about going into the military. At first, she was thinking national guard. It will be three years this Christmas that she and Norman went to Georgia. Both Martin and Stephen was stationed down there so the four kids were together, their first Christmas for a long time, and so they talked it over. They all of them told her they didn't want her in the national guard, and Martin didn't want her in the army, and the air force offers girls a lot of opportunities and education."

We go to the dining room where she shows me the photograph of a fresh-faced young woman.

"While she was in high school, she was busy. She worked two days at the newspaper office and four or five days at Sandy's Cafe. She was constantly busy, but that wasn't what she wanted to live her life for."

Laura points out that, in order to live differently from the young women with whom she had graduated from high school, Susan had to leave Clyde.

Laura remains in close communication with all her children; she obviously approves of them and likes them. Susan, she tells me, had met a young man in training and accepted an engagement ring from him, but then had second thoughts and gave it back. "She said she had too many things she wanted to do before she took on a husband," Laura adds, and I see that she is proud of her daughter for this decision.

In partial explanation for why three of her children have left the area to adventure in the world, she says that all her children were great readers when they were growing up. She and Wesley always had books around the house. She shows me her latest book purchase: a complete set of the works of Laura Ingalls Wilder, author of *Little House on the Prairie*. Willa Cather is another of her favorites, she tells me.

When I leave Laura's house this afternoon, I am thinking of
Susan Vytlacil, on Guam, "half a world away," as Laura put it. I
wonder what of this land she carries with her, whether she
dreams at night of the fields of grain stretching out to the horizon,
whether she misses Sandy's Cafe and her high school friends. And
I think how lucky she is to have parents who are so concerned
with her welfare.

The Troublemaker

There are girl children in these small towns whose lives turn
out much less happily than Susan Vytlacil's. Their parents are
poor, sometimes plagued with illness or alcoholism, unable to provide the support that more fortunate parents give to their children.
They live uneasily in these communities, struggling to earn a living and make a life for themselves, planning self-improvement or
escape. Sometimes they have a child, the product of a relationship
with a man with whom they may have been in love, who may
have drunk too much, beaten them up.

Such a woman works as a waitress at the Kountry Kitchen
cafe in Concordia. I sit in a booth here, thinking how ironically
close we are, only a few blocks, to the tree-sheltered houses of
some of the town's oldest inhabitants, those people whose grandparents or great-grandparents laid out the first city lots. They
form the social foundation of the town, firmly embedded, while
here, waiting on counter at the Kountry Kitchen, is a young
woman who bobs on its surface, lightly attached. They live their
gracious, ordered lives while each day this woman, with very little
support or encouragement, struggles to acquire the basic necessi-
ties of life, to build her self-respect and envision a future for herself that will not repeat the disasters of her past.

Richae Colby is just the age of Susan Vytlacil. Born in Beloit,
a town to the west of Concordia, she is the seventh child in a
family of ten children, and the first in the family to graduate from
high school. That graduation seems an enormous achievement,
given the circumstances of her life. For Richae, from the age of

ten, has made her way from institutions to foster homes and back, from drugs to liquor to violence, in a growing-up chaotic enough to rival the experience of any big city street kid.

The disarming sweetness of her round-featured face, the gentleness of her large brown eyes, make the story of her childhood seem remote, even unlikely. She was, as she describes it, "a little troublemaker" who was sent away from home when she was ten years old and has never been back. She lived in foster homes and correctional institutions, and she began drinking.

"I guess it was just me," she says, and her eyes cloud with pain. "I wanted to get in trouble, so I did. I regret what I did, now. When I was sixteen they took me from a foster home in Belleville to put me in Topeka State Hospital as an alcoholic. I didn't think I was, but the tests they run on me showed I was. They knew more about it than I did. I was just a dumb kid. I don't remember much about that stay. I was pretty out of it, really. And then they put me in, like, a halfway house after I got out of Topeka. I was in the state hospital for two months, in a halfway house for six months, and then they put me in another foster home."

The noises of the cafe reverberate around us—crashing of pans in the kitchen, rise and fall of voices, silverware clinking on china—as Richae tells me how she began using drugs.

"I weighed 152 pounds when I started, and I was four feet six inches tall. The kids at school pushed me down just to see me roll. I got teased about it all the time. I'm four foot ten now. See, if you take speed or acid, you don't eat nothin', or else you'll get sick. Three-fourths of the time I was always on 'em anyway so I couldn't eat. And the other fourth I didn't eat very much 'cause, you know, comin' down off of them makes you tired and you want to sleep."

I notice that she is not now overweight, her body well-proportioned in the white waitress uniform she wears to work.

"I got caught with drugs twice. I was taking chemicals: speed, acid, stuff like that. Once I got somethin' bad in my system, I don't know what it was, it was too strong or somethin', and I got real sick and they ended up takin me to the hospital and I was in there for about two weeks just goin' nutty in the head. Ever since then I won't even look at it. Scares me even to think about it."

With her arrival in Concordia, after she was released from Girls Industrial School in Beloit, her life took a turn for the worse. She was living in a foster home, and began to date her foster mother's nephew. Richae did not know that this young man was a heavy user of drugs until one evening, without provocation, he attacked her.

"I went over to his apartment one night," she says, "me and a friend, and he told the friend to go get some beer and he turned around and beat me up real bad. He's in jail for it now. Then two months later I found out I was pregnant with his kid. He had good parts about him but he had bad parts too. Then before he went to jail he was supposed to have done something to my little nephew, and they proved him bisexual too. It was a big mess. It bothers me bein' here because the people I run around with are all related to him. My boyfriend now is his cousin. They all know about it, they all feel sorry for me, but I don't want to be felt sorry for. It was in the past, and I made the best out of it I could."

This she says with a kind of weary stubbornness, looking down at her small hands on the table and then up at me with those large brown eyes. I ask her how she managed to finish high school.

"Well, part of it I did myself," she answers, "but my foster parents really helped me a lot. I went through school my junior year when I was pregnant, and, you know, nobody teased me. I thought I was going to get teased. And I kept my little boy for eleven months, and then I started going out on my own. They put me on an independent living course, and there wudn't no way I could've afforded it at all. So I put him up for adoption. I know where he is. His adoptive parents write to me every month and tell me how he's gettin' along.

"Sometimes I regret what I did. You know, it just goes back and forth in my head. Like, my foster parents said they respected me for doing it, 'cause I thought of him before I did myself. When I think of it that way I see it as right, but when I think of it

another way ... you know ... just givin' up your kid.... My
mom don't like that at all. But there was four of us that got sent
away in our teens and never was home. I didn't want him to be
that way."

Where are her parents now? I ask. She tells me about her
stepfather, who lives in Beloit. He is eighty years old. She and the
youngest two children have to take care of him. Her mother, she
tells me, has "cut down a lot on her drinkin'. My stepdad and my
mom are still married, and my mom's in California and she's
livin' with another guy. You know, it's just like a little soap opera."

This is the first bitterness I have heard in her voice since she
began her story. She shrugs in her white uniform blouse, turns to
glance at the counter to see if she is needed.

"My mom and I weren't gettin' along when she left for California," she says. "When I put Joshua up for adoption we got in a
big argument. I got kinda mad and I turned around and hit her,
and she placed assault and battery charges against me. They put
me in jail for three months."

We sit impaled on the implications of this story. I do not know
how to respond, or if she expects anything from me, and Richae
adds, "You know, the juvenile jail in Salina." And then she states,
with perfect detachment, "Salina, Wichita, and Kansas City are
about the only places they got juvenile jails at."

This part of Richae's story hurts especially. We let it settle for
a time between us, and Richae looks sideways to check the situation at the counter again, finding a way to slide out of the dilemma she has raised here: mother versus daughter, a frenzy of guilt
and rage, a repetition of betrayal.

This evening at twilight, as I come out of the apartment house
where I'm staying onto Washington Street, I am feeling Richae's
story. I walk south toward the park and the outskirts of town,
hearing the sounds of children playing, the buzz of a motorbike,
pickups accelerating. From the center of Concordia where the big
old frame houses stand, I wander into the streets where low,
ranch-style houses are set next to each other on neatly mown
lawns. Along the side of State Street for three blocks stretches the

cemetery, the stones silhouetted against the sunset. Just beyond it
I approach the junior college, a new, square, brick building set on
a rise, sterile corridors harshly alight, all doors locked.

Richae told me she would like to get work as a welder, and
someday she wants to go to college so that she can become a
counselor for teenagers. I stand in the gathering darkness of the
college grounds, remembering her telling me of the efforts she has
begun to make to get support for the schooling. But as she told me
about it her voice trailed off, and I felt how overwhelming it was
for her to think of making this step. Her past seems a heavy
weight to carry out into the world of college students.

As I return toward the center of town I see the high bulk of
the Nazareth Motherhouse, convent of the Sisters of St. Joseph,
imposing against the sky. One window glows yellow in its spire.
The cicadas buzz in this night that is so strangely warm and
gentle for October. I walk on into the center of town, Sixth Street,
to see what will be open at this hour. The movie marquee advertises a Barbara Streisand film. The young woman in the bright
ticket booth stares out into the empty street. Around the corner on
a side street two liquor stores, situated cattycorner from one another, show their small neon signs. A few people go in and out of
a store marked "Discount." Two pickup trucks, extravagantly
painted, with twin aerials bent back and fastened in gleaming
arcs, pull up to the stoplight at Sixth and Washington. Motors
growl and, when the light changes, one pickup takes off while the
other bucks and bounces like a bronco, tires screeching in a dance
of power.

One of those drivers could be Richae Colby's boyfriend, I
think. He owns a four-wheel-drive pickup, and for entertainment
she and he ride around the town and countryside in it. But her life
is mostly just work at the cafe, going home each night to her sister
and brother-in-law's, where she lives.

I go on with my walk, past the moviehouse, until a clacking
commotion from an open doorway draws my attention. Inside,
behind the front counter piled with folded newspapers, I see
printing presses and two men at work. This is *The Kansan,* letters

on the window announce. (The *Blade-Empire* around the corner is locked up tight.) I go in to pick up a copy from the counter and leave a coin, unnoticed by the two men, and come back out to go slowly toward my house.

Walking the night streets of this town gives me a 1930s feeling. Shades of Sherwood Anderson, Ernest Hemingway accompany me. The newspapermen working at night are both real and remembered images from an Edward Hopper painting. The closed-up bank and drugstore and barbershop stand equally in time and in the pages of books read long ago.

I turn off Sixth and walk up Washington Street for two blocks to the courthouse, a stark brick structure with lots of glass and metal railings, obviously not the original courthouse. Surrounding it, set among a few apartment houses and small office buildings, are the gracious homes in which live the descendants of the town's first families. It is they who own the downtown property where the businesses stand, they who live a measured life innocent of the grinding worry about money. I think once again of Richae Colby. Surely she and they must pass each other on the sidewalk occasionally, perhaps look curiously at one another, wonder about the other's life. These people's figures are securely woven into the pattern of the town, while Richae is a shadow crossing the weave, her very existence a questioning of the most basic tenets of this small society.

"Everybody Dies Here Is Your Friend"

Of life in Clyde, a much smaller community than Concordia, Virginia Racette says, "Sitting in the restaurant at noon, everybody that walks by, you know them. You know their family, their parents, their kids, you've lived with them around you all their life, and if anything'd ever happen there isn't a one of them that wouldn't run if you called for help." Living in such a town one has the opportunity to observe the span of lives, from that first notice in the paper of a baby's birth through the years until the old tired body is laid in the grave. Uncle Earl in his eighties remembers the names of every one of the players on his high school football team. An old woman recalls selling the first readymade dresses in a drygoods store. To people who have lived their whole lives in a town or in the countryside surrounding it, the past remains tangible. Each day for eighty years they have driven down the same street, turned at the same corner. While human time washes in a great slow wave over the buildings and trees and landmarks, carrying away much that they knew, the *place* remains the same, containing the past.

One who is in a position to view this performance of change and stability intimately in a town is the funeral director. She belongs to the town as does the doctor, the druggist, the minister. She responds to the needs of the townspeople in their times of greatest grief. Her duties may exceed the bounds of a mortician's service, until she becomes a mistress of many different ceremonies, a sort of priestess presiding at the great life changes. Such a woman is Laura Vytlacil's employer, Alexine Chaput, who might have been a friend to Richae Colby if Richae had lived in Clyde, as she was to many young women who grew up here.

"Oh yes, I help with weddings and christenings," she tells me. "I help with everything. I'm just, well, I'm just, see, I have a lot of friends who are young girls. Oh, I've had close friends, girls that come and talk, they'll come maybe and talk, they used to, now they don't do it so much anymore 'cause most of these girls have grown up and married, but I saw them all through their weddings, decorated for their weddings and helped them, and they used to come and stay all night at my house. One time I . . . the girls wanted to use my house for a slumber party, it was always open to whoever wants to come, you know, but I've always had a lot of close friends that were young girls, and oh, they just come over to the house, maybe to talk, or tell me about their troubles, maybe one comes, she had boyfriend trouble, she couldn't talk to her mother, so she'd come and tell me about it, and then, that's just the way my life has been, just helping others, but I've enjoyed it."

Alexine Chaput accepts my presence graciously here at the Chaput Mortuary on the main street of Clyde. An old man's body has just arrived; Alexine and Laura Vytlacil expect the family any minute, and the flowers soon after; but she will take a few minutes to talk with me. In her dark blue dress and checkered jacket, with a jaunty scarf tied about her neck, her hair fluffy and newly done, Alexine looks younger than her seventy-five years. She is gravelly voiced, majesterial in manner. She says she remembers me from that spring day two years ago when we came in to inquire about Uncle Earl. Oh yes, of course she remembers. She talks to me in that deep, scratchy voice, tells her stories without paying much attention to me, her eyes traveling the room to assess what needs to be done.

The Chaput Mortuary is a long shadowy room with folding chairs set up in rows and an open coffin on a wheeled carrier placed before the white-draped back wall. In the coffin lies the body of an old man, a peaceful, undemanding presence. An ancient tape recorder sends out the strains of unctuous organ music.

"You do a thousand things for people," Alexine tells me. "When you're involved with them in this way, there's so many things that they need help with. We put in so much of our time doing things for these people, I think maybe they get dependent on you. And you don't forget about them.

"You realize that everybody dies here is your friend, in a town this way, and some way you're involved. It kinda works on you a little bit but then you don't . . . I couldn't stay in this business if I really thought those people were dead! But I never imagine them as dead, I just feel like it's a new beginning for them. And I try to look at it as joyous instead of sorrowful. That's the way I try to go through this because otherwise, if you let yourself, you could go to pieces, you know, if you let yourself think they're dead, that you're not going to see them again.

"Of course, I'm Catholic. Laura here is a Methodist. But I think I find people with faith are very easy to deal with. For instance, a couple here celebrated a golden wedding and then she

died, they found her dead, I believe, the next day, in her bed. It
was hard for me to believe. They belonged up here at this old
Swedish Church but they had *much* faith, much faith. Remember
that family?"

She turns to Laura, who nods in recognition.

"Oh, I thought, to go to the family, that's the hardest thing.
That's what my husband used to tell me, and I didn't realize, and
in his later years he wouldn't go to the family unless I went with
him. I know now what he was talking about. That first break.
How can I enter that house?! You know, it took everything I had
to walk in that house. There was all the Golden Wedding gifts.
We had to move the table, cards and all, to get to the bed . . . you
know, to the bedroom . . . and the daughter-in-law was there and
the husband was just as calm. And the daughter-in-law says,
'Well, she's gone to her Lord.' "

The street door opens to admit a middle-aged couple and a
young man with puffy, reddened eyes. Alexine turns away from
me to rise and meet them, clasp their hands. Then she leads them
down between the folding chairs to the coffin where I hear her
murmuring. "Doesn't he look nice though . . ." and "Yes, I think
you made the right choice." My glimpse of the young man's griev-
ing face brought to me the import of the body in the coffin, who
seemed until now to be no more than part of the furnishings.
"The flowers should arrive soon," Alexine's voice comes softly
from the back of the room. "We'll have everything ready for the
viewing tonight."

It has been many years since I went to a funeral, saw my
brother lying in a gray-blue suit in a coffin. I was not yet twenty,
still living at home. For two days I stood with my parents to
receive my brother's friends; at his wife's request I lifted his hand,
cold and hard as wood, to slip the wedding ring on his finger. I
was terrified, touching him, that he would sit up and throw his
dead arms around me.

Laura leans close, speaks in a low voice, telling me about the
children who visit the funeral home. I come out of my thoughts to
look at her, such a large, comfortably fleshed woman, her eyes

kind. She must be reassuring to the children, as she is to me now, her very solidity and good humor almost making death seem an illusion.

"Since I've been working here I think every kid in town has been in," she says, "because when I started here my daughter Susan was twelve, she was still in grade school, and a lot of the kids would just come to the door with her, at first. She had permission from Alexine, that if the kids would want to see the caskets, she could show them the caskets. So Susan told the kids they could look but they musn't touch, you know, because there might be filthy hands or such, and so eventually, I think, through her, she's gotten about every child in town to come in, and finally they came in to view the bodies in the casket, when we had someone here, you know, and they weren't so timid anymore. . . ."

Soon Alexine has ushered out the relatives, with many comforting murmurs. Now she joins us once again, and it is Laura who must jump up, to receive the flowers that are being delivered at the back door. Alexine takes a few minutes to give me a tour of the back room in which the empty caskets are displayed. She shows them to me with a mixture of gravity and a saleswoman's pride in her wares. Inner linings of lime green cloth, of peach, of white show over the sides of the coffins; the material is gathered in tucks and ruches, satin pillows lie cozily at the top. How comfortable they look. How uneasy I am made by these boxes stately and rich with brass, as if we transgress a taboo in viewing them so casually, and yet it tickles me that one has such a variety of linings to choose from. This deciding among pastel shades is like shopping for a nightgown.

Now we come back out to help Laura, Alexine talking all the while.

"We're giving courses in death, death courses here. Well, I haven't given any in Clyde, but Belleville's getting them, Concordia's getting them. All the funeral homes are doing this. Now we have put some books on death in the town library, and that's helping people a great deal. And we give tours for the school. The school calls every year."

"I think it's their psychology classes," Laura says.

"And then we take them over to Concordia," Alexine continues, "and they tour the whole mortuary. Then when it comes to
the embalming room, the children are asked, 'Any of you that
would like to go see the embalming room? Those that don't, you
can sit out!' And every one of them come in. And I thought Joe
was very good 'cause he had a chart on the wall . . . of all the veins
and blood vessels and all, you know . . . and explained the embalming to them . . . what takes place, and then the questions
come up. 'Well, do you have to be embalmed? Well, why do you
have to take the blood out?' you know, everything. All those questions come up, and so it's really really educational. . . ."

The two women set up the baskets and sprays of flowers on
standards as they talk, finding the metal stand that will fit each
arrangement, discussing its placement near the body. The coffin
about which they are working is a black, dignified model with
gathered white draping inside. Lying in its snowy interior, the old
man is absolutely still, his eyes and mouth sunken in his head,
absent. I watch him, thinking that my father will be the next one
of mine to be packed neatly into a box like this. Already he is ill
and very old, his body broken down from hard work.

Resting for a few moments, Laura turns to look at me and
picks up where Alexine left off, to tell about the course in the high
school. "It's more or less a psychology course explaining death,
what happens, and, you know, because they have known cases of
people who have died for five, ten seconds, and these people have
swum around in the horizon, more or less, and have looked down
on the bed where they lay and then they've come back to life and
told about that . . . and so it's more or less a psychology course that
explains what happens in death . . . and what happens to the
body."

Periodically, Alexine and Laura stand back to view the arrangement of the flowers, then move forward again to shift the
position of a stand, move a basket. Suddenly Alexine freezes, staring down at her hand, her mouth dropped open in horror.

"Laura! A *fly!*"

I am suddenly enlightened as to the decorum of funeral parlors. In this sugary atmosphere what could be more expected,
more appropriate, than a fly? Yet its very being speaks, I suppose,
of decay.

Feeling lightheaded, I think of the section of Richard Selzer's
Mortal Lessons, in which he details the preparation of a body by a
mortician, a description most disturbing to anyone who harbors
respect and tenderness for human flesh.* I remember my waking
dream of my brother's decomposed body brought from its grave
and left on the bed in his old room down the hall from mine.

The music swirls slowly, like dark syrup, in the room. Alexine
becomes serene again, and goes about her business with the flowers, leaving it to Laura to chase and corner the offending insect.

Survivor

On Sunday in Clyde the streets are quiet. Farmers and townsfolk alike, after they do the chores, after they go to church, spend
the rest of the day eating, visiting, resting. Despite the innovations
of microwave ovens, waterbeds, and color televisions, Clyde citizens spend this day much as did the earliest inhabitants of the
town: they visit family. Grown children come to their parents'
homes from neighboring towns, bringing carloads of grandchildren for dinners of beef fresh off the hoof and homegrown vegetables. Siblings visit aged parents in the rest home at the edge of the
town. Nephews and cousins gather to check up on each other, tell
stories, watch the football game.

On Railroad Street, around the corner from Sandy's Cafe and
the Chaput Mortuary, is the dormered and turretted Victorian
house in which Ann and I stayed two years ago. It seems much
the same, except that several blond children stare at me from its
porch and the yard is littered with toys. I recall the days of our
visit, when we searched for reminders of her mother in this town,
and encountered the bleak vestiges of Amanda's life.

---

* Richard Selzer, *Mortal Lessons: Notes on the Art of Surgery* (New York: Simon and
Schuster, 1977).

Recently Ann went back to Clyde, and wrote me a letter from the Clyde Hotel:

I got in around noon, went straight to the South Side Cafe where I found Uncle Earl sitting, eating. Same crew of women there, and back in the kitchen was Ruth. It was a great surprise—everyone very happy to see me. Earl just beamed. Sat right down, bought "dinner" for me.

I visited with Ruth after the crowd left. She's older, eyes still giving her trouble, and has the Cafe up for sale. Is 65.

Says she's tired—just wants to rest.

An hour ago when I drove into town I saw that the South Side Cafe is closed, its plate glass window broken and partially boarded up, equipment piled inside. The sight of it brought me the memory of Ruth Chaplin behind the counter busy at the grill, cooking pancakes and sausages for the farmers in the morning, heavy lunches of fried chicken or beef and noodles, thick gravy on mashed potatoes, white bread with margarine; serving up coffee in mugs of different colors, ringing up the tabs behind a bright bouquet of plastic flowers. The South Side Cafe was one small, narrow storefront, counter stools cramped right up near the scarred wooden booths. Ruth told us it had been a speakeasy during prohibition, with curtains on the booths so that no one would know who else was there. From sunup to sundown she was hard at work at the South Side Cafe. I wonder how she is, now, without that constant labor.

She lives on Washington Street, the main street, a block from the cafe. Her rented house is very old and rather small, the white paint wearing off to reveal the red of the bricks underneath. A house trailer stands nearby. The front windows look across to a coin-operated car wash where the farmers come to hose the mud off their pickups.

Ruth is enjoying herself on this leisurely Sunday, dressed up in a pantsuit with a flowered top, sitting at her table doing nothing much. When I enter she enfolds me in a welcoming hug and introduces me to her daughter Claudia, who has come to visit. Claudia gives me a steady sharp glance, as if to make sure I mean no harm to her mother. She is a sturdy woman who wears a look of dissatisfaction, something distracted about her as she nods to me and settles her arms more firmly on the tablecloth.

Then we are all seated about the table, where Ruth has been sorting through some old papers while talking with Claudia. I look once again at Ruth's large-planed face, remembering how much it affected me when I first saw her in the cafe. It is a face carved by pain, etched deeply with worry, massive and enduring as if hewn out of rock. There is kindness in it, love, but no joy. It has settled in lines of resignation, the flesh relaxing as acceptance has come: this is the way things are.

We talk about her French background. Both her mother's and her father's people were French; as far as she knows, she is "full-blooded French."

"Wasn't your mother's maiden name L'Ecuyer?" I ask, pronouncing the name in the French manner.

"Li-kyoor," she corrects me. "The French pronunciation is Lay-coo-yea, but they always called them Li-kyoor."

She continues. "Yes, my mother was one. She was born in a sod house up around Concordia. The L'Ecuyers—I suppose they came originally from Kankakee, Illinois, like everybody else around here.

"When my parents were first married they used to talk French to each other, until my oldest sister started to school, and she could not talk English, so she had quite a time. Well then, Dad and Mom started talking English and they never did talk French again. We all understand it, but I can't really talk French. I could keep from starving in a French community, but to carry on a conversation and to make sentences, I couldn't."

Claudia sits listening, nodding occasionally, her hands quiet on the table.

Ruth tells about coming in from her farm home to go to high school in Clyde. Because there were no buses at that time, the students had to rent rooms in town and live there while they went to school. All eight children in Ruth's family attended high school. During her student years, she roomed in town with the Chaput family.

"So you know Alexine?" I ask.

"Oh yes, she's just like family to me.

"That was in 1928 that I started high school," she continues. "I didn't get to graduate, 'cause by then the depression was going real good. My folks in the meantime had pretty well lost everything they had and moved to town. So I was living with them at home. We were all living at home, all my brothers and sisters, and we all had jobs. Some of us of course were going to high school, and the reason I quit was to help some of my other brothers and sisters through school. They all went on through school but me, but then nevertheless that was the way it was."

I feel her acceptance of "the way it was" and wonder if she was not more comfortable helping the others than she would have been pursuing her own education.

"I stayed on working at the variety store here in town for ten years, and helped five of my brothers and sisters get through high school."

Two of Ruth's sisters live in Clyde, and she maintains close relationships with them. All of her seven siblings are living. She comes of a long-lived family, her mother having died at ninety-three, her grandmother at one hundred.

"So you'll last a long time too, huh? I ask.

"Oh, I think I probably will. I imagine ... " She laughs. "When I went to the hospital last week they found out I had an ulcer, bad ulcer, but my blood pressure was okay, and ... "

"They let you drink coffee?!" I ask, peering meaningfully at her cup.

"Huh-uh. This is tea. I can drink weak tea."

From the end of the table her daughter Claudia snorts. "She won't pay attention to that diet!"

Ruth first looks annoyed, then ignores her.

We discuss herb tea. "No I have never tried that," Ruth says. "You get that at a health store?" I promise to bring her some.

"Now I drink that Kava," she says. "It's not the greatest but it's better than nothing." She laughs. "I've drank coffee for years and years and I know that I drank too much of it. I know that but you know, when we were at the cafe I didn't have time to eat, most of the time, and I think it was the stress and the way that I was eating and then, see, I've had this operation, you know, on my lower bowels. I had part of my lower bowels out and part of my colon out, and then pretty soon this ulcer got to going. I would get so sick I was vomiting every day about noon, I would just get so sick, and so one morning—wasn't it Claudia?—Claudia came in there and I had been sick for about ten days and I don't know if she talked me into it or if I had just made up my mind."

Claudia interrupts. "We ganged up on her."

"Well, so I said, this is it. This is my last day. It was fourteen years I ran the cafe, and I had four major operations while I was in there."

"Do you have social security to live on now?" I ask.

"Uh-huh. Yep."

"So you can make it all right."

"Oh yeah, I can make it. There's always welfare, I guess, if you get to starving. No, I think I can make it okay. I'm gonna try anyway. I might get a little job, you know . . . "

Ruth's voice sounds as if she chews her words in the back of her throat, and her laugh bursts out each time like a surprise. She is enjoying this visiting, the luxury of having time to sit and talk. She tells how in 1939 she went to Oregon at the urging of her married sister, who lived there and felt she needed a change after working ten years in the store.

In Oregon Ruth married, and in 1942 she started having her babies—"boom boom boom," as she describes it.

"Well, let's see, when Mary Lou, my fifth child, was born, Phyllis, my oldest, was not yet six years old."

Claudia interjects, "And Chuck and I were both born the same year—he in January and I in December."

The sixth child was born when Ruth had returned to Clyde, after a seven-year break from childbearing.

"It was 1954," Ruth says. "I had my five kids and I was six months pregnant when I came back here."

Claudia gets up to go into the living room, and returns with her sweater and purse.

"Mom, I've got to go now," she says, and I wonder if she has been made uncomfortable by the direction in which the conversation is going.

Ruth breaks off her story to tell me that Claudia lives in Concordia where she works at one of the Boogaart supermarkets. Looking distracted, Claudia stands waiting for her to finish, and then tells us both goodbye.

When she has gone, I ask Ruth what happened in Oregon in 1954. "Did you break up with your husband?"

"Well, he had taken off with another woman so I guess you can call that breaking up." She gives a harsh, flat laugh. "He was *gone.*"

She begins to describe for me the events of those early years, the first great blow that struck her.

"My husband had disappeared, I didn't know where he was for six or seven weeks. This happened in May of 1954, I guess. I've sort of forgotten dates, I mean that's how far back this has gone in my mind. Then finally after seven weeks he called me and he was down in Klamath, California, so I flew down there and talked to him and he told me all this big rigamarole, that he had met this woman, so on and so forth, and he was so in love with her he couldn't see straight or hear or anything else, he was just really taken by this gal. So I came on back to Medford, Oregon, that's where we lived. He was working in Klamath, but he didn't send anything to us." Her voice lowers to a soft dead tone. "And then after a while I ran out of money so I had to go to the welfare, which was ... it really about killed me ... but that's what happened and what I had to do.

"I think that was about in August. Well, he had traveled all over and then he called me from Colorado and said he was coming home. So okay, he came home, and he was there for about three days. But he couldn't get this woman off of his mind, and so that was the end of the rope right there! So he went on back to Colorado and he told me, 'Why don't you go on back to your people?' He said, 'I'll try to get myself straightened up and then maybe we can take it from there.'

"The minute he left I knew I didn't want him in the condition he was in, so I went to the phone just as soon as he drove out of the yard, and called my brother here in Clyde and told him I was coming home. I had my five kids and I was pregnant. Well, I don't know ... when you have to do something you just do it, period. So I sold out all of our furniture, packed all the things that I wanted for here and shipped all that back, sent some by freight and then brought all I could on the train. And we traveled, we had sleepers and we got along just great. We were on the train three nights. The kids were getting a little bit restless, I can tell you. When the train stopped and I said we're getting off, they did really take off. But they were real good. I can't complain really ... it was a ... well, my family had been wanting me to come back here. They said, 'You come back here and we'll help you' and so. . . .

"Everybody was great to me really. Then I had the baby. And then he had called me not too long before the baby was born, from Colorado. So he came home for Christmas and then he went on back there. Then I think it was in February of '55 that he decided that he would come on back to his family.

"So he came back here. And he was here for ten years. He's a mechanic. Well, in fact he is a lot of everything. I mean he's a smart person, he can do all kinds of things. He has a lot of good things about him. He's a jack of all trades, but he's good at all of it. He's also a construction worker. So they rebuilt and relocated this creek that used to go right through here after the big flood that we had in 1958, and he got started on that and worked on that and followed this construction company to another job. Well, anyway, he got mixed up with another woman." There is something loose in her expression, bewildered, a wonderment that her life could have been devastated once again by the actions of this person she loved, that she could have been hurt once again so deeply.

"So then that was the end of everything. I mean, *once* you could forgive more or less, but not forget. That was me. Maybe it wasn't the right thing but I never could forget it. So then we just finally come to the end of the rope and he went on to California and I didn't hear from him for three years.

"He never sent the children any money or anything. My youngest boy was eight and Mary Lou, my other girl, was in high school. She would have been fifteen. Claudia was probably seventeen, Chuck eighteen. They never did get over it. You don't know how that affects a family." I realize now why Claudia left so hastily.

"I did sue for a divorce not long before he left," Ruth continues, "but I cancelled it after he left because I didn't have the money to go ahead with it. That's the way it's been: I mean, we really aren't divorced, but then what difference would it make? Nineteen sixty-three was the last that I heard from him. I've talked to him on the phone several times. Even if he's married and committing bigamy I never would do anything to him. If this gal can make him happy, more power to her, because it seems that I couldn't."

Was there no rage, I wonder? Was there no fury at this man whose wandering caused such anguish to herself and her children? Ruth's face looks grave and suffering as she tells the story.

"So then I was sick. I was so *down* from this. I went to work at the liquor store and I had to apply for Aid to Dependent Children."

She sits in silence for a few moments, and I look away from her face out the window. In a town of one thousand inhabitants there is no anonymity. She must have read the knowledge of her predicament in every face she met on the street, in church, across the counter of the grocery store; in the eyes that looked at her she must have seen pity, curiosity, now and then disapproval, a veiled contempt, or a secret delight in another's pain.

Ruth goes on matter-of-factly. "Then in 1965 when I got on my feet to where I had some strength, I took over the South Side Cafe. My son is the one that bought it for me. I paid him back a long time ago. The cafe took care of everything for me—I mean, any loneliness or insecurity. To know that I was going to get the rest of my kids through school. It was the answer to a lot of things. I'm a Catholic and I firmly believe that prayers are answered; there is a gain for every loss. So that was just the thing that happened to me.

"I had worked in another cafe across the street for a year, but I had never done any cooking, and I had never had anything to do with the business end of it. But I didn't find that hard. When you have a family, you learn to manage at home. I cooked in the cafe just like I cooked at home. I made bread and made rolls. I kept all my tickets and all my stuff like that and then I turned it over to this lady and she kept my books. I didn't have time to do that.

"When I got the restaurant the kids were pretty well grown up, all but the little one. I had a phone here that rang from the restaurant and I'd call him, you know. His clothes were always ready and he would get dressed and come down there and eat and go on to school. It was no big thing. I was *always* there.

"I never had any problem with anyone in all the time I worked there, never ever any trouble or words with any of the girls or anybody that ever worked for me. We all ended up just great friends. I built up a real good business. We had all we could handle, and there were four of us working there all the time. I enjoyed it down there at the cafe. If I felt well, I'd have never given it up."

The farmers, she says, would bring their crews into her cafe to eat, because many of the wives were working and were no longer available to cook for the crews. She used to feed the high school football team, too, with early supper at four in the afternoon before they went to their out-of-town games.

Had she ever considered marrying again? "I have never thought about it," she says. "I was so busy I wouldn't have had time to. Now as far as going anywhere, I never ever. I worked and that was it. I was so tired when I got home. Which is all right. I mean I was not unhappy doing this. My kids were all around and I have a lot of friends here. Oh I would go once in a while to a show or something like that. As far as ever going with men, I

never ever did. And it isn't because I don't *like* men. I mean I like
men okay, you know. It's company. I love to talk to men and
they're a lot of nice people. But I had been so hurt that I never
ever wanted one more minute of what I had. And it's no sign that
anybody would've done that to me *again,"* She laughs, "but I just
didn't want to stick my neck out."

"I think I was forty-eight when he left. If I had been a younger person, it might have made a lot of difference. But also I had
six kids by this time. It's hard to find a husband that wants to
come into a family with six kids. And then I always felt like I
would never want my children to have a stepfather, so . . . it just
plain did not enter my mind to look around for another person.

"But I was not feeling sorry for myself, that was not it. I just
wasn't going to give anybody any opportunity to hurt me again.
I'll always remember how that hurt, see, it was a real sad thing for
me."

Religion was some consolation during the worst times, she
says, although most of the time she was working so hard she could
not get to church.

"But that doesn't keep you from praying. I mean you can pray
while you're working. And then of course my mother always
prayed for us too; she was very religious. I think the good Lord
understands what your problems are, you know, and I didn't feel
guilty that I wasn't going, 'cause I would work six days a week
and put in I don't know how many hours and by Sunday I was so
tired I just couldn't make it. But you know, I still have my faith.

"So anyway, I'm a happy person. I don't feel sorry for myself
and I am not a lonely person. I can live with myself. It doesn't
bother me at all to be alone. I like to read and it makes me mad
that I can't see good enough to really stay with it now. My eyes are
conking out on me. I get the *Book Digest.* It's a real good little
thing; it has all the latest books, comes every month. Then I read
a daily paper, and I subscribe to this magazine, *Harpers.* I don't
like it. I'm gonna cancel. Then I subscribe to a movie magazine
and keep up on what's going on out there. And I took *Other
People* magazine for a while and then I let that run out. I just kind

of like to know what's going on in all departments!" She laughs.
"And I know a little bit about everything and nothing about anything.

"Now, my kids, well, Claudia, of course, works at Concordia,
and then my youngest son is assistant in the meat department at
Boogaart's there. He's a butcher. He's getting along just great, just
climbing right up there. Mary Lou, my youngest daughter, works
at the Elk State Bank right here in Clyde. She's doing real well,
has two lovely children. I see her most every day. And I have a
daughter in Indiana, my oldest daughter. She has five children
and she works in the meat department in a big Kroger store. She
has a real good job, they pay real good, I think seven dollars an
hour for the type of work she does. Then my son John, that's my
oldest son, is a foreman on a construction company. He makes real
good money too; he lives here. My other son is out in Reno. My
youngest son got married this last spring, a lovely little girl. I just
think she's the greatest little thing ever."

"What will you be doing now that you're out of the cafe?" I
ask her.

She smiles at me, her eyes dim and strained behind her glasses,
her big face gradually livening with anticipation as she talks.

"I don't have any plans. I just want to be home. I want to be
home here 'cause I've got so much to do. I've got to completely
clean my house and do a lot of sorting, and just take it easy and
do what I want to do at least for two or three months. After that
I don't know. I'm not even going to think about what I'm going
to do or let it bother me at all. I'll just let things happen. My
daughter wants me to come see her in Indiana. She called me the
other night, wants me to come. And I told her well, maybe spring,
I might. And then I'd like to visit my sister in Oregon. I mean,
these are things I'd *like* to do. If I don't get to do it, okay. And
then I have a friend who wants me to go to Florida with her. And
oh, just junk like that. I may not do any of it."

For years her relationships have been limited to her children
and the clientele at the cafe. The physical arena of her life has
been bounded by that one block between the South Side Cafe and

this small worn house. Her sisters are among her closest friends.

"My sister Chy, she lives right across that alley back of the restaurant. Now she and I are very very close, and every night when I'd close up, she'd come over to the cafe. We always would visit for about an hour. Doe would come too when she could. That's my other sister."

I remember the evening we spent in the cafe, Ann and I, Ruth and Chy and Doe, and Doe's daughter Jolene. I ask about Jolene, recalling how she had challenged the older women, and Ruth tells me she lives in Hays, a town many miles southwest of Clyde. She was here with her husband and children this weekend, Ruth says, visiting Doe. I probably just missed her.

She goes on with her enumeration of her friends. "Alexine Chaput is a very close friend of mine too. And Anna that used to work in the cafe. And I have a real good friend in Concordia."

We talk about how much more opportunity she will have now to see her friends. But she thinks she will want to "just do nothing," saying how lazy she is. She does not feel compelled to do much housework. Piled around us in the dining room and kitchen are utensils, dishware and other objects brought from the cafe when it closed. Ruth says it's a shame I should see her house this way, but she's waiting until she's cleaned the kitchen before she finds places for all the things.

"I'm not going to let it bother me. I like to just set! I can just set and think about this and that, to just kind of meditate I guess, or read. I've never watched TV much. I'd come home, I'd read and I'd go to bed. I know I led a funny life, probably worse than some of the nuns." She laughs with great satisfaction.

"Well, when I get my house cleaned up, there'll be a lot of the girls I'll invite down here for coffee and visits and one thing and another." Her face softens. "And I think I'll get out every day and go up to the cafe when it opens up again and eat my breakfast at least. I don't do a whole lot of walking because of this bad leg of mine. I had that operation on my leg, that cancer taken off, and all the glands and stuff through here ... " She pushes her chair back from the table to lay her hand on her leg. "They took a lot of tissue and veins out of my leg and so it's swelled all the time. I wear a rubber stocking, a real heavy one, starts clear down at my toes, comes all the way up through here. I have to wear that all the time or I can't walk. I'll walk uptown if I need groceries, that type of thing, but I'm not too whippy. I wished I could say let's go for a walk, and walk out to the river bridge or something like that, but I couldn't do it anymore."

We talk about Clyde in the old days, and Ruth admits to a certain nostalgia for the first twenty-six years of her life before she married, when, as she remembers it, she had a lot of fun. "Of course, after I got married I mean it isn't that my fun stopped, I don't mean that. But my life changed, you know, with having children so fast.

"There have been a lot of changes in Clyde, businesswise, since I was working in the variety store back then. We would open that up at seven o'clock in the morning and we were there until eleven o'clock at night. The grocery stores would stay open until 12:30, one o'clock, on Saturday night, and this was a busy busy town. You'd go downtown on a Saturday night, you couldn't get through, there were so many people. That was the big treat for the country people, see. That was the only time they came to town. They'd get all their groceries, and bought all their supplies and that was the highlight of the week. Meet their friends and their people and go in and have a hamburger. They had a show here and the kids would go to the show and it was all the big treat. It was that way when I left in 1939. Then when I came back, I did notice a big change. By then people were working only eight hours a day and they had a coffee break. There was no such thing as that, you know—to have a coffee break—before.

"It's altogether different now. I think there are fewer people here. And the lifestyles are all different. People get in their cars and they go, you know. The farmers and all, they go to Concordia to eat at the Moose or the Elks, or the country club, and most of the people belong to private clubs.

There are a lot of widows here—a *lot* of widows—and they were all left, you know, with plenty of money. They all have new

cars so these gals they just get together and they go out to dinner
and they go to shows, you know, or have card parties at home, or
that type thing. And they have a lot of fun, just the women. I call
them the Merry Widows!" She chuckles, pleased with her joke.
"You know, there are a lot of things you can do if you have
money and a car, one thing and another and a lot of good friends,
good women friends. You can have a lot of fun with the girls, you
know."

Here in Ruth's house on a Sunday afternoon, I am content, as
if I have known her all my life. I feel a great fondness for her as
she tells me that she has never been inside the door of Sandy's, the
other cafe in town.

I laugh in astonishment. "Ruth, you mean in all these years
you never once went there for Sunday dinner even?"

"Huh-uh, not at all. I never. I worked in the cafe so long,
eating out was no big treat to me. No big treat. Now I would
enjoy it. I don't have anything against her, you know, that I
wouldn't go in there. I just hadn't even thought about going down
there."

I wonder what may be behind this, whether there was a competition between the two eating establishments, patrons lost, un-
kind words repeated. But when I ask her, Ruth assures me, "Oh,
I had nothing against her whatsoever. I didn't go there, but I
didn't go anywhere else either. All my hours were spent in my
own cafe." And she adds, "I always wanted to make it in business.
At the same time I wanted everyone else to do the same."

Would she let me take her to dinner at Sandy's cafe? I wonder, and imagine asking her to go with me this evening, when she
tells me, "I'm due at my sister's real soon for supper. I was going
to ask if you would drive me over there in your car. It's not far."

As we leave the house to come out into the evening, the car
wash across the street stands dark against the sky, an open-ended
metal barn that frames the sunset.

Ruth sits beside me in the car, faintly smiling, her face softened and relaxed. She directs me the several blocks to her sister's
house, and when I stop the car she says, "I enjoyed our visit."

"Me too."

For a few more moments she sits beside me, a look of puzzlement on her face. Then she turns to me to say, in a tone of surprise, "Why I don't believe I've ever told my life to anyone before!"

Catherland

It is a cold, dark morning of pelting rain as I start on my journey from Concordia to Red Cloud. Driving up Route 81 toward the Nebraska border, I hear on the radio that pheasant season begins tomorrow. Semis splatter my windshield as they roar past. The morning is bleak out across the harvested fields, all color reduced to a dull brown-grey. The voice from the radio says that Topeka sweltered in summerlike heat this past Sunday, while in northwest Kansas a storm swept down out of the Rockies to deposit two inches of snow. My destination—the town in which Willa Cather grew up—makes me think of the women in her books, who had to face such weather with none of the tools and conveniences we have now.

Driving down toward Riley on Monday I had encountered a most unusual sight. Out in a field was a windmill bent double, its long supports folded neatly in the middle, bringing its wheel to rest on the ground next to its base. I stared at it, puzzled, and kept the picture in my mind for the rest of the day. Then on the way back home I picked up *The Riley Countian,* and saw on its front page a photograph of the ominous black funnel poised in the distance. Inside the paper were photos of a truck lying on its top, a pile of wreckage that had once been a trailer home, a storage shed turned on its roof.

I snap off the radio to concentrate on my driving, feeling melancholy. Once again the pioneer women in their muddy sod houses or dugouts come to mind. What a test of the human spirit was forced upon them by this land, sometimes so wild and unfriendly, as if it heaves and thrashes in the attempt to throw off its human inhabitants.

It was these people Willa Cather wrote about, the Bohemians and Swedes who broke the sod of the prairie near the town of Red Cloud, just north of the Kansas border in Nebraska. In *O Pioneers, My Antonia, Obscure Destinies,* and others of her novels and books of short stories, her women characters especially stand out large, women of great strength, whose portraits are drawn with immense love and fascination. I have cared about Willa Cather since reading her in college, introduced to her by a woman who dared to teach a course featuring Gertrude Stein and Willa Cather.

Now, as I drive up over the border into Nebraska and turn west, I think of the young Willa Cather growing up in Red Cloud before the turn of the century. The friendships she made there lasted all her life. The Nebraska prairie was subject matter and mother to her creative gift. As she grew older in the artistic and literary world of New York City, she clung more steadfastly to her friends of Red Cloud days.

This land is much like Kansas. Driving through the rainy morning, I see the same prairie, perhaps rolling a little more right here, the same tall grass and far horizon. Ahead of me, the town of Red Cloud appears abruptly, like a mirage in this emptiness. Old red brick facades, strict and angular, are softened by window arches and copings of white or brown granite. Weathered frame houses stand behind small square lawns, the cottonwoods shine golden in the wetness. There is a small tract of retirement housing at the edge of town; on a street near it I see an old man in overalls riding a giant tricycle.

Red Cloud was named for the great Sioux Indian Chief who, as far as anyone knows, never came anywhere near it. Called by other names, in many of Willa Cather's books, it is "the 'Sweetwater' of *A Lost Lady,* the 'Frankfort' of *One of Ours,* the 'Haverford' of *Lucy Gayheart,* the 'Moonstone' of *Song of the Lark,* the 'Black Hawk' of *My Antonia,* and the 'Hanover' of *O Pioneers.* It is the village of 'The Best Years' and the several villages of the stories in *Obscure Destinies.*"*

---

*From Mildred R. Bennett, *The World of Willa Cather* (Lincoln/London: University of Nebraska Press, 1961), p. 94.

Present-day Red Cloud is as securely Willa Cather's town as when she lived here or when she lived in New York and wrote about it, for the town has been turned into a Willa Cather historical park of sorts by certain industrious townsfolk. This public honoring of the Cather reputation was superintended by Mildred R. Bennett, author of The *World of Willa Cather* and a respected authority on Cather, who is also—and proudly—wife of the town physician, Dr. W. K. Bennett.

In small towns it is generally the wives of the doctors and lawyers who preserve the culture. Often better educated than their neighbors, they have more leisure time and a perspective that allows them to see past the exigencies of daily life to the broad historical or cultural significance of what surrounds them. But this is only a more public version of the role played within most families by women. It is women of all classes, in the humblest farmhouse as well as the governor's mansion, who save mementos, keep photo albums, write in diaries. They are the unofficial historians, who pieced together a quilt to commemorate a wedding or a birth, to mourn a death and tell of the deceased for succeeding generations. The lived quality of the time since settlers first came to the Great Plains, the thousands of hours of the days of the years of feeding and clothing, giving birth, marrying, working, suffering, celebrating, growing old; all this is alive in a thousand attics, in the objects collected, carefully folded and put away by women who knew it mattered that the story of their families survive.

Operating within this tradition, Mrs. Bennett, with others, was able to acquire and restore the house the Cathers had lived in, to stake out the other locations in town and the surrounding countryside that figured in Willa's life and in her novels, and to convert the old Farmers and Merchants Bank building into the Willa Cather Pioneer Memorial.

Inside this tall, narrow building is a tiled lobby where the teller's booths are still intact. A portrait of Mildred Bennett hangs in a place of honor near the entrance: because of the formality, the finality, of this tribute, I at first surmise that Mrs. Bennett is dead, and do not think to ask to meet her.

Behind the grille of the teller's booth works a woman who is pleased to take me on a tour of the Cather house several blocks from here, at Third and Cedar. We bundle up in our coats and scarves and go out into the cold. As we walk the half block over to Third, the block to Cedar, I discover that Dorothy Mattison is native to this area, and lives on a farm eight miles outside of Red Cloud. A woman in her mid-fifties, she conducts herself with that stiff seriousness that is often a mask for shyness. But her enthusiasm breaks through as she tells me that even though she and her husband are retiring as farmers, and will move to town, their farm is of such historic value that it will be bought by the State of Nebraska to be developed into a museum someday.

"That kinda takes the sting out a little bit, when you know it'll be preserved," she says.

"We are nearing the story-and-a-half old frame Cather house now.

"What's historic about your land?" I ask Dorothy.

"There was an Indian village there, and three Indian burial grounds, and it's where Zebulon Pike lowered the last Spanish flag in the United States and raised the American flag." Proudly stated.

We ascend the steps to the Cather porch, and Dorothy unlocks the door. An entranceway opens into a living room ringed with heavy dark furniture and dominated by a great nickel-trimmed stove.

"When Willa's parents died, the family had an auction and sold all the stuff in this house," Dorothy tells me. "Then when Mrs. Bennett and the others started to restore this house, back in the fifties, people would bring back the things they had bought. Except the woman who bought the piano just refuses to give it up."

We wander through the rooms, listening to a taped male voice describing in rich, fruity tones how the Cather family lived here. Sometimes the voice issues from a couch, sometimes from a bed, a bureau. In the kitchen the stove speaks to us, in a deep and stove-like voice. On its top sits an old metal basin and kettle mottled blue and white; looking at them, I am carried into an awareness of my grandmother's house, smell the sweetish-tart odor of the medicines she drank in spoonfuls all day long, feel the softness of her dress as she held me, unwilling, on her lap.

But the stove has no patience with this reverie. It directs Dorothy and me up the narrow back stairs to the second floor.

We climb to a long attic under the sloping sides of the roof. Chimneys of red brick dominate each end of the space. Opening off the north side is a little low-ceilinged room containing a bed, a washstand, and a glass case of seashells. This was Willa Cather's room. A narrow window lets in light on wallpaper, small red and brown roses on a yellowish background. The basin and pitcher stand serenely on the washstand; the towel hangs as if left there, this morning, damp from Willa's use before she went off to school. The ceiling slants down to meet the walls on either side, giving the room a strong sense of enclosure, a comforting privacy. Here lived the child who would become the artist. In this room she must have found her measure of solitude, the door closed against her many brothers and sisters. Here, commanding this small space for herself, she must have studied and dreamed and planned her future. This room holds an immense attraction for me.

Dorothy stands with arms folded, patiently waiting for me, her head turned to look down the length of the attic to the window, beyond which dance the bare, topmost twigs of the trees. The voice has long ago died away. It is time to go.

When we come out into the cold again to walk back to the Memorial, I ask Dorothy what the townspeople thought of Willa Cather.

"People around here used to tremble when another of her books came out, for fear they'd be in it." She pulls her coat tight around her, looking ahead to the yellow leaves strewn across the sidewalk. "She wasn't too kind, you know. She told the truth."

"But she had many friends here, didn't she?"

We have turned the corner onto Webster Street and I see the tall red bank building before us.

"They say you either liked her or you *dis*liked her," Dorothy says. "There was no middle ground."

Back at the memorial, Dorothy and another attendant, a slender, pleasant woman named Sue Fintel, settle me at a wooden table at the front of the bank and bring me the folder of Willa Cather's letters to Carrie Miner Sherwood. Mrs. Sherwood was Willa's oldest, dearest Red Cloud friend. She lived into her nineties, and helped to preserve the Cather reputation in the town. I asked for these letters because I want to understand more of Willa's relationships with the women here. In these letters to Mrs. Sherwood she reveals herself as one does only to the most trusted friend. They are written in a neat, not very legible hand, from 5 Bank Street, New York City, Willa's home for many years; from Europe; from a second address in New York; from California, where she went to be near her dying mother; from Grand Manan, the island in New Brunswick where she and her companion Edith Lewis kept a home. They are filled with the details of her daily life over the years, and in them she grows older. Eventually she writes of the deaths of others, the sorrow of losing them. The last letter is dated a few months before her own death.

I sit back, hearing the clock tick from the wall behind me, and especially I retain a sense of that New York environment in which Willa lived, the apartment where she worked and entertained friends. I remember my own New York, in which I first experienced the power of Willa Cather's work. While publicly delighted with this fast-paced new world, privately I felt buffeted and lacerated by it. In truth, I was lonely, and burdened by a deep, wrenching homesickness. I was reading Rilke and Carson McCullers, Thomas Mann, Herman Hesse; was in love with the grotesque, the highly wrought in art. But my ambivalence showed itself one day when I decided that, since I had grown up in the Midwest, I would return to that great writer of the plains, Willa Cather. I went to the library for a stack of her books and, in the next few weeks, I read three or four of her novels. When I had finished I thought I retained nothing of them except vague impressions of women, farm life, a prairie setting. I had come to expect the complexity and intensity of the Southern or European sensibilities. Measured against them, Cather seemed decidedly bland. She took her time, she seemed to leave open spaces, the novels moved with the rhythm of seasons and years. It was as if the land were the principal character and the people existed secondarily. But those very qualities caused the books to affect me at a level deeper than I recognized at first. They soothed, they comforted me, and Willa Cather became a special person to me. We shared something. Though it was many years before I came to appreciate fully the mastery and the magic of her writing, her prose wonderfully spare and yet rich with significance, her rendering of this region and its people deep and compassionate, from the time of that first meeting in New York, I cherished her.

Now, in the big, shadowy bank building, as the light grows murky outside the window, I get up to wander into the rear rooms where glass cases hold Cather memorabilia, where photographs and paintings of Willa decorate the walls. She gazes resolutely down at me, her wide mouth now and then curved in faint amusement, her eyes clear and wise.

When I return to my table, Sue Fintel joins me. Can she help me with anything? she asks, and I put aside the letters to talk with this woman who is one of the caretakers of the Cather reputation.

"I didn't know anything about Willa Cather other than that there had been a woman author who lived in the town of Red Cloud," she tells me. "I had never read any of her books until I moved here. But because I've lived around so many places in the country, why I've always tried to avail myself and find out a little bit more about the place that I was going to be calling home. So the first winter I checked out all of Willa Cather's books and I read them. The first time I was in the museum was a cold cold December 7, her birthday. I was fascinated and intrigued that I lived in a town where all this went on years and years ago. That was long before I ever thought that I would be working here."

Sue is forty-eight years old, with fluffy graying hair and dark eyebrows. She has been a secretary for many years. Her husband, a Nebraska native, was a railroad man. They lived and raised their family in several large cities, but in 1977 they moved to Red Cloud to be near his widowed mother in Deshler, Nebraska. Now her husband runs an upholstery shop, while this job at the Cather Memorial is perfect for Sue, she tells me, because she can combine her secretarial experience with her love of antiques.

"After that first cold winter I spent reading her books, I've reread almost all of them, and I found an awful lot more in them the second time through. Her writings are such that they're down to earth, but yet she can write in six lines what it would take me six paragraphs to write." She pauses thoughtfully. "I don't think I read into them as much as some people do, but I read for enjoyment. I am not studying her literarily, so to speak." I reflect that Sue and Dorothy must feel intimidated by some of the professors and graduate students who come here researching Cather.

Surely, working in this place, Sue must have a special view of Willa, who in our talk we refer to simply as "she." Now I ask, "If she came to visit, what would she be like?"

"I've tried to picture this," Sue says, and her high forehead creases slightly in thought. "She didn't like change. She'd probably be very upset with Red Cloud. I think she'd be upset when she found, for instance, that the farmers have airplanes. I think that the hurry-scurrying that even people who live in small towns do . . . she wouldn't like that if she was to be here today. For instance, changing that storefront across the street, that would be upsetting to her, I feel. She just didn't want things done any differently than they always had been."

"How would she be personally?" I inquire.

Sue ponders for a moment, looking down at her crossed hands.

"I think she was, in a sense, demanding. But anybody that has a certain talent—if they are, so to speak, *in their works,* then they feel like everybody should see them as an artist. Edith Lewis, who lived with her, talks about how on Friday afternoons they used to have tea, and she used to receive people. But I have an idea that the type of thing that was done was all about her writings and the like and what *she* was doing."

She pauses, still gazing at her hands on the table, her eyes intent and thoughtful.

"I would say that she was a very regimented person, if she made up her mind; and very strong-willed, so to speak. If she was going to spend four hours writing, then that's what she did."

We sit pondering this assessment for a time, and then look up to see Dorothy Mattison approaching the table. Dorothy looks enthusiastic, as if she brings good news.

"Would you like to talk with Mildred Bennett while you're here?"

Quickly I move past my surprise to answer yes, and Dorothy goes to the phone.

Mrs. Bennett is author, scholar, researcher, known throughout the world for her work on Cather, her importance amply acknowledged by Dorothy and Sue, humble workers that they are. There is something Virginia Woolfian about Mrs. Bennett. Like Mrs. Ramsey's spirit hovering over the family in *To the Lighthouse,* Mrs. Bennett's presence broods over this memorial, organizes it, gives it its serious and somewhat scholarly tone. She is spoken of in the reverential tones reserved for a great personage. Now that I know she is alive, her figure hovers in the wings, threatening to appear at any moment. I experience a flutter of trepidation at the thought, and vow to study *The World of Willa Cather* tonight in preparation, for Dorothy has come back from the telephone to tell me Mrs. Bennett will see me at eleven tomorrow morning.

Exhausted by this long day, I drive to the edge of town where I park to enjoy an unobstructed view of the sunset. The land stretches away, empty, endless. The roads are tracks of slick red clay up and down rolling hills. In an earlier trip here, I innocently drove out in the rain to visit the cottonwood grove and river bluff, cemetery and school house of the Willa Cather historical tour. My car skidded out of control on the slippery rutted roads. It seemed certain I would slide into the ditch, so I abandoned the tour to drive in first gear, shoulders clenched, through this treacherous, rain-tormented wilderness to the nearest paved road. Now I look up from the land to a violence of color bursting through great banks of cloud. The sky is bloody and burnt, as in the aftermath of a battle, swollen with raging reds and yellows. A strong, icy wind shakes my car. Grass, leaves of trees, bare earth—all glow red under that immense, rending sky.

I turn from this eerily magnificent scene to drive back through town to the McFarland Hotel where I am staying. Its lobby is high-ceilinged and as randomly cluttered as a warehouse. Today, when I arrived, the pheasant hunters had taken all but one room, and I was led to a room opening onto the lobby. All evening now I hear the blare of the television set through my door. The furnishings appear to be castoffs from someone's house. The radiator under the window knocks periodically, very loudly, in no rhythm I can follow.

Here in my room I think of Willa Cather's writings, her vision of this Midwest that was so much a part of all our growing up, whether we knew it or not. There is something wholesome, romantically American about Willa Cather.

But I must prepare for my meeting—should I call it an "audience"?—with Mildred Bennett. I prop myself in bed and open *The World of Willa Cather,* which I soon find to be a graceful, readable volume describing the sources, in Red Cloud, of many of Cather's major fictional characters and settings. Now seventy years old, Mildred Bennett has lived in Red Cloud for more than thirty years, I discover in the author's note. Besides having written this book, she edited *Early Stories of Willa Cather* and contributed the introduction to *Willa Cather's Collected Short Fiction 1892–1912.* She is president of the Willa Cather Pioneer Memorial and Education Foundation, having labored for years in its development.

Today, when I left the Memorial, I went a few doors down the street to talk with Viola Borton of the Willa Cather Historical Center, a companion institution to the Memorial. She told me that

Dr. W. K. Bennett is her family doctor, and she spoke of the Bennetts with great respect. Although Mrs. Bennett has done some of the most important historical research on Cather, her contribution is often not properly acknowledged, Viola said. "Many people have used Mrs. Bennett's material without crediting her." And as I think about it, it does seem logical that the professors and graduate students who consult Mrs. Bennett's work would be tempted to steal her material. She is not, after all, a professor or literary critic, operating out of a university or large city. She is a small town doctor's wife, a cultivated and accomplished woman, yet one who moves in the very circumscribed sphere of life in Red Cloud, with visits to the university community at Lincoln. It would be easy for members of the literary establishment to take bits of the biographical information in *The World of Willa Cather* and Mrs. Bennett's articles without thinking to credit the woman who gathered and organized that information.

When fatigue forces me to turn off the light and get some sleep, I have read almost all the way through the book and feel that I now know something about this woman's work.

In the morning, at the Memorial, I await Mrs. Bennett.

She arrives. A tall woman in a long coat, her light hair swept back from her forehead, she hurries in, clasps my hand briefly and, looking sternly at me, informs me that she has guests at her house and must return soon to cook lunch for them and Dr. Bennett.

"We can talk for an hour," she says, and beckons me down the stairway to the basement.

When we have seated ourselves in a corner of the quiet basement room where earlier I had watched a slide show of local sites, Mildred Bennett regards me suspiciously. Who did I say I was? What exactly do I want from her?

She has a large face, her mouth thin-lipped and pulled down at the corners. Her eyes are wary, sensitive. There is an air of tension about her, the tendons of her long neck prominent in their tightness. She seems younger than seventy years in her erectness and in the bright, intense focus of her energy.

Our conversation jerks along at first, tentative, reluctant.

"I notice in the recent forward to *The World of Willa Cather,* you mention that you've done a lot of research since the book came out," I begin.

She looks steadily at me, her expression a little sour.

"Yes, that shows up in the footnotes mostly. Well, of course, not all of it. There's a lot that isn't in that book."

And then she waits, offering nothing further.

"Are you writing another study of Willa Cather?" I ask.

"Well no, not right now."

Again she is silent, and I wonder if she really does want to talk to me.

"How did you get started on your Willa Cather work?"

"I came out to teach in Webster County in 1932. Some of my students in high school were descendants of some of the people who were friends of Willa Cather. One of my senior girls, Charlotte Lambrecht, brought me *Shadows on the Rock,* which had been autographed to her grandmother. That was the first Cather book I read. And then I saw the grandmother, a little old German lady who could barely speak English, and I became fascinated by the friendship between this little old immigrant lady and this well-known New York author. And I have been interested ever since. It kind of became a life project with me."

I begin to feel a little easier, for I sense the storyteller in Mildred Bennett, impeded for the moment by the strictures of her caution.

"I didn't really get down to work on it seriously until 1946," she continues. "I went to a writers' conference in Omaha, and Dr. Jacks of Creighton University said, 'Willa Cather is going to die one of these days, and the first person who comes out with a good biography on her will make a mint of money.' And I thought, 'That's for me.'

"And . . . I haven't made a mint of money, but I've made some beautiful friends all over the world and had a lot of fun traveling and researching."

"When did she die?" I ask.

"April of '47," Mrs. Bennett answers. "But I had already started reading everything I could get my hands on, in '46. My husband was just back from the war, and we were in Omaha with his parents until we decided where he would locate. We were thinking of locating in Alma, which is about forty-five miles up the river from here, but the people from Red Cloud came up there and begged him on bended knee to come to Red Cloud. He said finally to me, 'Well, what shall we do—stay here or go to Red Cloud?' And I said, 'Well, I'd rather go to Red Cloud because I can learn more about Willa Cather in Red Cloud.' So we came here in 1946, and I've been working on Cather ever since."

The atmosphere in the room has changed. While she sits as straight as ever, Mrs. Bennett's face has relaxed and brightened with the beginning of excitement. I feel from her the enthusiasm that has motivated her in these thirty years of research.

How was she able, I ask, to gather the material she has presented in *The World of Willa Cather?*

"There were a lot of oldtimers left in the area," she explains. "The Lambrecht family was still living, the girls that Willa had played with. Carrie Miner Sherwood, who was a good friend of hers, helped me enormously. And Mary Miner Creighton was still alive. There were a lot of contemporaries of hers who were still alive."

"How did you begin?" I ask.

"Carrie Sherwood said the first thing to do was to go through all the newspaper clippings—she had a collection of clippings and things that she had kept—and find everybody that ever knew Willa Cather and write a letter to him or her. Which I did. Among those people to whom I wrote were the Menuhins."

Willa Cather had been a staunch friend, Mrs. Bennett says, to the children in that great musical family. Child prodigies all—Yehudi Menuhin the most famous—they had responded to the attentions of this mature artist, and she had maintained relations with them over a number of years. Mildred Bennett found the Menuhins living in California and communicated with Mrs. Menuhin, telling her when she would be on the West Coast.

"She called me up at my folks' place in California and said, 'Come on up, we'll be delighted to have you.' I said, 'I have a four-year-old son,' and she said, 'We love children. Bring him along.' And the next day I got a telegram saying 'Don't come. Can't talk about Willa Cather. Have nothing to say to you.'

"So I then discovered that she had talked to Edith Lewis, who had lived with Willa Cather for thirty or forty years, and Edith Lewis had told her not to have anything to do with me. And then Edith Lewis wrote to everybody she could think of—all the relatives and everybody who had ever known Willa Cather—and told them to have nothing to do with 'that wretched Mildred Bennett.' My friends have told me they've read some of these letters in the collections in different libraries.

"Anyhow, this posed a problem. I had a manuscript written out by 1948, and I went to see Alfred Knopf, Willa Cather's publisher. He took the manuscript and read it and he said, I'll get you an appointment with Edith Lewis."

Mrs. Bennett leans back slightly in her chair, her eyes looking past me. I imagine she has told this story often. It is as if I disappear and she is talking to herself, reciting the past.

"Well, this was probably on a Thursday that I saw him, and after that my husband and family and I drove up to Rhode Island to see some friends we had known in the war. The wife of the dentist that we went to see—she and I decided to drive up to see Willa Cather's grave in Jaffrey, New Hampshire, and also see Dorothy Canfield Fisher if we could."

Dorothy Canfield Fisher, the novelist and short story writer, was a friend of Willa Cather from their youth, Mrs. Bennett explains, when Dorothy's father was chancellor of the University of Nebraska.

"So first we went up to Jaffrey and saw Willa Cather's grave. There was no tombstone yet. They were erecting a house between the gravesite and Mount Monadnock, and the place was all muddy. I had a big new Packard, and it got stuck in the mud. Finally we got out of that, and we started over toward Burlington, Vermont. I decided I better call Dorothy Canfield Fisher and see if she were home before I drove over there. I got her husband, who said, 'Dorothy is down at the commencement exercises of Marlboro College. I don't think she'll talk to you because she's had a letter from Edith Lewis … unless you get Knopf's permission to talk to her.' He said, 'I think it's a lot of foolishness! But I don't know anything about Willa Cather, so I can't help you. But anyway, you call Knopf, and if he says okay, you go on over to Marlboro and catch her there.'

"So I called Mr. Knopf. He said, 'What are you doing way up there when I have an appointment for you with Edith Lewis on Monday!" This was Friday, I think, and it was all of two hundred miles away! And I said, 'Don't worry, I'll be back.' Somehow in New York distances are a lot different from out here. Two hundred miles is nothing out here. And he said, 'I don't see any reason why you shouldn't talk to Dorothy Canfield Fisher. Go ahead and talk to her.'

"So I thanked him and hung up. And I got in my Packard and started for Marlboro, Vermont."

I relax once and for all now, realizing Mildred Bennett has worked up momentum and is purring along briskly, not needing any further urging.

"When we talked to Dorothy Canfield Fisher, she said, 'Anything I can do to help you I will be very happy to do. You write me and ask any questions you want.'

"She was a great help to me. I wrote her a number of letters, and she answered all my questions and gave me permission to quote from her published articles about Willa Cather. I wrote her some questions that she received when she was on her deathbed. Her husband read the letter to her, and she answered the questions and he wrote and told me what she had said. She died soon thereafter. She helped me right up to the very end."

She pauses briefly, gazing at me from behind her glasses, while I ponder Dorothy Canfield Fisher's generosity, and wonder about the Cather relatives. Were they also cooperative?

"Willa's sister Elsie, who lived in Lincoln, wouldn't have anything to do with me." Mrs. Bennett answers. "I called her up and tried to talk to her and she wouldn't talk to me. Then when I was working on the manuscript, one of Elsie Cather's friends here in Red Cloud, who is still living, wrote to her, 'Now Mildred Bennett is going to do a good piece of work. The book is going to be published whether you like it or not, and if there are mistakes in it, it's going to be your fault because you have refused to help her. Then the word came to me by grapevine that if I would call Elsie Cather I would get a better reception. So the next time I was in Lincoln I did call her again, and she said, 'Why yes, I would be very happy to help you. You plan to come out and spend a week with me, and we'll go over the whole manuscript! So I went out and I stayed with her. She was a teacher in Lincoln and she was retired. Nice little house in Lincoln. She had prepared for my week there. She had cooked a smoked tongue, and we ate smoked tongue for the whole week. We didn't do any cooking or anything else, we just worked on that manuscript. She helped me a great deal, clarified things and corrected things and so on. She was so happy with what the book was, when it came out, that she bought one for each of her nephews and nieces."

I interrupt the flow of her talk to ask, "What had been her objection at the beginning?"

"Edith Lewis had written to her," Mrs. Bennett answered, frowning, "and she said she didn't want to hurt dear Edith. Edith had written all the nephews and nieces too, and one of the nieces wrote to Carrie Miner Sherwood, who had been Willa's good friend for so many years, and said, 'Don't help Mildred Bennett.' That made Mrs. Sherwood furious. She said, 'I guess I know what is right and what isn't right, and they don't need to tell *me* what to do.' She was a very imperious old lady, who was very clear-minded up into her hundreds. She went with me on all my speaking engagements after the book came out and was the life of the party. She was the most remarkable woman."

I remember the photograph I had seen of the young Carrie Miner Sherwood in a dark tailored dress and top hat, looking brighteyed and resolute, and can imagine she stayed that way until her death.

But I am still wondering about that meeting with Edith Lewis in New York, arranged by Alfred Knopf. Now I ask Mildred Bennett if it ever took place.

"Yes, I met with her, and she was very nice except whenever I mentioned Willa Cather she was very adamant. She said, 'Who are you that you think you can write a book about Willa Cather when even *I* wouldn't write a book about her!' In every respect aside from Willa Cather she was very sweet to me, asked me about my family and about my little boy. But every time we talked about Willa Cather she twisted her handkerchief into just a . . . well, she practically tore it to shreds, she was so nervous.

"She was the executor of the estate—executrix, I should say, in this day of women's lib. Anyway, she had the say about all the publication of the books. She appointed E. K. Brown as the official biographer for Willa Cather, but she would not let him look at any original material. He came out here, and he told me he was having a terrible time with her. She didn't want Willa Cather's original birth date, which was 1873, to be put in the book. We had a birth certificate from Virginia, where Willa Cather was born, and other evidence—letters from the family indicating that she had been born on December 7, 1873. But Edith Lewis persisted in putting up a monument with '76 on it."

It was the relationship of thirty years and more between Willa Cather and Edith Lewis that had left her in this position of power. Partnership, love affair, friendship: no doubt it was all of these. "One realized," wrote Elizabeth Shepley Sergeant, "how much her companionship meant to Willa."* As Willa Cather aged, she grew more and more reclusive, Edith Lewis cooperating with her desires by protecting her from the demands of admiring strangers. Willa Cather had always wanted to be known strictly for the work she produced, not for the manner in which she lived her life. And two women living together in so intimate a relationship had reason to guard their privacy closely against public attitudes. So the habit of extreme discretion was established. After Willa's

* Elizabeth Shepley Sergeant, *Willa Cather, A Memoir* (Lincoln: University of Nebraska Press, 1953), p. 202.

death, Edith still acted out of loyalty to her, carrying out her wishes in a manner consistent with their life together.

Mildred Bennett persisted in her researches here in Red Cloud and elsewhere until her book was finished and published by Dodd Mead in 1951. It sold well, and led to her meeting Cather fans from many countries. The Japanese, she says, are very interested in Willa Cather, and she speculates that it may be Cather's feeling for heritage and her symbolism that attract them. So many people are drawn to Red Cloud by the Cather Memorial that Mrs. Bennett and its other caretakers have organized a yearly conference, the first week in May, in which a Cather authority comes to Red Cloud to discuss a particular book.

So in this town, where yesterday I heard the women in the cafe discussing waterbeds, where an old man rides a big-wheeled tricycle down the street, and the cafe advertises "Pheasants dressed, we keep all feathers"—here the ghost of that forthright young woman, that distinguished novelist, hovers all year and is respectfully summoned in the spring. Yet how ironic is this public notice, when the artist developed in secret, the young Willa Cather storing up material all unaware, letting it settle inside her in the long days of childhood. If she were here among us now she would listen, watch; and one day Dorothy and Sue, possibly the dignified, loquacious Mrs. Bennett, might reappear as characters in a book of hers, where she would tell their lives as they never could themselves. And they might, as did some of her contemporaries in the town, resent this intrusion.

"There were a lot of people who hated her," Mrs. Bennett says, "because she was different and because she was famous, and because she had written things that obviously were Red Cloud that were not complimentary. She had written *A Lost Lady* about Mrs. Garber. That made people in Lincoln very angry, because Mrs. Garber had been the governor's wife and they'd been very fond of her. Willa Cather was very fond of Mrs. Garber too, and she wrote in the autographed copy that Mrs. Sherwood had, 'Wasn't she a flash of brightness in our lives' or 'Didn't she have a lovely laugh,' or, I can't remember the exact quotation, but any-way it was very complimentary. I think she had no intention of doing anybody any harm. In an interview she said she didn't write the story until there was no one left who could be hurt."

"Did she visit here often?" I ask.

"Yes, until her parents died. Then in 1931 she came back to help close up the house. She wanted Elsie to keep the house open as it had been when the family lived there, and Elsie had her own life to live and she wouldn't do it. So they had an auction and closed up the house, and sold it eventually, and it became the first hospital in Red Cloud. When Willa found out it was to be a hospital, she was furious and she wrote to Carrie Miner Sherwood and told her how unhappy she was, and Carrie wrote back and said, 'Now just calm down. We need a hospital and there is noth-ing that would be a better use for that house than a hospital.' And Willa sent a thousand dollars for the hospital with the provision that nobody know that she sent it. Carrie could always manage her, but I think there was nobody else who could. Carrie was four years older. She encouraged Willa a great deal, and had a great deal to do with her growing up, and knew her probably better than anyone else in Red Cloud, and probably better than anyone else in the world. She had the kind of a mind that understands. And it was most fortunate that I had that long fellowship and friendship with her.

I'll tell you how I happened to get in so well with Mrs. Sher-wood. Our little boy was four and he went around the block knocking at all the doors asking if there were any children he could play with. He came to Mrs. Sherwood, and she said no, she had no children, and he said, 'I like your house, can I come in and look at it?' She said, 'You certainly may,' and she took him from top to bottom of her house, and they had a big conversation. She loved him, and was his friend, you know, remembered his birth-day and his graduation and anything else as long as she lived. He had opened the door for me, because I was the mother of that charming little boy."

I see how her work on Willa Cather grew from an immediate involvement in the town and with its people, so that while her endeavor extends out to touch readers and scholars in distant cities, reaches even to Japan, it is rooted in the intimate details of life here in this small town.

Mrs. Bennett, who has been glancing anxiously at the stairs, looks down at her watch, now, her eyes opening wide in alarm.

"I should be going soon. Yes, it's almost noon."

But I do not let her go quite yet, wanting to know what she thinks about the burning of most of Willa Cather's letters before she died. Did Willa Cather and Edith Lewis burn the letters to get rid of information that might have compromised Cather's reputation? Were Willa and Edith destroying evidence of those passionate relationships with women that Willa maintained all her life? I phrase my question carefully, placing my words like stepping stones through a mined terrain.

Mrs. Bennett stops putting on her coat to peer sharply at me. I suppose everyone asks her some similar question.

"I have no way of knowing," she answers, "so why should I make a statement!"

And she gets up to pull her coat around her and button it. Her desire to be across town tending to her guests and husband is so strong that she seems already to have left this room. But she returns for one last commentary.

"I think all the facts are out that are going to come out. I don't think anything about Willa Cather is hidden. I don't think the burning of the letters has confused or confounded anybody too much, because Willa Cather wrote herself so definitely into everything she did. She wanted to be judged by her books. I think she told everything in her books."

We say goodbye, Mildred Bennett brisk and defended once again. I watch her go up the stairs, her body angular, imposing, and then I sit for a time in the quiet basement, thinking of this woman who displayed such persistence in her research, such sensitivity in her writing. I realize that it was the achievement of Willa Cather that allowed Mrs. Bennett to work and develop herself in this setting; that we are linked, down through time, woman to woman. While the services and accoutrements of this memorial are sometimes a little pompous, still this tending of the roots, this examination of the first soil in which a great writer began to develop, protects a precious heritage.

Mrs. Bennett has performed this work with assiduity for many years. She is obviously a gifted and highly intelligent woman, and I wonder what frustrations may have assailed her in her life here as a small town doctor's wife. This we could probably never talk about. Perhaps in the context of Red Cloud and the Memorial, it is enough to know her accomplishments.

I walked out into a stretch of unbroken prairie near Red Cloud, the wild red grass taller than me. It hissed in the wind, moving as if with a life of its own. I disappeared into it as completely as the pheasant who came flapping up next to me, making me rear back, heart pounding, and then swooped off to plunge into another portion of the grass with the abruptness of a pelican dropping into the sea. I feared I was lost. I could see nothing but the slender stems moving around me. So many grasses here—I had seen them labeled: Buffalo grass, Blue Grama, Prairie Dropseed, Sideoats Grama, Little Bluestem, Switchgrass, Indiangrass, Prairie Cordgrass, Big Bluestem that can grow over nine feet tall, Eastern Gamagrass, Reed Canarygrass. The wind whipped the grasses, its cold stiffening my cheeks and making my ears ache. I liked being here in this undulating world. Next to my narrow winding path I saw milkweed plants, their pods split open, the snowy fluff bursting out, and I remembered the field next to our house where I spent my days as a child. The grass and weeds sometimes reached above my head. I was alone in my world, and I laid the silky milkweed fluff across my palm, smoothing it as I did the pelt of the rabbit we kept in a hutch in the backyard. I blew it up away from me, watching the individual seeds float on the wind and wobble slowly down into the grass. Willa Cather

must have done that. On this prairie I strode forward, looking for
a way out, noticing the shrubs now in among the grass stems. So
many varieties: did she know their names? Probably she knew
them all, for she said there was one book she would rather have
produced than all her novels, the Clemens botany describing the
wildflowers of the west.

I came out of the grasses changed, as if I had journeyed far
back in time to the unbroken prairie, where buffalo grazed, native
people hunted, the weather raged over a nearly empty land. In
just this way I used to emerge from the field, carrying with me
intimations of the secret existences of rabbits and mice just
glimpsed, the occasional snake that slid among the grass stems.
Smelling of growing things, of earth, I would enter my mother's
kitchen, my mind still wide with the vastness of sky seen while I
lay on my back in the tall weeds.

I found this same wonder in Willa Cather's writings. So much
she gave to us of her own love of the Great Plains, her understanding of the lives of the generations preceding hers. Less re-
nowned women have also passed down this knowledge, through
women's crafts and arts, preserving the culture in the larger world
as well as in the privacy of the family. In the small towns I felt the
women's interest in and respect for their heritage; and often I
experienced a vivid remembrance of my mother as she had been
when I was a child.

The towns are dwarfed by the prairie; life there is intense,
turned inward as on an island. There is no escaping one's mistakes, which are present in the memory of one's neighbors, called
to mind by a tone of voice, an inclination of the head, a look that
says *I* know who you are. Alexine Chaput, in her half century of
burying the dead and encouraging the living, has seen her neighbors rise to heights of socially beneficial behavior, has viewed their
most petty and ignominious acts. She carries this depth of knowledge with appropriate gravity, and will no doubt pass it on to
Laura Vytlacil, if Laura stays in the funeral parlor. Richae Colby
in Concordia must live daily with others' awareness of her misfortunes, must carry the burden of being "felt sorry for." The hard

times are lived through in full view of the community, and in the shared experience over a long period one may perhaps come to know more fully what it means to be human.

One who fulfilled a harsh destiny among her neighbors and family is Ruth Chaplin of the South Side Cafe. She told me her story so ingenuously, she lives each day that is given her without apology and without expectation. Her life as she told it confronted me with a difficult question: how much of what happpens to us do we invite, design, seek out; and how much occurs by chance? How did Ruth participate in the disasters that befell her: was she simply a victim or was she an individual working out a complex destiny in which loss and pain served specific purposes?

Her own theory is the Christian model of an all-knowing God who giveth and taketh away. "Prayers are answered," she said. "When one thing is taken away, something is given back." Her belief in this balancing-out has allowed her to work her way through to acceptance of what she has had to endure, to resignation in the face of all she could not control. But resignation is hardly a joyous embracing of what is. It requires the deadening of much that lives in us; it is a patient submission to that which cannot be changed. I hear Ruth's voice saying, "I'll never give anybody the opportunity to hurt me that way again," and I feel how, out of fear, often, or the habit of restraint, I too hold back from experiencing the deepest, simplest joy; hold back from a trust in human beings that would let me live my life to its fullest. This also is a legacy from our foremothers.

There is a price for surviving. The women of the heartland know it well, descended as they are from those who held fast against enormous odds on the frontier. Willa Cather wrote about those women; Mildred Bennett preserves their heritage in her honoring of Willa Cather. In their relations with young women and children, Laura Vytlacil and Alexine Chaput transmit this intimate, essential knowledge. Richae Colby is the wayward daughter, the heir.

My own mother harbored a reticence comparable to Ruth's; we rarely saw an expression of her feelings. I wonder now if she learned this from *her* mother, a woman who was continually ill for all the years I knew her. My grandmother sat all day in a rocker, her left arm shaking with palsy, her voice weak and gently complaining. She was locked away inside her illness. Though I was asked to love her, to sit on her lap because I was her littlest granddaughter and presumably she loved *me,* I could feel almost nothing for or from her. She seemed like a whiny child, patiently tended by my grandfather, aware only of her own needs.

On the day my grandmother died, my mother fixed dinner for us as usual. As we ate, my sister and I began to argue. Suddenly, we realized my mother was crying. My sister, my brother, my father, and I stared at her in amazement and distress. Her face contorted, tears slid down her cheeks from her reddened eyes, her hand fumbled in the pocket of her apron for her handkerchief. And when she had left the table, we sat in stricken silence, and I understood: this was *her mother* who had died.

That evening my washing of the dishes, my picking at my homework, were permeated with an intense awareness of my mother and myself. When she came downstairs later, her eyes red-lidded, I watched her with a new, shy tenderness, for I felt the larger sweep of her life now, had seen her opened to herself in her grief.

Bon Marche store, Concordia

Richae Colby at the Kountry Kitchen Cafe

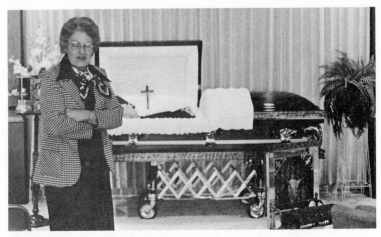

Alexine Chaput at the Chaput Mortuary

Ruth Chaplin

Sue Fintel and Dorothy Mattison with portrait of Willa Cather, at the Willa Cather Pioneer Memorial, Red Cloud

Entrance to meeting hall, Cuba

Washstand in Willa Cather's room

Cultures Side by Side

Standing Deep in Time

The capacity for hard work, the resilience, independence, and pride of the white women in this book are rooted in the experience of their forebears who came to homestead the land in the second half of the nineteenth century; these qualities in the women of color come from more ancient sources. The white women arrived from many European countries and from the states farther east, while black people came from the American South after the Civil War. Native American foremothers were born on Kansas land or came from the states to the east, many from Great Lakes territory, not willingly nor with the pioneers' hopes of a prosperous future, but pushed west into reservations by the inexorable movement of white settlers and a federal government that saw them as a "nuisance," needing to be placated and controlled.

All who came in the early days to Kansas Territory found a vast prairie of undulating, tall, tough grasses, across which the wind blew almost without ceasing. A young woman of this time notes in her diary each day the direction and velocity of the wind, sometimes several times a day if it changed, until the roaring, sighing, whining, whispering, or shrieking of that great force becomes an environment in which the writer and her family live. Reading, one searches with growing anxiety to learn each day of the wind's moods. When she writes, "light breeze from NE," one can relax; when she notes, "It blew so hard last night we all went downstairs," we know a tornado was feared.*

The settlers found heartstopping heat in the summer, numbing cold in the winter. They were plagued by droughts or excessive rains, relentless winds, prairie fires, hordes of insects who ate crops to the ground. White and Native American peoples coexisted uneasily in a balance that often tipped over into violence. A murderous battle raged between those settlers who would make Kansas into a slave state and those who wanted her to extend freedom to all her citizens, regardless of color.

The homesteaders dug their homes out of the soil, burrowing back into hillsides to construct dugouts, or building houses of blocks of sod lifted up off the prairie. "They were warm inside," remarked Uncle Earl, recalling his grandparents' accounts, "but muddy."

It is not hard to imagine the privations and particular sufferings of the women who bore their children in these houses while the wind raged outside. Some of them died in childbirth, a few went crazy, some went back East. But many pioneer women thrived on the challenge of frontier life, sharing the vision of a prosperous civilized territory on the midwestern plains. Part of that dream for Kansas women was equality with their men, and the women were so active in their own behalf that, when the state constitution was drawn up, they won the right to acquire and possess property and to retain equal custody of their children. Fifty years later, the state was among the first to ratify the woman's suffrage amendment.

Each new wave of immigrants brought its own mores, its particular requirements about the roles of men and women. The Scandinavians, the French, the Germans, the English, the Scottish, the Czechoslovakians—all brought their old country customs to transplant in Kansas soil. Most saw them, over the years, trans-

---

* Diary of Olive Capper, Miscellaneous, Manuscript Department, Kansas State Historical Society, Topeka, Kansas.

muted by circumstance; saw the relations between men & women altered, too, by conditions. But many of the towns established by particular groups of immigrants retain their ethnic definition even today. Lindsborg is a Swedish town, where every other year a Svensk Hyllningsfest brings out the inhabitants in their embroidered vests and long skirts, knee breeches, peaked hats, to play host to the countryside for three days of celebration to honor the Swedish pioneers who settled the Smoky Valley area. There is ample evidence in the town of Cuba that it was established by Bohemians. Nicodemus was an all-Black town, and keeps much of its racial character today.

One very powerful segment of the influx of settlers was the New Englanders. Many were recruited by the Kansas freesoilers, who hoped to keep slavery out of the territory, and offered land very cheap. Often it was professional men from New England, mostly bearing Anglo Saxon names, who founded the towns and formed the upper crust on the great stew of pioneer society. But many humbler New Englanders came as homesteaders and remained farmers, their wives having given up the more civilized life of the East for a new home on the prairie. One such woman, Chestina Bowker Allen, came at the age of forty-six, with her husband and five children, from Massachusetts. She kept a record of her first few years in Kansas Territory, in a journal written in a neat, graceful hand. At one point she mentions that as she sits by the fire, snow blows through the chinks in the wall to fall on the page on which she writes. New England restraint reins in her expression, yet those snowflakes settling on the paper speak worlds about the hardship of her condition.

In this new life provisions were often scarce, the situation near desperate. On March 22nd, 1855, Chestina recorded,

Mr. Morgan and son from Brooks, Me. desired supper, lodging and breakfast, and two more [men asked] to cook their own food and lodge in our little hut, to which I assented. Morgan wished to sell a bag of flour, as the scarcity of timber and the expense of moving conspired to make him conclude that he had better return to Maine. By us this flour is considered a God send for we were out and could buy none in Juniatta. We lacked a dollar to make enough to pay for a bag of flour and the price of their entertainment just made it.

In her years on the prairie, Chestina traveled the countryside to aid in the births, illnesses, and deaths of the settlers. Of one such errand she wrote: "Mrs. Esq. Dyer and I go to Mr. Eubanks on horseback, Mrs. E. confined with a daughter the day before." Mrs. Eubanks, she noted, was "the strongest pro-slaveryite I have met with." One wonders if they carried on a political discussion at the bedside. Negro slavery presented itself in the flesh one day when "Booth Fox with his slave woman passed by. The poor creature had no covering for her head but picked up a cast off cap while in the neighborhood and went off running after her master and his ox team." Again and again Chestina Allen recorded the fighting between antislavery and proslavery proponents, these last chiefly from Missouri. In June of 1856 she wrote, "Hear that Col. Lane had come into the Ter. with some say 800 and some say 2200 men, that he has destroyed the town of Franklin and gone to Lecompton. It seems a mighty strife for freedom has commenced."

Although the native people in the area occasionally fought back against the settlers overrunning their land or took the intruders' stock or goods, Chestina never admitted to fear of them. On May 31st she wrote of a large drove of sheep and herders passing through on their way to California. "News came that when 40 miles beyond here on the Republican, the Comanches and other Indians had killed four of the men, wounded one, taken women and children prisoners and got the sheep. Some people are alarmed, of course." This last bland assertion leads us to believe that she did not share in that trepidation. In another instance, when Potawatomi and Cheyenne warriors clashed and the white settlers became frightened for their own lives, Chestina kept her sense of humor. She described the emergency meeting of the settlers, noting "O! they did watch to see the first pop of an Indian!"

Although Chestina Allen was often in contact with other pioneer wives, there were periods in which she suffered the acute isolation known by those who venture out beyond the edge of civilization. What it meant to her in these times to be visited, tended, by another woman, is felt in her brief notation of her feelings regarding the death of a Mrs. Carrol in the town of Wildcat. "[She was] the only woman who visited me in my lone two months residence and sickness there. This dear woman walked 3 mis. to comfort me in my affliction. A Mormon by profession and fared hard."*

Most of the women fared hard. But many, like Chestina, survived to a satisfied old age, having seen their lands and fortunes prosper, their children grow up to take over the farm and carry on the work of building a life on the prairie. The Native American women lived a different reality, their experience unfolding within the culture of their people. The black women, despite the racism of the society, survived to hold positions of respect within their communities. There are women alive now whose grandmothers told them of the struggles, the losses, the indomitable courage of their foremothers; these stories inform the present experience of midwestern women and link them with the past in all its violence and difficulty as well as its record of fortitude.

Proud Granddaughter

Golden leaves fall from the cottonwoods onto the sidewalks of Concordia on this warm October day. People go about without their coats. Just across from the courthouse, on the southwest corner of Eighth and Washington Streets, stands a small, dark-painted house closely sheltered by trees. The home of Marion Ellet sits high on the bank and is nearly invisible from the sidewalk, except for its square plastic doorbell button illuminated by a yellow light.

Even in this sunny afternoon, shadow surrounds us in Marion's living room as she sits watching me with indulgent interest. I have been sent to her by Marguerite Lasnier through Marguer-

* Diary of Mrs. Chestina Bowker Allen, 1808–?, History, Pottawatomie County, Manuscript Department, Kansas State Historical Society, Topeka, Kansas.

ite's granddaughter in California. The Lasniers' recommendation makes me respectable, but Marion scrutinizes me as she talks, and I sense that we are to maintain a strict decorum. She is a small, thin woman in slacks and sandals and a bulky sweater. She seems tired, leaning a little sideways in her chair, speaking steadily but without much energy, now and then dropping off into a silence to observe me. She has the quietness of one who is much alone; her long, serious face is set in lines of thought.

This morning I bought a *Concordia Blade-Empire,* the daily paper, to read what Marion Ellet had to say in the column she authors. She wrote about leadership, delineating its difficulties in "this era of total civil disruption," citing the particular dilemmas of the President and Ayatollah Khomeini as examples. Her column, which she has been writing each day for over fifty years, is called "Mugwump Musings." A mugwump is defined as (1) a Republican who refused to support the party ticket in 1884; and (2) any independent, especially in politics.

Republican, yes. Independent, most definitely. She is not only a spinster but a Christian Scientist, both of which definitions set her apart from her neighbors.

I arrived at her house having been told only that she was a newspaperwoman who might help me gather information. I had expected her to be at least thirty years younger than she is.

"I'm going to be eighty-one soon," she tells me, smiling. "I'm going to start my life over again on my birthday. You have a choice, at my age: you can give up and wither away, or you can begin again."

She speaks with satisfaction, with a certain proprietary interest, of the history of Concordia. My former experience of Concordia had been a visit to the stock auction barn on the edge of town and the Kountry Kitchen cafe on the main street, both the hangouts of overalled farmers, and my most recent encounter was with Richae Colby. Now, as Marion Ellet talks, I begin to get an inkling of another dimension of the town's life, for I realize that I am in the presence of a member of one of its first families.

"Concordia really is a New England town," she explains. "The

New Englanders arrived here before the French, and about the same time as the Swedish farmers. There were two types of influx: the peasant class, who came to homestead—they were mostly Swedes; and the New Englanders, highly educated people who came to establish professions in the town. The French came a little later. The Lasniers and Betourneys, the LeSages and LaRocques: they came as merchants from Canada. Some of them were known as 'black French'—they were dark complected because they had mixed with Canadian Indians."

Her people came in 1872, the year the town was founded. Her grandfather, whose name was Sturges, was a lawyer from Connecticut. Her grandmother came from New York City. "My family has lived over one hundred years in this very house. Of course it didn't look like this when they came. It was a 'bank house' that a German had built. A bank house is hollowed out of the side of a hill, so that it has ventilation on three sides but is protected on the fourth. That original bank house is now the cellar of this house. When my grandfather arrived by stagecoach with his two young sons and my grandmother, who was pregnant, he bought the house from the German and planned to build rooms above the original room before winter hit. But the blizzards came on too quickly, and my grandmother gave birth to my mother in that original house."

Marion pauses, and I wonder what it feels like to possess such firm knowledge of one's history. My own awareness of lineage has come to me in bits and scraps, a few stories, a few doubtful accounts. Her heritage exists right here where we sit talking.

"I've heard my grandmother speak of that birth," she continues. "She said she could not cry out because they were in that one small room. 'There was nothing between me and those two little boys except a curtain across the room,' she told me. 'I couldn't cry.'"

As if listening once again to her grandmother's voice, Marion gazes off into the shadowy corners of the room. I look around me, searching for a feeling of the antiquity of the house. The living room is not large; the old furnishings, which for all I know may be valuable antiques, seem modest and even a little shabby.

When Marion glances back at me, her gaze is clouded.

"Her best friend *died* in childbirth out here, during that first winter. It was a great blow to her. Grandmother hated this pioneer life. She wanted New York City. Only her loyalty to her family kept her here."

She muses for a moment.

"My mother, too, wasn't fitted for her life. She was a beautiful and talented woman. She should have been an actress. She should never have married or had a child."

There is sadness in her voice, no doubt partly for her mother, but also, I imagine, for her own growing up with such a woman. Was she perhaps given to understand that she would never be as beautiful as her mother, never as talented? Did she feel as if her presence prevented something?

"Have you always lived in Concordia?" I ask.

"I can't imagine what could interest you in *my* story," she counters, smiling uncomfortably. Her smiles are rare, lighting her long, serious face, making her seem vulnerable and young. "Don't you want to know more about the town?"

"I'm interested in your life too."

She glances sideways at me for a few moments, and sees I am not going to give up.

"Well, no, actually I grew up in Kansas City, Missouri." Her father's family had been settlers in Kansas, she says, but he went into the shoe business in Kansas City, so she and her mother had to live there. "I hated it. The years that I went to school in Kansas City, those were the years the locust ate. Each summer I was allowed to come to Concordia. Then, after I went to Barstowe prep school and Smith College, I came back here and broke into newspaper writing."

Pausing, she remembers silently, until I urge her to tell me how she began her career. She talks reluctantly, amused that I want to hear this.

"I hadn't intended to work on a newspaper. At that time at Harvard there was a remarkable drama program called the Harvard 47 Workshop. Smith had a similar workshop, and my plan was to do graduate work in that program. But on my way home from college a friend offered me a job on a newspaper; I took it and never got to the workshop."

"And you've been here ever since?"

"Oh no. After one year I decided to go to New York City to learn my trade. So I went there. I worked on the school page of the *Sun,* and wrote book reviews for the *Times,* and became a reporter on the night desk of the *Brooklyn Eagle.* That was the paper that Walt Whitman used to write for. I learned a great deal there."

Immediately I feel a kinship for Marion Ellet, realizing that even in the 1920s young writers from the Midwest made pilgrimages to New York City. I wonder what that city could have been like for her, and ask her whether she met difficulties entering such a male-dominated field as newspaper writing.

"Oh well, I never felt any sexual rivalry with the men," she answers. "They were all very nice to me, very helpful. I guess that's why I never became a feminist. You see, I came from a lawyer's family. I had an intellectual background in which people discussed ideas, often argued about them. I was always allowed to express my views, but I knew they would be challenged, and I had to take responsibility for knowing what I was talking about. Having had this kind of training in my family, I could always hold my own with men, and so I never had any trouble with them."

She seems to see herself as exempt from the common lot, as many exceptional women do, so that "women" are referred to as "they," a race apart from oneself and subject to separate rules. It is disappointing to hear that Marion does not identify with Kansas's proud feminist history. With her self-confidence and educational advantages, she would have been uniquely fitted to defend the rights won by her predecessors. Kansas women, from the 1860s on, traveled the state in open wagons to speak in schoolhouses and churches, meeting halls and parlors, on the cause of woman's suffrage. Ratification of the woman's suffrage amendment by their Kansas state legislature took place in Marion's lifetime.

I see her, Smith graduate, proud granddaughter of a prairie

patriarch, traveling the night streets of an Eastern city. She would take the subway home to Manhattan each morning at 2 or 3 A.M., she tells me, from her job in Brooklyn, riding the trains alone, standing in the stations without fear. Once she thought to ask a policeman if there was any danger. He assured her there was not, but if she were at all anxious she should carry a whistle. "If anything seems strange to you," he told her, "just blow the whistle and we'll all come running."

"I stayed in New York about four years," she explains, "until I realized the competition was so heavy that there was very little opportunity to break into editorial or feature writing. It was then I decided to come back here, where I could have more chance to do the kind of writing I wanted to do."

I wonder if Marion knew, in 1925, that she was making a commitment that would last the rest of her life.

She came back to Concordia and got a job on the daily paper. For the first year she did reporting and anything else they asked of her. Then the city editor, who had written a daily column, died. Marion asked her boss if she could do a column to replace it, but he was skeptical. In order to convince him, she offered to write for free. He finally agreed to let her try. That was 1926. In a short time, her writings began to be picked up by other papers around the state, and after a year the paper began to pay her. She has been writing "Mugwump Musings" ever since. Now it appears daily in the *Emporia Gazette,* the *Great Bend Tribune,* and the *Concordia Blade-Empire.*

"How would you characterize your column?" I ask her.

"It's pretty much political, critiques, human comment, some travel reporting."

I look at her with respect for her perseverance in this daily labor for over fifty years. I ask, because I imagine everyone in Concordia is married, "I suppose you married and raised children here?"

"No, I never married." Said matter of factly.

I'm surprised, and my view of her changes. She is no longer the elderly materfamilias surrounded by children and grandchildren, a distinguished old husband looking on from the side room or beyond the grave.

"How has it been, how is it, in this town, to be a single woman?"

She answers with surprising readiness.

"There is always discomfort. Society goes in twos. There are places where I am not welcome because I'm a single woman. It's difficult, always has been. But I don't feel any deep sorrow around that."

I wonder whether she has had loves over the years, and what these may have been. She mentions in passing a newspaperman with whom, she said, "I was in love, or thought I was in love." Were there others? But I don't ask.

Instead, I inquire about change in Concordia in all the years she has known it. She gazes intently at me.

"The general social character of this town has changed very little," she says. "It has always been intellectual, artistocratic. Outsiders call it a snobbish town. I don't know. There has always been very elegant living here."

I am fascinated. My own view of Concordia is of a community that exists to serve the farmers coming in from outlying farms, descendants, no doubt, of the "peasants" who had arrived here at the same time as the New Englanders. True, it is the county seat and has a country club, community college, Catholic convent, and hospital for its 7,533 citizens; but where the elegant living may take place, I do not know. Marion makes clear to me the social hierarchy in Concordia, the patrician heritage of which she is beneficiary.

She speaks of the "old families": the Thurstons, who have a place three miles southwest of town; the Kennet family, whose patriarch was a law partner of her grandfather.

"But isn't the town very dependent on farming?" I ask.

"Oh yes," she agrees. "We are very close to the earth. Unless the earth prospers, I don't have tenants for my buildings. Unless the earth prospers, I don't have readers for my columns."

We speak of the great national and world upheavals in her time, and she tells me towns like this one on the prairie are relatively untouched by such influences. "Here people live a more level life."

This echoes the statement of one of the farm women, who told me, "We're aware of what's going on out in the world, but it's from a distance. It's not like, well, tomorrow I'm going to have to get up and live my life different because something happened fifteen hundred miles away from me."

But the drought, the dust storms of the thirties, had a tremendous effect on this region. It was this natural disaster that drove thousands of farmers from the Great Plains and sent them principally to the West Coast to find a way to feed themselves and their families. Marion Ellet remembers this hard time. The dust storms were called "black blizzards," she says, and she describes the worst one she experienced.

"I was working in my study here in the house, right by the window there. It was midday; there was no wind. Suddenly everything went black as midnight. I remember looking out my window into that pitch dark. It was the dust settling."

"Did most of the farmers from around here leave?"

"No, not many from right here. They suffered terribly, but they stuck it out."

"Did your family feel the effects?"

"No, we had industrial property."

I am pulled up short by this casual reply, made thoughtful by the class privilege it expresses. So much is said about Marion Ellet's life in those few words.

When it's time to go, she asks where I'm staying, and says, "I would ask you to stay here, but I've been having a difficult time these last few days over a personal matter, and I need to be alone in the house."

We stand over the bookcase together while she looks for the book that is a history of Concordia. I notice her fluff of gray hair, her narrow shoulders, and her body, which is thin but not delicate. Strong seeming, adequate. *It Takes People to Make a Town,* the book is called.* She hands it to me.

"After you've read it, you'll know more about the town. You must come back and we'll talk again."

I promise to do so.

"It's my only copy," she says as we walk to the door. "But I'm not worried. I know you'll return it."

In the days that follow I find that Marion Ellet is much admired in her community. People in Concordia and Clyde remark on her columns, her rare public appearances. They respect her person, her intellect, her family's role in the history of the town. They are awed by her, the humbler among them admitting outright fear. When I asked Uncle Earl, who is Marion's age, if he had ever met her, he said, "Oh no, I'd be *scared* to meet Marion Ellet."

Walking or driving past Marion's house in the next week, I often think of dropping in. Even in our brief exchange there had seemed to be the possibility of some communication that might go deeper than the subject of Concordia history. But I am prevented from visiting by my awareness of the caution with which she guards her time, arranging her day to allow solitude and concentration for her work.

Finally, one twilight when I have just driven in from the countryside, I find myself lonely. The sunset is fading, and darkness clings to the trunks of the trees, crouches under bushes. I leave my car and take a walk on the streets near the courthouse, pondering my aloneness. I think of Marion, who seems a kindred spirit, and in the next moment realize I have a perfect excuse to visit her.

A few minutes later, I arrive on her porch to push the lighted eye of the doorbell. This time she takes me through the shadowy

---

* Janet Pease Emery, *It Takes People to Make a Town* (Salina, Kansas: Arrow Printing Co., 1971).

house into the kitchen at the back to share her dinner. The kitchen is filled with light, and its temperature is ten degrees warmer than the front of the house. In the corner near the stove is a narrow counter on which rest a typewriter and small TV set. A comfortable-looking chair sits before the counter. The other surfaces are piled with newspapers, magazines, books. Marion Ellet works and lives mainly in the kitchen of the house now, and goes there each morning very early to research and write her column.

Marion gets me settled in a rocking chair before the stove.

"I can't serve you at a proper table. I hope you won't mind eating off a tray."

I am delighted to be here with her in this study/kitchen, where the soup simmers on the stove. She has some bread she's made. It's not so good, she says, but is improved greatly by these sweet pickles she put up herself. She arranges two small plates with carrot sticks and dabs of mayonnaise. These preparations are made with small, gentle movements, brief, considerate questions as to my tastes. There is a sweetness and intimacy in this procedure.

I watch her moving about the kitchen, struck by the change in her aspect since she opened the front door a few minutes ago. She had seemed a very old woman then, her eyes dim, her movements hesitant, looking out first at my feet and then up at the rest of me, bewildered. For a few moments her long grave face remained puzzled. Having seen her before when she had been alert and focused, I was surprised, and felt a flash of protectiveness toward her. But in the next few moments, as she recognized me, seeing that I held the book she had lent me, her body drew together and her eyes cleared. This was a visible process, as if she brought the elements of herself, which had been spread like a mist about her, back into the contour of her body to arrange in a familiar pattern.

Now, as she pushes the wheeled table over to my knees and goes to the stove for my soup, I see that she is completely herself again. She wears slacks and a plaid flannel shirt open at the throat. She looks slightly flushed, and her steady eyes meet mine as she arranges the tray on the table before me.

As we eat, I am reminded of my great aunt, one member of my mother's family whom my mother revered. My maternal forebears, of Scottish origin, came from New England. They were preachers and teachers originally, though my grandfather was a handyman, and they were tough, long-lived, redheaded people who neither bent nor broke under adversity but endured in tight-lipped silence. My great aunt Agnes lived alone in her old age, refusing the help of relatives, maintaining her autonomy and taking care of herself until she died. She was a tiny frail woman with snowy hair. To my mother she was the model of independence. Now, with Marion Ellet, I feel this same steady maintenance of her life, the same refusal to be defeated by age.

Marion questions me about my encounters with the farm women. Then we speak of a recent "Mugwump Musings" column, in which she commented on the political significance of the Pope's visit to the United States. This leads us to speculation on the Democratic nomination for president.

"Chappaquidick will be a determinant, of course," Marion says. "I've heard Teddy Kennedy say they should concentrate on issues, but it *is* an issue when a man runs away from an accident in which a girl is dying. It is an issue that a man values his reputation more than his integrity. Of course, it might be fortunate if he *were* chosen, because he'll be the easiest candidate to beat. All you'd have to do is go back and quote his voting record, which is simply appalling. It's strictly New Deal!"

She takes a small bite of bread and pickle, chews thoughtfully, watching me.

"I guess you've gathered by now I am quite conservative. The candidate I favor is Reagan. He's smart and he can think on his feet. They harp on his age, you know, but I don't think age matters all that much. Maybe I think that because I'm old myself, but he's vital, he's vigorous, and hardworking. He'd make an excellent president!"

We have finished the soup now, and she gets up to find the stewed apricots. These are apricots from her own trees. Fruit trees have a hard time in Kansas, she explains, because of the abrupt shifts in temperature, but if they do survive, the flavor of the fruit is superb.

"It's something in the soil."

She is right about the apricots.

"Would you like a liqueur with your tea?" Marion asks me. "Let's see, I have creme de menthe and brandy."

I choose brandy, and she pours me some in a narrow glass.

We talk of alcoholism, the "breakdown of the family." I have noticed, in her columns, that she considers the present to be an era of confusion and fear.

"You're not going to agree with me," she says, "But I think one of the major factors is the emancipation of women. When they began to go out to work, the family began to decline."

I wonder where she places herself in this dilemma, for she has certainly not fulfilled the conventional expectations for a woman. I decide to do battle.

"But women have always worked. They have always performed at least half of the labor."

She takes a different tack. "Well, I think this new trend is often the fault of the men. They don't hold the family together like they should."

"I don't think individual men have much power," I counter. "They're at the mercy of job situations and social pressures too."

The kitchen is steamy and comfortable, and now I am warmed from the soup and the brandy.

"Well ... perhaps ..." she says.

"Really, you can't invoke morality in isolation from economic factors," I insist. "We are all, to some extent, the product of our circumstances."

"That I agree to."

She tells about the family across the street, a divorced woman off at work, with sons who get into trouble. Marion has never seen the mother with the sons, so she assumes the mother must not care about them. I argue the mother's case: work responsibilities, fatigue.

Then she speaks of the "transient life" of the coasts. The

"crime and homosexuality" there, she states, are the result of people's not having roots.

I am moved to challenge her, to cite social and economic causes for the conditions she reads about in the newspapers, which I know firsthand. But I keep silent, left with my ironies; I am so much a part of that life of the coasts, so grateful for the latitude of behavior that is accepted there, yet all that formed me is here. Here I encounter the stern virtues, the questioning intelligence in Marion Ellet's being and her work. I see that, despite her family's affluence, Marion Ellet in her kitchen, in this writer's den, is a worker too, each day for so many years fashioning her opinions, her analysis, her particular personality, into something that speaks to other people. Stern she is, and disciplined, and asking still, in her eightieth year, a great deal of herself. Watching her, I allow my ambivalence to sink down.

A scratching begins at the back door, and Marion gets up to open the door and let in a tomcat, rather imperious and obviously a great favorite, who would like me to disappear so that he can have my table. He tramps about on my tray, a large creature with thick, glossy, black and gray fur, while Marion watches him fondly.

"Usually, he sits on that table," she explains. "Just push him off."

I set the cat on the floor and lean to scratch his ears, thinking that here, with Marion Ellet, there are subjects I can discuss and others I automatically censor. In that moment it strikes me that she must feel the same, seeking out topics that are proper, possible, with this near-stranger from California. But I am curious about her spiritual life and tell her so, asking about her involvement with Christian Science.

"Well, in your studies, did you become familiar with the work of Schopenhauer?" she asks.

"Not really."

She puts down her cup and turns in her chair to face me fully, her eyes intent on mine.

"Schopenhauer held, and Kant before him, that all this that we see around us is illusion. But it is the illusion of something that is real. And he said it is possible, though very difficult, to learn to see that reality. It's pure transcendentalism, you know.

"Well, Mary Baker Eddy took it one step farther and said, if you see that world of real forms, you are healed. This was the basis of Christ's healing. You remember the Bible story about the woman who was hemorrhaging for many years and no doctor could help her? Well, Christ looked at her and saw behind her the form of the whole woman, and in seeing that, he created it, and she was healed."

"Do you mean to say that disease is an illusion?"

She nods, her expression inward and absorbed.

"Mary Baker Eddy says that God's law is harmony. All that is inharmonious is illusion. God did not create disease; he did not will it; and so disease is illusion."

"But, in practical terms," I ask, "suppose you become ill, what do you do?"

"You consult a practitioner, someone who is better able to see your condition than you are. And the practitioner helps you to understand your true condition."

Recently, some health concerns began to worry her, keeping her up nights. She called the practitioner, who told her, "There is no such thing as hereditary disease. Nothing comes from your family: everything comes from God, so let go that fear." Earlier, during a period of loss and sadness, the practitioner told her to turn her thoughts in a different direction. She objected, "Well, that's easy to say, but it's difficult for me not to think about those things." The practitioner countered, "You say it's difficult because you don't want to do it." She understood she was hugging those things to her, she didn't want to let them go.

We speak of loss, and Marion, with a wondering sadness, says, "Something I find difficult to understand is loss of *feeling*. Both in oneself for another and coming from someone else—how you can care one day, and the next, all feeling is gone."

I seek in my own experience for this phenomenon, I who tend to keep on caring no matter what. I remember Proust's painstaking delineation of the ebb and flow of passion, the moment when indifference arrives like a clammy ghost, and you wonder, What could all that commotion have been about? I mention him to Marion.

"Does he explain how that can happen?" she wants to know.

"No, he merely evokes it."

"I've been told I would enjoy Proust. I used to read a great deal, when I was in my thirties, but then I began to find *people* more interesting. I began to pay attention to what was going on around me."

I share her desire to know about living people, their activities, their motivations. We talk about my encounters with the women in the Concordia and Clyde communities, and I tell about my visit with Ruth Chaplin several weeks ago, how she shared her life so openly with me.

"When you talked with *me,* did you think I was holding back?" Marion asks from the sink where she had taken her tray.

I feel a strong surge of affection for her, even as I search for a diplomatic answer.

"Well, you're a much different person from Ruth Chaplin, and very cautious."

"You're right," she says with satisfaction, "I am *very* cautious."

But she takes me into her confidence a little later that evening when she tells me about the novel she wrote many years ago, which was never published. Entitled *Black Blizzard,* it was an autobiographical novel based on her family. Might I read it? I ask. Later, I walk from Marion's house into the brisk night air, carrying the prologue to *Black Blizzard* under my arm.

The pages of the manuscript are brown and crumbling at the edges. The voice that speaks from those pages in the first person tells of a town called "Compton" and a farm at Scandia where a dignified, gracious life is pursued. "In their simplest living there was a vibrance," states the narrator, and I think of the kind of gentility that one feels from Marion, in which physical vigor and intellectual passion are as important as the gentler virtues of tact and courtesy.

Reading on, I find Marion Ellet vividly present in these pages; the language measured, graceful, precise. Her strength and limita-

tions, and especially her loyalties, lie open to view. That she has
written exactly the kind of novel one would expect her to write is
wonderfully symmetrical and satisfying.

Our last encounter takes place on the concrete walk up to her
house. She is just returning from somewhere, bundled up against
the cold, and I have rushed from watching a magnificent sunset to
bring her *Black Blizzard*. She takes the manuscript in her gloved
hands, gazing intently at me. She is elegant in a fur hat and
fur-collared coat.

"Do you think I'm better at this style or my analytical style?"
she asks me.

"It seems," I answer, "That you are more comfortable with
the intellect than with the emotions."

She nods. "Yes, I suspect that." She glances down at the
manuscript thoughtfully, as if pondering the disadvantages of this
ascendance of mind over feeling.

Then, before I leave, her face opens briefly in a smile that is
warm, friendly, almost tender. She says she has enjoyed knowing
me, a sentiment I share in regard to her, and we turn in opposite
directions, she to ascend the steps of her house, I to go off down
the street to the place where I stay. I turn back to see her, an erect
old woman moving to open the door of this house that has sheltered her for so many years.

First People

On this prairie, long before Marion Ellet's family arrived, lived
the native peoples. They remind me of how much life had taken
place here before the first covered wagons wore tracks across the
grassland. The ancient people left their bones in communal burial
grounds, some of which have been uncovered by white excavators.
At one such monument, near Salina, I encounter the skeletons of
146 people, lying on separate pedestals of dirt in a pit that has been
dug around them. They lie on their sides, curved in the fetal
position, bones shiny with brown lacquer.

Near the concrete side wall of this pit rests a being by itself. The shallow bowl of hipbone curves like an elk's magnificent antler, the leg bones bend in a tight crouch. The rest of the skeleton is only fragments up to the skull, narrow and intact, grinning with a set of perfect young teeth. "Female," reads the sign balanced where the ribs once were, "age about sixteen." Looking for a long time, I feel how the flesh must have sat on the bones, how the skin covered the flesh, hair cushioned the head as it was laid in the hole. Perhaps there were clothes of hides, perhaps moccasins, jewelry. Eaten by the earth, becoming the earth—flesh and fabric, skin of animal and human, thick black hair.

I look at these people in death, remembering lines by Barbara Deming: "I lie in bed, knees to my chest/ (as we were buried when death/ was known to be the Mother)."* These people with their legs drawn up and hands placed close to their faces, laid under the earth so long ago to be hidden forever—here exposed to the eyes of other humans, charged admission for, written up in a pamphlet. These people in that most sacred of transitions. These so-vulnerable bones.

I wonder what contemporary Potawatomis think as they drive the highway, seeing signs advertising "Prehistoric Indian Burial." These particular bones, however, cannot be the remains of their actual ancestors, for, like most other native peoples now living in Kansas, the Potawatomis come from a different part of the country. They were driven out of the eastern states, while the peoples native to Kansas were pushed west to make room for them. They live now in an eleven-mile-square reservation near the town of Holton in the northeastern part of the state.

Today I am driving out across the bleak open land of this reservation, on a road so deeply rutted that my car lurches and thumps like a foundering boat. I am on my way to the O Ketche Show O Now center (a name pronounced, to my Anglo ears, nothing like its spelling), and since I must drive so slowly, there is plenty of time to ponder the remembered weirdness of that burial

* Barbara Deming, "Death Song," in *Sinister Wisdom* 10 (Summer 1979).

site. How different it was from the Indian burial mounds in Ohio where my parents took us when we were children. I remember playing on the sloping grassy sides of the great Serpent Mound, which stretches for thirteen hundred feet in the shape of a snake, its tail coiled in two complete turns, an oval mound representing its heart. There I felt the mysterious presence of people whom I imagined to be ancestors, for one of my father's many stories was that we had traces of black and Indian blood in our veins. I don't remember how my sister and brother received this information, but I know I was thrilled. It seemed so American, so right, to me to have a mixture of blood, and it allowed me to view myself in a new way. Crawling through the weeds of a field in search of small animals, I would imagine I had inherited the Indians' alertness and stealth.

A pickup truck filled with brown-faced people comes roaring past me, and I ponder how ill-equipped I am for the task ahead of me. Even my car is barely adequate to this road. I have no personal contacts on this reservation; I am sent by no one and have no credentials to make me welcome. But I am determined that I will talk with some Indian women to discover what I can of their lives.

I pass two white men standing next to the road, talking to each other, and I recall that at the office of the Prairie Band Potawatomi in Holton I had been told that some of the reservation land is leased to white farmers. Before my visit to the office I had studied the several accounts of the Potawatomi's history, reading the anthropologists' descriptions of the life the Indians lived in their original home on the shores of the Great Lakes, their decline in power over the years, and their final removal to Kansas.* That tale gave me little insight into the lives of the women I met in the tribal office, one of whom is head of the tribal council. The books stated that, in the Potawatomi villages, the

---

* Historical material on the Potawatomi in this section is taken from James A. Clifton, *The Prairie People: Continuity and Change in Potawatomi Indian Culture, 1665–1965* (Lawrence: The Regents Press of Kansas, 1977). Other books on the Potawatomi are Ruth Landes, *The Prairie Potawatomi: Tradition and Ritual in the Twentieth Century* (University of Wisconsin Press, 1970), and R. David Edmunds, *The Potawatomis: Keepers of the Fire* (University of Oklahoma Press, 1978).

women functioned as producers and nurturers of children and
tillers of the soil. The women, however, may have exercised a
power and influence among their people that was invisible to
those newly transplanted Europeans who wrote about them, and
from whom contemporary anthropologists have drawn their
information. Anthropological sources claim that when the
Potawatomi made an alliance, the men generously sent some of
their daughters and sisters as gifts to the village of the other tribe.
Before the arrival of horses, brought in by the French, the women
were the burden-bearers, along with dogs. So say the
anthropologists. Still, they tell us, now and then a woman might
become a priest in the Midewiwin (Spirit Doings) or Medicine
Society. How I wish there were a history written by the native
people themselves that I might read.

Just when it seems that I will go on driving out through brush
and empty fields forever, I reach the turnoff they had told me
about back at the office. As I drive down the road I see the Oh
Ketche Show O Now center, a large square building set in open
land.

A few minutes later I enter the library of the center, having
been told to wait here by a woman named Margret Mahkuc until
she will be free to talk with me. Already I am unnerved by the
people in the lobby, who spoke a language strange to me, who
observed me closely.

Now I stand in the doorway of the library, where an older
woman sits at a desk. She looks up at me, and her eyes shoot fire.
I take a step backwards, shocked, as she begins to rail at me in her
native tongue, in words whose meaning I do not understand but
whose venomous intent is unmistakable. Surely rage might be
expected in people who have been so consistently betrayed and
harmed by members of the white race, but I am shaken, not
knowing whether her reaction comes from a generalized abhor-
rence of white people or whether it has something to do with me
personally. Stupidly, I stare at her as she harangues me, and my
instinct is to bolt and run. The car is still warm in the parking lot;
I could be gone in a few minutes! But Margret Mahkuc has told
me to wait here.

Suffering the words that fall on me like stones, I walk toward a library table, and I determine that I will not be driven away. Sitting down, I place my arms on the table and stare straight ahead. After a few minutes, the woman stops speaking. Sneaking a glance at her, I meet a withering stare. Such hatred is frightening. Sitting here, I have never felt so Anglo nor so alien, and I experience a wistful longing for the taken-for-granted American society I have just left, in which I know the rules and the language and where, if someone attacks me, I generally know why.

When Margret Mahkuc comes to get me, I am more than grateful. She leads me out of the library, glancing curiously at the librarian's angry face, and suggests that we go in the basketball court to talk because it is the only place where we will not be disturbed. I would like to ask her why the librarian was so furious with me, but I am afraid to, imagining that the explanation might make us both so uncomfortable that my visit here would be ruined.

We sit down next to the shiny floor of the court, and the lofty ceiling draws Margret's voice out in echoes. She is a director of the center, she tells me. She spent many years going to college and living in the white world, being active in Native American political endeavors. Now, at age thirty-five, she has brought herself and her children back to the reservation to live in a more traditional way.

Her long, glistening black hair falls down over the shoulders of her dark smock. Her face is round, serious, with dark eyes and full lips. She describes growing up on the reservation, raised by her grandparents. "They taught me a lot of things, including the native language and how our people believe—religion. I never knew the outside world, which I had to get exposed to, and it was hard on me because, being with old people, I never had contact with white people. Then when I went off the reservation to public school it was real hard for me ... I don't know, I felt like I was an outcast most of the time. Back then I thought it was kinda hard growing up."

Margret gazes out across the glistening blond wood of the floor and is silent for a few seconds. Then she tells me about her years in California and other states, her decision to return. Her people, she says, have maintained as best they can their traditional way of life. Unlike the Citizens Band Potawatomi, a branch of the tribe that chose to assimilate, the Prairie Band follows the native religions, preserves the language and customs.

Our conversation progresses unevenly, as sometimes I ask a question and Margret does not answer but is silent for a time and then picks up where she had left her own thought, and continues speaking. During most of our talk she does not look at me, and I am disconcerted by this lack of eye contact, only later realizing that this avoidance is probably a customary practice among her people. She corrects me several times, as when I ask about the peyote cult and she says it is not a "cult" but a religious practice that ought to be given the same respect as any other religion. As she speaks of the coherence and inclusiveness of the Indian view of the universe, I am aware of the distinct cultural differences separating her world from mine, making it hard for me to know her as I knew the farm women, the small town women. But I feel she has spoken straightforwardly to me, and with good will.

The cultural differences that separate Margret and me are essentially the same as they were when the Potawatomis saw their first white people, the Frenchmen who came to establish New France in the Great Lakes area in the early 1600s. At first, the discrepancies in culture did not prevent the two peoples from establishing a mutually beneficial relationship. According to the anthropologists, the Potawatomi traded furs to the Frenchmen and fought for them in the war with the British, and they expanded their own territory to occupy large parts of Michigan, Indiana, Wisconsin, and Illinois. But their dependency on European technology was to be their undoing for, by the late eighteenth century, the animal supply in their forests had been so diminished that they could not trap sufficient furs to trade for firearms and other goods. By this time, also, no one wanted to hire them as soldiers. In order to acquire from the white man the items they sorely needed, they began to sell the land on which they lived and hunted. This again is the story as told to us by white men, in which the role of the Potawatomi women is barely mentioned.

When the Potawatomi began to sell their land, a chain of events was begun that brought them ultimately to this piece of Kansas prairie.

Earlier, at the headquarters of the Prairie Band Potawatomi in Holton, I heard about the present-day ramifications of this history. Behind a rustic facade of stained and weathered wood was a suite of offices where a number of people were busily at work. Here I talked with Vestina Durham, chairperson of the Tribal Council. She was put in office by a formal tribal election, and as leader of the tribe she presides at council meetings, signs all contracts and negotiations sanctioned by the council. Fifty-one years old, she has spent her life on the reservation, member of a family active in tribal affairs.

Vestina Durham was a brisk, attractive woman with short curled black hair, wearing a light-colored pantsuit with bright blouse. Her manner was professionally smooth, but she let her annoyance show when she saw the book I carried under my arm.

"You like that book?" she asked sharply.

I glanced down at the cover, which read "The Prairie Potawatomi by Ruth Landes."

"Yes," I answered.

Vestina regarded the book with irritation. "I don't know where she got all that stuff she put in there. Someone must've been making up stories!"

She motioned me to a chair, and I sat, but she remained standing for the duration of our talk, her eye on the bustling activity in the office. Now and then we were interrupted by someone who came to ask her a question.

Vestina told me there had been only one other female head of the Tribal Council.

"Is there any problem with your authority being accepted?" I asked.

"Well, I think some of the older people may still feel that a man should have the job."

"Are there other women on the council?"

"Two women, five men," she answered.*

Although she was very busy, Vestina was willing to talk briefly with me about tribal affairs. With the adoption of their constitution and bylaws in 1976, she told me, the tribe began to push for self-determination. That does not, she said emphatically, mean termination of the tribe's association with the government

"Termination would be a disaster. It just wouldn't work, because we have so many very poor people who would not be able to pay taxes."

I thought about the way in which this dependency came about, for originally the Potawatomi had been a unified and sovereign nation that had dealt with the French and the British as equals. Under the Indian Removal Act of 1830, the Potawatomis were among the 10,679 people from the Eastern United States who were uprooted and transplanted to Kansas. After this period, the Potawatomis never again assembled as a whole in one place.

The first indication, to American eyes, of the social and political power of women among the Potawatomi was the appearance of a few women's names on some of the final treaties in which the nation sold its land. The significance of this to the people themselves cannot be known. But there is no doubt that the survival of both men and women was at issue. Preyed upon by traders and missionaries, infiltrated and exploited by white businessmen, surrounded by white farmers, the Potawatomi struggled to retain their cultural heritage.

They are still struggling, on the reservation and in the Prairie Band office, where Vestina Durham told me about the economics of survival. Federal and state programs employ some people on the reservation, she said, but the majority of the Potawatomis commute to Topeka to work. She spoke of a comprehensive program that would allow for taking back for their own use the land the tribe now rents to white farmers. Under an HUD program,

* In 1979.

houses are being built, thus allowing people like Margret Mahkuc to move back to the reservation. Some Potawatomis are on welfare, but, "Indians are proud," said Vestina. "They don't like to do that. They help each other, their families help. Only as a last resort will they take welfare." Although many tribal members live in Topeka, they, like most Native Americans, come regularly to the reservation to visit relatives and participate in celebrations; their home ties are strongly here.

In the senior citizens room at the O Ketche Show O Now center, a large American flag hangs on the wall, a plant in a macrame sling dangles near it. The room is large, opening into a kitchen at one end where long tables stand in rows. At the other end of the room, Minnie LeClere and Cecelia Jackson pull tufts of yarn through the border of a coverlet they are making for an old man. They move about the quilt frame on which the coverlet is stretched, working, ignoring my presence, while a large, round-faced woman named Coralene Potts talks with me.

Coralene, who is fifty-nine years old, is actually a Kickapoo, and was born on that people's reservation, a five-mile-by-six-mile rectangle a short distance up Route 75 from here. She tells me she understands the Potawatomi language, but can't speak much. She is so friendly that I consider asking her about the incident with the librarian, but again I feel uncertain and cannot bring it up.

At my urging, she tells me a little about her schooling at the Haskell Indian Institute in Lawrence.

"Now Haskell is an Indian junior college," she says, "but then it was an all-Indian boarding school."

"What did you do after you got out of high school?" I ask.

Coralene looks embarrassed. Although she wants to visit with me, it is clear that my questions make her uncomfortable.

"I got jobs doing housework . . . in various towns."

"And then?"

"Then I got married. That was 1942. My husband was in the army and he went away for four years to the war."

"Did you live on the reservation?"

"When he came back we lived here, and had our seven children."

That life had its difficulties, Coralene tells me. Her husband worked at temporary construction jobs when he could find them. For a while, the house they lived in did not have electricity.

She is a member of the drum religion, as are her children. "That's hard for them sometimes," she says, "because the services are in the native language and they don't understand it."

This talking about herself has made her anxious, her hands clasping and unclasping nervously, and she changes the subject to tell about Minnie and Cecelia, the two women at work on the quilt frame.

"Cecelia is just great at needlework. She's a real artist!"

Cecelia goes serenely on with her work, pulling the yarn, smoothing the coverlet, her face impassive, her broad back communicating that, as far as she is concerned, we do not exist.

"And Minnie, now, she could tell you some stories about the old days. She's been around a long time."

Minnie, a wrinkled woman with a delicately curved nose, looks up to blink peevishly at us.

"I'm not *that* old," she mutters.

These three women are paid employees here at the Senior Citizens Center, from which each noontime a van is driven out into the surrounding communities to pick up old people who want to eat at the center. Coralene and Minnie and Cecelia prepare the meal for these people and the center employees and guests. Their life experience is fairly typical of Indian women of their generation, and corresponds to the experience of other women of color, who traditionally have been relegated to domestic work or low-paying service jobs.

I ponder the lives of the women I have met here. Margret Mahkuc, coming back from years in white society, wanting to return to the traditional ways of her people, to give her children an Indian identity and way of life. Vestina Durham, seasoned politician and now leader of the tribal council, trying to protect and advance the cause of the Potawatomis in the world of legal maneuverings that is the Native Americans' official modern arena. Minnie LeClere, Cecelia Jackson, and Coralene Potts at the senior citizens center, doing useful work, attending to the needs of old people like themselves. These women have given me some inkling of what it means to be Native American in a culture that denies the humanity of native peoples. My discomfort among them, I realize, is nothing compared to the alienation they must feel in an environment that is hostile to their very existence. My sense of their present situation deepens with the awareness that they are the descendants of a people who roamed freely in great areas of woodland and lakeshore; that their estate has shrunk to a claustro-phobic eleven-mile-square tract of prairie, and even this they must vigorously defend, for their land is surrounded by white farmers who covet it, and already lease and farm many acres of it.

This evening, as I leave the Potawatomi reservation to drive south to Topeka, I am heavy with fatigue, produced by the strain of having been all day in an environment foreign to me. I recall the sound of the Potawatomi tongue being spoken by the old people, and especially the words hammered at me by the woman in the library. There was none of the easy familiarity that I feel with the farm and small town women with whom I visit—as different as our lives may be, still we come from the same cultural root. With the Potawatomi, I frequently overstepped the bounds of decorum out of ignorance, like a clumsy child. I know that what I learned of Margret and Vestina, Minnie and Coralene and Cecelia, was limited and distorted by this ignorance. Silence would have been more appropriate than my questions, I realize. To begin to know the Potawatomis at a deeper level would take weeks of sitting quietly in the senior citizens room until someone spoke to me of her own accord, days of simply being there until I might become a trusted person.

Now I see the lights flicking on in the buildings on the hori-zon, which I am fast approaching. In a few minutes I drive down a wide, brightly lit avenue into Topeka, the state capitol, as dark-ness swallows up the prairie behind me. I feel I have come from a different time back there, where people live in a different spiritual relation to this Kansas earth and sky. For a moment I entertain the fantasy of an American population and government respectful of native peoples, receptive to their beings and their rich heritage, but my knowledge of the reality overwhelms this fragile dream. The streets through which I drive bear witness to the supremacy of a culture antithetical to much that is sacred to the first people. Here are neon signs, telephone wires, used car lots and motels, where once lived buffalo and deer; here is the blat and rumble of traffic where once only the wind was heard in the tall grass. It is easy to understand Margret Mahkuc now. Having spoken with her, I see this glossy, swift environment with new eyes, and feel estranged.

They Came to Teach and Heal

Hollywood movies and most historical accounts would have us believe that white pioneer women were either wives, daughters, or whores. They have not shown us the women who came on their own or in the company of other women to stake claims. Sisters and groups of two or more female friends sometimes lived and worked together to carve out a farm on the prairie. Others journeyed here in the service of a religious calling, their heads covered by wimples rather than sunbonnets.

The Nazareth Motherhouse in Concordia stands as a monument to these last. It is the home of the Sisters of St. Joseph, who came to the United States from France in the early 1800s and journeyed across the country opening schools. These convent boarding schools were disseminators of culture not just for Catholics, but for other citizens who wanted their daughters to receive a solid and genteel education. It was by default that the Sisters of St. Joseph arrived in Kansas in 1883. Sr. Stanislaus Leary and two other nuns were on their way from New York to Florence, Arizona, to open a school, when in Kansas City they heard news of "Indian troubles" in Arizona. Afraid to continue their journey, they offered their services to the Bishop of Leavenworth, just upriver from Kansas City. He appointed them to Newton, Kansas. No doubt they often wished they had gone on, Indians or not; for in their first year at Newton, the Sisters suffered "the sting of hunger and privation," and the presence of a priest who, in the words of Sr. Stanislaus Leary, "has shown marked unkindness to us." But they went to work, and a school was opened to which over one hundred pupils came. The next year they were transferred up to Concordia, and the Motherhouse was established.*

It is a majestic structure on a hill. Seven stories high, built of red brick with a circular stained glass window in the front and scallops of white stone above the rounded windows, it sits back in a landscaped lawn. It is a building of much dignity and beauty, and the great old trees surrounding it stand like friends to its weathered brick. Oak and blue spruce and elm, redbud, magnolia, and evergreen trees dot the front lawn, branching out above neatly clipped hedges.

There are over four hundred Sisters in the order now, of which a hundred live here at the Motherhouse. Inside its walls are a chapel, an auditorium, a giant kitchen and dining room, even a swimming pool, whose use is shared by members of the Concordia community. The Sisters here and in other towns work in the five hospitals, twelve elementary schools and five high schools maintained by the Sisters of St. Joseph; they also operate Marymount College, which was founded by the Order.

I am led about the grounds of the convent by Sister Marie Chaput who, in her street-length dress and nylons, looks less like a nun (to my naive and un-Catholic eye) than she does an elderly school teacher. Although she is reluctant to speak personally about herself, when I ask if she is related to Alexine Chaput in Clyde, she says that she comes of the same family as Alexine's husband. We walk through the orchard and the cemetery, where the Sisters are buried under identical headstones. Other Sisters pass us, some in full habit with a blaze of white starched collar under the black

---

* The full story of the Sisters of St. Joseph of Concordia can be found in *Footprints on the Frontier*, by Sister M. Evangeline Thomas, Ph.D. (Westminster, Maryland: The Newman Press, 1948).

shawl, a strict white headband across the brow. A few wear habits with short skirts and small soft collars. Still others wear dresses, their only religious identification the crucifix hung on a cord about their necks. Sister Marie introduces me to them, and they speak to me in rich accents—German, Irish, French.

We stop at the greenhouse, where two old cheerful nuns are at work. This glass enclosure bursts with well-tended plants. The two Sisters observe me, their faces smooth, their eyes clear. They smile at me, nodding, and when Sister Marie introduces us, they greet me in thickly accented English.

She tells me the plants are the special love of Sister Eva Marie, who stands beaming at me.

"She talks to them," Sister Marie says. "They grow wonderfully."

Then as we leave the greenhouse to walk near the tall, dignified Motherhouse, Sister Marie points out a foot-high slender statue set on a pedestal.

"You see that statue of Mary? A tornado came through here. It uprooted a big tree right next to the pedestal and never touched the statue."

We gaze at it, marveling in her case perhaps at the power of faith, in my case at the vagaries of tornadoes.

"The building was damaged in that one," she says, looking up at it with an expression full of concern. "Windows blown out. The structure weakened."

I feel her love for this place where no doubt she will live out her last vigorous years of service.* The lives inside this building are shared ones, strictly circumscribed, imbued with humility. What an antique virtue "humility" seems in this age of assertiveness. As Sister Marie admitted, hers is hardly the most sought-after lifestyle at present. Still, there's a secret in it. There is a selfhood beyond ego. And the Sisters of St. Joseph, who have

---

* I was wrong about this. In her last communication to me, Sister Marie wrote, "In a short time I will be leaving the Motherhouse. I hope to bring the 'Good News' to the sick, poor, elderly, etc."

existed for three hundred years carrying the responsibility of teaching, nursing, administering schools and hospitals, have surely developed an identity resilient enough for any worldly tests. I look up again at that building with its great mass and presence—a mother house indeed.

We talk of the early students of this school, many of whom live in or near Concordia still. I have had a long and cordial visit with one of them. Teresa Mahon, an eighty-six-year-old farm woman, told me it was her father, Charles Lasnier, who with his brother started the Bon Marche drygoods store in Concordia in 1886. Her brothers went to college, but "I would never have thought to ask to go to college myself. My father was a strict Catholic, and he feared having his daughters away from home. We girls were fortunate to go to high school at the Nazareth Motherhouse."

Like the other young women who first studied here, Teresa's life spans some of the most difficult times this part of the country experienced. After graduating from the convent school, she worked in her father's store for many years. She did not marry until she was thirty-nine. It was the mid-thirties, hard times, when her husband took her to live on a farm on the Republican River some miles outside Concordia. The drought had turned the fertile Great Plains into the Dust Bowl.

"It wasn't such an easy life when we were first out here on the farm," Teresa told me. "There were the dust storms, the drought, that terrible heat. My first daughter was a little baby then. I'd put her in the wash basin and just sponge her off with cool water, as often as I could during the day, so she wouldn't suffer so much. A poor little baby like that.

"The river went dry, but the earth here must have had a little moisture left in it because my husband was able to raise a few stalks of corn to feed the stock. The rest of the area was so bad off that people came from as far away as Beloit to try to buy corn from him."

She shook her head, remembering.

"And then in 1935 came the worst flood in history. A neighbor called to tell me, 'There's a wall of water coming down from Nebraska, and it'll be here on Sunday.' When my husband came in from the fields I told him this. I remember it so well. He just fell on the couch and laughed. And then he said, 'There's never been any water in this house and there never will be.' I begged him to help me take up the rugs and pack the other things and move them upstairs, but he wouldn't believe it could happen. So I got the baby ready and took what I could carry and went on into town alone.

"Well, at noon on Sunday it hit. One and a half foot of water in the house. Damage so bad we couldn't live in it for a year and a half. When it hit, the men were here trying to make some preparations. They had to run to their cars to get away. And they never even thought to move the tractors up onto the railroad bridge to save them!"

Her disgust with the men is apparent; forty years have not wiped it out.

"We had hard maple floors. They were warped so bad he had to nail them back board by board. My cedar chest was wet. The rugs. It took a long time to clean and dry everything.

"After that, we built a dike between the house and the river." True to the indomitable spirit of those who survived, they planted lilac bushes on it, and cottonwood and elm there and around the house. Teresa and her husband made something beautiful in the aftermath of destruction. "In the spring the lilacs were so lovely that people would stop just to look at them," she said.

Her memories of her schooldays at the Nazareth Convent were as lucid as those of her later life. "My sisters and I were day scholars," she told me, "but it was a boarding school. The girls came from as far away as Denver. Everybody spoke French in school, teachers and students. The studies were in English, but for everything else we spoke French. And the nuns taught us music! There was one sister who played the violin so beautifully!"

It was at commencement exercises that students showed off their musical and linguistic skills. The first of these celebrations took place in 1885, and featured several young L'Ecuyer's singing songs and reciting French dialogues.

Vestiges of France are still present on the convent grounds. Sister Marie Chaput and I stand now in the grotto built of dark, pitted rock, a replica of the famous Catholic shrine of Lourdes. At the end of a corridor with arched openings, a near-lifesize statue of Sister Bernadette kneels to gaze up in wonder at a statue of the virgin poised above her with folded hands. I glance at Sister Marie, who seems perfectly at ease and proud to be showing off the features of this grotto and the splendid grounds that surround it.

As we walk toward the Motherhouse she reveals that she is, as I had guessed, a teacher. Now retired, she taught all the grades and junior high, for many years, in cities other than Concordia. This is just about all she cares to tell me about herself, her manner impersonal and a little dry, her eyes inscrutable behind her glasses; it is as if she accepts my presence and is willing to give out information, but her true attention is focused elsewhere.

Sister Marie and I pause behind the building and turn to look out across a long, gentle rise of grass and then wheat field, to distant Route 81 with its stream of semis and pickup trucks. Here with the Motherhouse towering over us, in the silence of these enclosed grounds, this dispassionate Sister and I seem to exist in a separate world, as if that activity out there were a dream. Yet, as she and Teresa Mahon and others in the town and surrounding farms have let me know, this institution is bound with deep ties to the community that surrounds it, and persists as a center of energy in the secular lives of its neighbors.

Bessie Caldwell

Salina, fifty or so miles south of Concordia, throbs with activity. An airport, bus station, and major interstate freeway bring many outsiders here. On the streets of Salina, I see black and brown and yellow-skinned people as well as white; and many young people, some of whom must be students at Marymount College, the institution run by the Sisters of St. Joseph. From its bustling downtown section the streets fan out, the houses becoming farther apart, until they give way to cultivated fields. Salina seems metropolitan at its heart, yet its edges frazzle out into the open space of prairie, whose vastness seems to mock its self-importance. I like the feeling of the town.

In a neat, ranch-style house midway between the glossy restaurants of the main drag and the stubbly fields of the outskirts, I sit talking with a woman who has taught at Marymount College for many years, and has taught independently even longer.

"Now the dance classes I have here in my home," explains Bessie Caldwell, sitting across from me in her living room. "I have a studio in the basement. And I have been teaching, I would say, for at least twenty-five years. Perhaps a little bit longer. Because we've been married almost thirty-five."

A small, slim woman, Bessie has a high forehead and gently rounded cheeks, soft curly short hair, an easy smile. My friend in Kansas City had told me about her: "There's a wonderful woman in Salina you ought to see. I used to take tapdancing lessons from her when I was growing up." She told me the Caldwells had been good friends of her parents for a time. "And I never was able to figure out how my mother, who was one of the most prejudiced women I knew, could be such good friends with a black woman, but she was." At the time my friend knew them, Bessie and her husband were both active in the NAACP, and since then he was elected the first and only black mayor of Salina. This was all she knew of Bessie and Bob Caldwell, whom she had not seen in many years.

When Bessie met me at the door I was at first confused by her youthful appearance, for wasn't she my friend's teacher when she was a child, and now if my friend is almost forty, wouldn't that make Bessie ... ?

"At Marymount, I'm in the physical education department," Bessie offers, "teaching health, teacher education, methods in physical education, and all the dance classes, which would be modern, social, tap, ballet, gymnastics. I coach the pom-pom girls. . . ."

She laughs, perhaps at this ambitious range of activity, and goes on to tell me how she began to dance. During her childhood in Kansas City, Kansas, she and her sister learned ballet, acrobatics, and tap from a woman named Mabel Williams. "On Saturday we spent our day at the dance studio," she says. "We would go early in the morning, 'cause she didn't mind if we worked out with any class we could work out with. So we would go about nine o'clock and get back home about five in the evening. This was because we *wanted* to. I took from her, I guess, about six or seven years. And then I took from another lady. Then when I went on to college, well, I took every dance class I could. It was completely different to what we had before. They offered modern dance. This was the University of Wisconsin, and I'd never heard of modern dance until I went there and I was just carried away with it. I loved it."

She smiles, and I hear almost a child's enthusiasm in her voice. As we go on talking I notice that this happens whenever the subject is dance. I look closely at Bessie, seeing her lithe, strong body, the smooth brown skin of her face. She has told me that she is sixty-two years old, but in her presence there is none of the sag or inertia of age. Instead, her body communicates a sense of energy calmly contained.

"When I was growing up, our home was situated in a good location," she goes on. "We were within four blocks of the church we attended and four blocks of the playground, and at that time the WPA had regular playgrounds, you know, for the kids. So we lived at the swimming pool and at the playground and did all of these things just in the neighborhood. I guess once you become involved you just continue. My brother used to tapdance, and I loved watching him. Then when we were able to take lessons, we went on. And I never stopped. After I went on to college I'd go to classes wherever I could afford to go, even after I married. I was married when I went out to California to study with Lester Horton and then I went to a Colorado college to study with Hanya Holm. In Milwaukee I studied Martha Graham's technique."

As we talk about her schooling, I reflect on the issue of racism, a persistent theme for any woman of color in white society, no matter what her class background or present status.

The black presence in Kansas today seems to be confined to the cities.* Their absence in Clyde, for instance, is conspicuous. In the entirety of Cloud County, population 13,560, there are two minority individuals: two sisters of Mexican descent, married to white farmers. One of the older women in Clyde told me the story of the time a black man was brought there as a laborer to help build the school house. It was unthinkable that he should stay in any of the townsfolks' homes, as did the other laborers. So they pitched a tent for him in the schoolyard. He lived in the tent until the job was done.

As late as 1970, a law in a town in the southwest part of the state specified that no Negro be allowed to stay the night in town. The black veterinarian was permitted to ply his trade within municipal boundaries, but he had to make his home in the surrounding countryside. I recall the casual remark made in Clyde, that Darlene Tate had been hired at Northern Natural Gas so that the management would not have to hire a black man.

While the extraordinary insularity of small farm towns may provide some excuse for these stories, they are manifestations of a racist culture that exists throughout Kansas (as it does in every other state in the union). Within this environment, however, there are black people like the Caldwells, whose lives are relatively secure, who are solid and respected members of their communities, whose income allows them to live comfortably. They are the descendants of those Southern blacks who came north in the first great wave of migration to Kansas after the Civil War.** In 1874

---

* By 1976, black people in Kansas numbered 125,000, 5.6 percent of the state's total population of 2,253,000. While this might not seem a large percentage when compared with northern states like New York (12.5 percent black) or Missouri (11.8 percent black), still it shows a much more substantial black population than most of the West North Central states and many Western states.

** The first Kansas blacks were brought to the Kansas-Nebraska Territory as slaves, like Booth Fox's slave woman whom Chestina Allen glimpsed, and pitied, in 1855. The census in that year showed 193 slaves in the state; by 1856 the number had increased to four hundred. The slaveholders were among those who fought so bitterly to have Kansas de-

and 1875, a great number of blacks from Kentucky and Tennessee arrived in Kansas; then, in 1879, a mass exodus from the South to Kansas occurred. This movement was not one primarily of individuals, but had a communal character. Some of the "Exodusters," as the refugees were called, arrived destitute and were housed in temporary camps by the white populace; but many came organized into "colonies" and founded their own all-black communities on Kansas land. At one time, eleven black towns existed in Kansas. Reflecting on this, I wonder how fully the Exodusters' dream of autonomy, opportunity, dignity has been realized in Bessie Caldwell's life.

In her family there were five children. Her father ran a grocery store, her mother did "day work"—that is, she cleaned, cooked, and washed for people in their homes. Of the children, only Bessie and her oldest brother went to college.

"I first went to school at Wisconsin because my brother was there and I could live with him," Bessie explains. "I had never been in a mixed situation before. I had always gone to an all-black school. There at Wisconsin there were very few blacks. The people were very nice, very warm, we could participate in anything that we wanted to be in, but . . . there was not enough social life for me, I guess. So then I told my mother, and she says, well, where do you want to go? And I had quite a number of friends who were going to school at Kansas State college at Pittsburg, Kansas, so I said, well, I'd like to go there and try it. So I went there and I liked it. There were not a lot of black students, but there were just enough where you could enjoy yourself. The difference between the two was that in Wisconsin you were not excluded; in Pittsburg, all activities were separate. If the whites had a party in the gym, then the blacks had a party in the cafeteria. We were not allowed to swim in the swimming pool except

clared a slave state. While Kansas remained free, most blacks would not have chosen to move there, for it stood next to Missouri; there was too much danger to a free black of being kidnapped and taken across the state line to be sold into slavery. Thus, by 1865, there were still only about six hundred blacks in Kansas. These figures are taken from *Blacks in the West* by W. Sherman Savage (Westport, Connecticut, London: Greenwood Press, 1976).

on Fridays, when they were ready to clean the pool anyway. This was in, like, 1935 or so. We were in regular classes with whites, but anything outside of school activities was segregated. When we marched for commencement, we had to walk at the end of the line."

Bessie speaks in a light voice, without apparent rancor.

I ask her, "What was the consciousness of black students at that time?"

"Oh, they didn't like it," she says quickly. "In fact, we had chapel every Thursday, and the blacks had got in the habit of sitting at the back, and the Kappas, which is a black fraternity, had a speaker come who told them that they should not be sitting at the back, they should be sitting wherever they wanted to sit. So at the next chapel, we decided we would sit in the center section, and we did. And the students started throwing books at us, papers, all of this, and one girl was hit by one of the books."

Bessie's pleasant expression does not change as she says this. She looks down to smooth the fabric of her slacks over her knee.

"They had a dorm for the women, but the black women were not allowed to stay in the dorm, so we stayed in homes in the town. We ate together in the cafeteria but we never sat at tables with them."

Them, she says, meaning the white students, and for the first time I feel uneasy, thinking with irony of my father's story of our trace of black blood. This possibly fictional racial mixture did not prevent my family from holding the usual racist views concerning anyone who was not as white as we. There were no black people in my neighborhood; the closest I came to an awareness of black culture was hearing my brother's boogie woogie and jazz records. My father worked with two black plumbers, brothers who were "good at their trade"; I remember his saying over and over how responsible they were and how skilled, and it occurred to me even then that he never praised white workers, that there must be something special, then, in a black man's doing a job well. I had graduated from Ohio State University before the 1960s and the civil rights movement, and had associated with perhaps two black people during my growing up, in a city in which there was a sizable black population. All this was part of the mental climate in which Bessie Caldwell, some decades earlier, had gone to college. I remember during the 1960s, when the civil rights struggle was at its height, my husband's father would always manage to use the word "nigger" when we were together, in order to bait us into an argument. Our rage at him, each time, must have come at least in part from our own unconscious participation in the attitudes that made that word so magically powerful.

Bessie goes on telling about her college experience, and laughs, unaccountably, as she says, "Oh . . . the thing that hurt me most, when they had a program and I wanted very much to be one of the dancers, I couldn't because I was black."

She gazes across her well-furnished living room, out the picture window to the lawn. "I don't know," she says, shaking her head slightly, "I learned an awful lot there. It was a good comparison, after Wisconsin. It helped me to get my values straight. Which is better for you? Do you want this separate situation or do you want an integrated situation? Well, I was very happy because I met my husband there and that's all I was thinking about at the time, so it didn't matter to me whether I did all these things, because mixing just didn't make that much difference to me."

After graduating from Kansas State she taught grade school for seven years in Kansas City. The Second World War was in progress, Bob Caldwell serving in the army overseas. He was wounded in England, spent some months in a hospital back in this country, and when he was well again began work on a masters degree. Then he and Bessie married.

"He was teaching here," she says. "He became principal of the all-black grade school. Then, after the schools were integrated, they closed that school and he did not have a specific job nor could they give him a job teaching. So he became playground coordinator over all the schools. I think he did that for two years. Then they built the new high school, and they had a printing department, so they put him in charge of printing, which was what he was trained for, and he stayed there until he retired. That was many years. Of course he was mayor, too, but that was recently. This is his second year of retirement, and he's still trying to get used to it. But he stays plenty busy, he really does."

I had met Bob a little earlier when he came through the living room to say hello. He was a tall man carefully dressed in sports jacket and slacks, tie, newly shined shoes. It seemed he had just returned from an appointment.

After getting married, Bessie tells me, she stayed home for a time to raise the first of her three children, but she taught dance and movement at the recreation center near her home, "just for fun." Meanwhile, she and Bob worked on their masters degrees in the summers in Pittsburg, Kansas, which was his home town. When they were able to buy a house in Salina, they built an extra room on the back, and Bessie began teaching dance in her home. At that time, also, the high school invited her to do the choreography for their musicals, and she did that for several years. Again, "just for fun." This was an integrated school, where blacks took parts in the plays along with whites, the taboo being that romantic parts could not be played by a mixed couple.

When Bessie took her job at Marymount College, once again she did the choreography for the musicals; but she found herself in a frustrating situation. "They would let the black kids dance and sing in the chorus, but they would never give them a lead in a play. So I told the chairman of the dramatic department, I said, 'Look, it's all make believe anyway. If they have a voice good enough to do the part, then I feel that they should have a part, regardless.' But he couldn't see my way."

She looks angry for the first time now, her jaw tight, her eyes intense. There is none of the detachment of her previous description of the inequities at Pittsburg.

"I told him all along that he was prejudiced, but I still worked with him until he just got on my nerves so much that I would no longer do the musicals for them. I told him, I just cannot work with you. I cannot accept the things you do!"

Bessie has taught at Marymount for almost thirty years; she is still the only black instructor there. She was for many of those years chairman of the physical education department. There are only about twenty black students among the under-one-thousand total enrollment at Marymount, and she tries to ensure that in all physical education activities blacks are treated equally. In Salina itself, she tells me, blacks make up only a small proportion of the population.

Bob joins us now, wondering if we are interested in lunch, and we tell him we are not quite ready. There is something official in his manner, a certain dignity and graciousness. I have no trouble imagining him as the mayor of Salina. When I ask him about his experience as mayor, he talks about the larger picture of change for black people, beginning with the civil rights struggles of the sixties. He mentions the first meeting in San Diego of mayors and city officials that he attended, where there were only fifty or sixty minority people. In the next two years, there were over two thousand minority people attending. Bessie had told me that Bob was the first black ever to run for the Salina city commission, from whose commissioners the mayor is selected. She said everyone in town knows him. He never gets angry, she said, won't hold a grudge. "We never have any fussing in the house. I can't get a good argument out of him."

Bob sits in a chair across the room from Bessie and me, his big hands spread on his knees, telling me about his work with the NAACP, for which he is chairman of the Political Action group, which is currently working to put a minority lobbyist in the state legislature. The Black American Citizens Organization of Salina recently caused some city funds to be withheld, he says, because blacks were not represented among the recipients. They succeeded in getting the funds extended to minority groups. I notice he uses the term "minorities" a lot, speaking the language of the politician, the public man.

I am curious about the fate of the town of Nicodemus, settled a little over a hundred years ago by blacks from the South.

"Yes, Nicodemus is still a black town," Bob Caldwell tells me. "It's one of the national memorials now. I don't think they have a post office or a school anymore, because they go into the surrounding towns to attend school. But it's still a small, thriving community."

He rests his elbows on his thighs, clasps his hands between his knees.

"They did have a Black Exodus celebration, you know, in Topeka this summer. It was one hundred years ago that the Black Exodus took place. They had quite a time over there. The governor spoke, and other officials. . . ."

We discuss the great "Kansas Fever" exodus, in which nearly six thousand black "Exodusters" from Louisiana, Mississippi, and Texas came north to settle in Kansas. So-called Kansas Fever was rampant among blacks in the South, for Kansas was known as a state in which there had occurred, as Chestina Allen described it while living through it, "a mighty strife for freedom." It was the home of John Brown, fiery abolitionist, a state that had never allowed slavery. By 1879, this "promised land" looked very good to southern blacks, for their situation was becoming more and more difficult. It was clear by now that the U.S. government was incapable of ensuring black civil rights in the South.

So, beginning in March 1879, black people gathered on the banks of the Mississippi River to take passage on boats going north, and came up to St. Louis, Missouri, from where they traveled overland to Kansas. Thousands left Louisiana and Mississippi between March and May 1879, their flight ending only when the steamboat captains refused to pick up more black passengers. Later in the year, more thousands of black people came overland from Texas to Kansas.

While St. Louis had been inhospitable to the Exodusters, leaving their care to the resources of the resident black community, Kansas welcomed its newcomers. The Freedmen's Aid Association, a largely white abolitionist organization, was formed in Topeka to house and care for the black people, many of whom were penniless. Kansas people thought of their state as the land of freedom, and accepted their new citizens with enthusiasm. The governor, the attorney-general, chief justice, prominent businessmen, and Susan B. Anthony, who happened to be visiting Topeka at the time, worked with the Exodusters' aid movement. Sojourner Truth, a former slave, radical abolitionist, and feminist who was by then very old, went to Kansas in 1879 and then toured the country, lecturing to stir up sympathy for the black refugees. She considered the Exodus "the greatest movement of all time." The Freedmen's Aid Association functioned for two years and was eventually run by Quakers, who helped settle the Exodusters and find jobs for them. They started a common school in Dunlap, Kansas, and in the process distributed over ninety thousand dollars in cash and supplies.*

By 1880 there were 43,110 blacks in Kansas. But the state must not have fulfilled the Exodusters' expectations of the "promised land," for black settlers' lives were hard in this rough country. Most of the all-black towns, unable to generate sufficient capital, or suffering the devastation of drought and other agricultural misfortunes, eventually failed. Still, very few blacks went back down South. They moved out into white society, taking the only jobs open to them: most of the women became domestic servants in white homes, the men did construction or railroad work. And some of them moved farther west.**

Bob Caldwell gets up to find the "Kansas Fever Bulletin" printed for the centennial, and a leaflet called "The Nation's Greatest Story of Racial Brotherhood." The publications describe the hopes and aspirations of the arriving blacks, their reception by white Kansas citizens, and their contribution to Kansas history— such as the election of a black, Edward P. McCabe, as State Auditor, in 1883.

We discuss the celebration in Topeka, Bob telling about the attendance at various events. It seems now we are trying to find a way out of that long, tumultuous history back into this pleasant living room. The import of that past profoundly determines much

---

* Historical information taken from *Exodusters: Black Migration to Kansas after Reconstruction*, by Nell Irvin Painter (New York: Knopf, 1977), which provides a thorough and compelling account of this movement.

** An excellent glimpse of the communities established by those black people who went west to Colorado is given in "Black Women and Their Communities in Colorado" by Sue Armitage, Theresa Banfield, and Sarah Jacobus, in *Frontiers (A Journal of Women Studies)*, vol. II, no. 2 (Summer 1977). The authors stress the role of the women in maintaining the social and familial life of these segregated communities within white towns and cities.

in our respective realities, yet we are also simply who we are now in this present, three people who are interested in each other, who are concerned that each of us is comfortable.

Earlier, when I had asked Bessie how it was that after Bob's long absence in the army they got back together to marry, she said, "I guess we just liked each other best." After thirty-five years they seem still to like each other, living easily side by side, involved in their separate pursuits, but together in a way that is supportive and strong.

Finally we arrive again at the subject of lunch, and Bob agrees to go out for Mexican food while Bessie offers to show me her studio. I follow her down the steps to the long, green-walled basement room where she teaches.

In the studio, I see a bar against the wall for practicing ballet postures, a large mirror on the opposite wall. A cluttered desk stands near a bulletin board. A pair of white tap shoes sits on the desk.

"Each year I say I'll stop teaching dancing here at home," Bessie says, "and each year the parents start calling. . . . This year I didn't start until October, a whole month later than usual. I have about a hundred students this year."

"How do you manage all that with your job at Marymount?" I want to know.

"Well, every afternoon after school I teach from 3:30 to 6:30, little kids, and then three classes of older girls. Ballet, jazz, tap, acrobatics. Jazz takes the place of modern. I'm through after 6:30, then I relax. At Marymount this semester I'm teaching ballet, modern, and tap. And aerobics—I love that! This year I decided not to have Saturday classes, but we're having a ballet so I'm teaching four groups their dances for the ballet, and that takes up my Saturday mornings."

I am breathless just hearing about this arduous schedule, but Bessie tells it casually, while showing me the various features of her studio. She puts her foot up on the bar to demonstrate a stretch. Then, with her leg out perfectly straight before her, heel hooked on the bar, she returns to the subject of her early study of modern dance.

"Lester Horton's style was primitive modern, Hanya Holm's was lyric modern, and both of them were very good. I loved Hanya's movements because they were more ballet oriented. I guess I liked all of it. I guess I just like dancing, you know.

"I would love to have performed, but at the time when I was in my prime it wasn't worth it. Black performers couldn't make any money at all."

She brings her foot down and stands easily next to the bar. "But in my teaching I use the parts I like the most, mix them all together. Of course with modern dance you just have to teach the students basic steps, and then they're supposed to create their own dances, otherwise there's no point in them taking modern dance. You give them a background and a basis for it, and if you haven't taught them enough that they can go ahead and make up their own dances then you really haven't done what you should in modern dance. I have kids in the fourth and fifth grades who can make up their own dances. Even in kindergarten and first grade, the things they do are very simple but they know how to move and they know how to experiment."

Bessie shrugs. "It's just hard for me to think of retiring. Each year by May I'm ready to do it. But then after I've had the summer to recuperate, I'll go back and I say, "This isn't so bad after all.""

Clearly, it is this unbounded enthusiasm for dance that keeps her so energized. There is no extra flesh on her small frame; her presence is casual and alert, wasting no gestures, harboring no buildup of emotion in her body.

From upstairs comes Bob's voice, calling us to lunch. Bessie smiles at me, and leads me out of the studio up the stairs into the kitchen. The three of us sit in the large dining area looking out on the back yard.

Eating our enchiladas, we speak of the Caldwell children. The older daughter, Toy, has a doctorate in clinical psychology and teaches at Emporia State University. Teree, the youngest child, is a student at Kansas University, working on her masters degree in public administration. It is not so easy to talk about Robert, their only boy and the first-born of their children.

When we have finished eating and Bob Caldwell has left the table, Bessie and I sit for a time, and she tells me about the day, ten years ago, when Robert was at home on vacation from college. He was driving not many blocks from the house when a car driven by a drunk plowed into him, injuring him so badly that he died after a week in the hospital. He was nineteen years old.

As she speaks of Robert, Bessie smiles gently, and I feel the pain of that time must have been lived through and left behind, for in talking of him she seeks to evoke not his death but his living.

But then she tells me that, after the funeral, the man who drove the other car came to see her. He wanted to say how sorry he was, to let her know he had stopped drinking. He told her he had been afraid to come. Bessie is not smiling now.

"I asked him, 'What did you expect me to do to you?!'"

In this I hear that bitterness is still in her. Bessie gazes at the middle of the table, her eyes fixed. I look at her slim, upright body, and match her silence, now, feeling this weight in the room.

From the last breath drawn by that young Indian woman who lies in her people's communal grave near Salina, to Bessie Caldwell's goodbye to me on this cold November day, there stretches a great wealth and complexity of lived human time. Distinct social realities exist side by side here on the prairie, and the past lives in its many manifestations, linking people who would never imagine their lives to bear similarities. In a town where, as one young woman put it, "heritage is what's important," Marion Ellet lives in the house where her pioneer grandmother gave birth to her mother. She honors traditional values; in her person and in her writings she actually embodies them for the members of her community. Some of the Native Americans are more fiercely traditional, hoping to survive by preserving as best they can their people's original ways, insisting on their separateness from white society. And it was the arrival of Marion Ellet's grandfather, of the Swedes, the French, and other immigrants, that began the assault on native people's culture and the theft of their ancestral lands. Both white and native people exist within certain ironies, certain cruel memories.

In my own family, South met North, my father's emotionality coming up against my mother's wintry restraint. Kansas history mirrors this same clash, as slaveholders from Missouri and points south battled abolitionists from New England. In Kansas I looked not for private history, but for some sense of the sweep of time with its generations of human beings; this I found, and saw in the women's lives a chain connecting each new life to those before it.

Many languages were spoken in the early towns and home-steads, many disparate customs followed. The Catholics came as missionaries to settlers and Indians alike. The Sisters of St. Joseph established Marymount College, where Bessie Caldwell now teaches. Quakers ran early mission schools and, later, helped the Exodusters find homes. Whites and blacks labored to develop the land and build the cities. My visit to the Caldwell home helped me to understand that the Midwest is still an uneasy or dangerous place for people of color. Potawatomi Margret Mahkuc, too, described the discomfort of her school years, in which she went off the reservation into an alien culture.

Out on the land, in the small towns and on the farms, the past most acknowledged is the experience of the pioneers. The struggle of their foremothers to survive and prosper in the new territory is part of what weds contemporary white women to the land, gives them a sense of themselves as competent, and in some cases even indestructible. Because their grandmothers or great grandmothers dared so much, they are able to know who they are and to think of themselves as truly belonging to the broad generous sweep of prairie.

The experience of disorientation in new surroundings that the pioneer women knew has in the succeeding years been endured by women from many disparate origins, from as far away as the other side of the world, for there are Asians, too, in Kansas. In the larger towns and cities people of different races and ethnic groups live side by side, and here and there the immigrant experience is lived out once again by individuals, some of whom, now, are Vietnamese or Cuban.

Skeleton of young woman at "Prehistoric Indian Burial," Salina

Judy Anderson and Vestina Durham at the Prairie Band office of the Potawatomi, Holton

Minnie LeClere and Cecelia Jackson in the senior citizens' center on the Potawatomi Reservation

Sisters Margarida Boucher and Leona Dinges of the Sisters of St. Joseph of Concordia

Teresa Mahon

Bessie Caldwell

City Life

Flight and Return

This morning, in my apartment in Concordia, I am pondering the difference between me and Virginia Racette, Jane Snavely, the women in Red Cloud and Clyde. Are they who I might have been if I had stayed here? It's true I grew up in the Midwest just as they did, it's true I was married for ten years as solidly as they are married, true I have lived with and cared for children: these are our similarities. But that lust for the experience of the "great world" that awakened early in me and guided my life for many years was apparently never aroused in them. This, perhaps, is the crucial difference between us.

Thinking of my life in the Midwest until age twenty-one, thinking of how I left the Midwest, I see the face of little Lana Lambert bent over her french fries that night in Sandy's Cafe, eyelids lowered, mouth slightly smiling, as her mother explained that she was a vegetarian, of all things! I suspect that I was such a mysterious, secretive child; I know that at her age I was absorbed in my inner life, already planning my future. By the age of nine I had decided I would be a wildlife photographer in Africa.

Later, when my ambition changed from naturalist to writer, I knew I would have to leave for New York City as soon as possible. But my parents insisted I not leave until I had finished my education, neither of them nor my older brother and sister having earned a college degree. So I lived at home with my parents on the outskirts of Columbus, Ohio, and went to school at Ohio State University.

In the spring of 1958, just before I graduated, I received word
that I had been chosen as a guest editor of *Mademoiselle*. Twenty
college women each year were selected from applicants through-
out the country, to come to New York and work on the magazine.
I had applied that year and the year before, without much hope of
winning: it seemed too glamorous and remote a possibility for me.
I was stunned. *Mademoiselle* had bought me a plane ticket to New
York and reserved for me a room in the Barbizon Hotel for
Women on Lexington Avenue, where all the guest editors stayed.
I held my freedom in my hand.

Thus I fled the heartland twenty years ago for what I believed
would be a larger, richer life. This was an irrevocable act, one that
led to my ability to communicate well with the women in this
section. They are all city women, and our rapport derives from an
awareness of social and political realities that to the rural women
come only as pictures on a TV screen. Just as the farm women
respond to the seasons, the weather, we adjust ourselves to the
changes, the shifts and flow of city life. We live with similar
threats and paranoias, similar challenges in the struggle to survive.

"The Earth Is Alive"

Not much more than a hundred miles from Concordia is the
town of Lawrence, Kansas, home of the University of Kansas.
With 46,000 inhabitants, it is not a very big city, but students and
faculty from all over the world give it a more diverse and metropolitan character than most Kansas cities. The proximity of
Topeka, with its Menninger Foundation, adds to this sophistica-
tion, for Menninger conducts scientific research in the field of
psychic phenomena and sponsors annual conferences of psycholo-
gists involved in the investigation of "alternative consciousness."
In the area of nontraditional spiritual inquiries and disciplines,
there is considerable activity in Lawrence. Two Zen groups flour-
ish; there is a Kundalini yoga class at the University; there is also
a dream study group. The Metaphysical Society posts its flyers on
the campus, and head shops sell alternative culture items.

I come to Lawrence to stay for a few days in a little white frame house on a street far across town from the university. The two women who rent the house have taken me in with no more formal introduction than my mention of the women of Iris Films in Berkeley, who visited here the year before. Their manner toward me is interested and casual. Bonnie, tall and cheerful, with a bright mop of curly blond hair, works as a cook in a restaurant, where she is learning to prepare complicated gourmet dishes. Marty is a few years older, darkhaired, intense. She is an artist/photographer/filmmaker who works at present as a clerk in an auto parts store. The family bursting the confines of the shabby little house is completed by an eager young dog and two cats.

Vivid saffron leaves lie strewn across the yard. The weather has turned cold, and Marty lights the gas stove in the crowded dining room. In the living room, which is crammed with books and records and green plants, we sit talking of the woman I have come to Lawrence to see. Marty and Bonnie know Denise Low not only for her poetry, but in her role as a psychic who gives readings and conducts classes in the development of psychic abilities. I had first heard of her from her sister, who works for the *San Francisco Examiner.* "My sister Denise," said this woman, "is a Third World poet." A puzzling remark, given that she herself is the model of blond, blue-eyed WASP looks.

Marty laughs. "Oh, she said that because Denise is married to a Chinese-American and she writes a lot about her Asian relatives."

I tell them that my interest in Denise Low stems from her seeming to embody much of the cultural change going on in the world today. In pursuing both academic and psychic work, she stands at a juncture between traditional knowledge and a more intuitive method of inquiry; culturally, she moves between white American mores and the experience of people of color. It interests me that she lives here in the heart of the country, far from most centers of occult and psychic activity.

The next day, a wild rainstorm hammers the roof of my car as I set out for Denise Low's house. Half an hour later I am sitting on a couch in a warm living room with a basset hound draped across my lap. Rain whips the trees in this neighborhood of smooth lawns and flagstones and French doors opening onto patios. Inside this house all is muted and discreet, not in the least extraordinary. The woman across from me fits smoothly into this setting. She is thirty years old, of middling height, with serious eyes behind glasses, mid-length pale brown wavy hair. She wears a flowered blouse and jeans, and looks like a young mother at home on a rainy morning after having taken her children to kindergarten. Which of course is what she is.

Denise offers to rescue me from the basset hound, who is very heavy on my legs. Then we settle once again into our separate couches and talk for a few minutes about her life as a college teacher, lawyer's wife, and mother to sons aged seven and five. I find her mild and somewhat hesitant at first.

"I would really like to hear about your psychic work."

She nods. "Oh, that began when I was a kid, when I started to have experiences for which I could find no explanation from anyone or anything." She grew up, she says, in Emporia, southwest of Lawrence. Her face is impassive, her voice quiet and calm, as she talks about these childhood experiences.

"What happened?" I inquire.

"I would have hallucinations," she obliges. "I would see pictures. That side of my consciousness was just very active."

I ask her, "Did you tell your parents about the pictures?"

"Oh no, I never told them about any of this. What is it—astral flight?—I remember when I was a little tiny thing astrally going and standing over the stairs, which seemed very horrendous when I was two or three, and flying down them. The next day, in the flesh, I went over and stood at the head of those stairs for an hour just trying to decide if I should fly or not. I don't think I mentioned that to my parents.

"Then as I grew up, I tried to put meaning to the pictures. Simultaneously, my oldest sister was having psychic experiences in Southern California. She eventually put me in touch with a psychic when I was visiting her once. I had a couple of readings, and then I realized that, as the psychic talked, I was seeing what she was about to say. And then also I had an experience, a visual sequence, with a real strong feeling that it was something important, here in Kansas. Six months later, when I saw the psychic again, she had seen the exact same sequence, so there were some amazing correspondences that helped me to have confidence in whatever it was."

Denise has since developed her psychic capacities and has begun to teach others to do the same. She offers a "Psychic Visualization Class," in which she helps students activate their inherent psychic abilities. She has investigated and teaches in many areas of the occult, including the ancient system of *chakras* or energy centers in the body; the practice of astrology, at which she is adept; the interpretation of dreams.

"Is there some relation between your literary studies and your psychic abilities?" I ask her. She has told me she has a masters degree in literature and is engaged in scholarly pursuits.

She nods. "Well yes, but it took me a long, long time to make the connection. I really loved literature and art, and then here was all this occult, bizarre experience that at that time was certainly outside the realm of what you studied in school. I finally put together that it was the same process: the visualization that went on in literature, eventually in my poetry, and the visualization in psychic reading. And you have to interpret psychic stuff, often; there is a certain amount of symbolism just as in literature. Then, when I was a senior at the university here, they had a program where seniors could propose courses to the college of liberal arts and sciences, and if it were approved you could teach it. I taught 'The History of Astrology' and 'The Occult in Literature.' I had been studying astrology on my own. I needed money at that point, and made some money doing astrological readings. I'm a Taurus, Leo rising, Pluto on the ascendant, Venus on my sun, moon in Libra with Neptune on it."

I relax into the couch, hearing the rain pound outside, the hound snuffle at my feet. This astrological information makes me feel at home, because so many of my friends frequently reel off

such data. The fact that I am not capable of interpreting it does
not interfere in the least with its soothing effect.

Denise goes on. "To do 'The Occult in Literature' class, I tried
to find places in traditional literature where an occult or mystical
perspective is being used, or an astrological perspective—as in
Chaucer. In his day, astrology was astronomy. He wrote a treatise
on how to use an astrolog. He was involved in that, and he was an
astrologer. The Wife of Bath's tale particularly: she's a Taurus
with Mars and Venus in Taurus, and so her sensual nature is
associated with the whole thing. Even *Troilus and Cressida* is full
of astrology. It was part of their world view at that time, which of
course you aren't taught in your regular classes, because people
just aren't sensitive to it. They say, Oh, this is just superstition
from back then, they don't see it as part of the nice, closed, secure,
Catholic world view that they had, where the stars fit into the
whole scheme, the whole chain of being."

Denise's mild manner, like a fire banked low, masks intensity.
She speaks casually, leans back in her chair as she talks to me, yet
I sense the urgency in her literary quest, in her endeavor to coor-
dinate her intellectual with her spiritual capacities. What does it
mean, I ask her, to be a psychic?

"Different things at different times," she answers. 'There is
spontaneous psychic work and then there is forced or controlled
psychic work. Spontaneously, I'll have a hunch or a flash or a
picture of something happening. Also dreams. I have prophetic
dreams, usually on a very personal and insignificant basis. I feel
the most whole as a person when I really pay attention to my
dreams. I feel my consciousness is like the iceberg, it goes underneath as well as on top. And I bring that strength into my day-to-
day life.

"I have a lot of energy. I think every psychic has a lot of
energy, physical as well as psychic, and you can throw it around in
your body. Through meditation, most people raise their energy
into finer vibrations; I think it's just a quickening. To me, you
just start vibrating on a finer, quicker level, and that feels very
peaceful and energizing. I started trying to meditate when I was

in high school. At that time nobody knew what it was, of course. I had found some books, yoga books, actually. Then eventually I came to realize that what psychics call raising their energy to a level where they can do their work is a trance. It's not blacking out and your eyes rolling back in your head, you know, it's just . . . I can feel I'm using a different part of my brain.

"In the right place, in the right frame of mind," she continues, "I can see auras, I can read chakras, I can read past lives. To do this, I have to go into trance."

She goes on to elaborate the complexity of this process. "Since the Seth material has come out, it has really turned the occult world upside down, because it's nonlinear."

Seth is a being, ostensibly a spirit, who communicates in trance with the contemporary writer Jane Roberts to deliver wisdom on the human condition and the nature of the universe. These communications are transcribed, and have been printed in books with titles such as *Seth Speaks* and *The Nature of Personal Reality.* Central to Seth's teachings is the concept that past, future, and present time all exist in this moment.

Denise frowns, pondering the difficulties this theory presents. "Traditionally you have one life," she says, "then another, in sort of an upward spiral; whereas the Seth material says that everything is happening all at once, that it's horizontal rather than vertical. So I've really been having trouble thinking about it. I can't really say I read past lives—I don't know what 'past' means —but I can read other personas that seem to have some kind of metaphorical significance to this one."

In all of her talking I notice an effort to be precise. She had spoken earlier about the sloppy thinking some psychics indulge in, and I see that she makes a point of applying certain standards of accuracy in her work. Perhaps this comes from being a scholar as well as a psychic, and it may derive, too, from being a poet, for poetry requires exactitude of language and a rigorous distillation of meaning. It is not unusual for poets to be sensitive to the realm of psychic phenomena, to perceive a spiritual dimension within experience. I wonder how Denise's psychic abilities carry over into

her writing. She has gotten up to prepare tea, now. I lean to finger
the basset hound's warm silky ears.

When she returns with teapot and cups, I ask about her poet-
self, who she may be as a writer.

"I'm very committed to midwestern poetry," she answers, settling into her chair. "By that I mean poetry of place, poetry that
derives out of geography. I'm definitely a midwestern poet and a
midwestern person. I feel a real direct relationship between the
land and my survival. In Southern California I saw tiny houses on
the beach that were worth a million dollars! It's just so unreal.
And I think of trying to grow anything out there in that sandy
soil! That's such an artificial economy. With this economy here in
Kansas I just feel more secure. I'm a city person, I don't want to
farm, that's a very hard life, but I have fruit trees. I'm very serious
about my fruit trees and my strawberry patch and my vegetable
garden."

Denise inherited this love of growing things from her mother,
who always gardened, and it is something the two of them share
now that Denise is grown. She wrote a poem, "Day Lilies," to
express the presence of her mother, through flowers, in her everyday life:

> When I moved my mother gave me
> iris and lemon balm, forget-me-nots
> and families of day lilies
> with names and ruffles, stripes,
> already in bloom:
> Edna Spaulding, Susie Wong, Day Queen.
> I poked them into the dirt
> and watched the dozen blossoms
> fall in a week.
> By August I had lost their name tags.
>
> This spring roots showed,
> tubers under rumpled brown leaves,
> huddling like bunches of onions
> as iris bloomed about them.

I remembered the day lilies
and the person I had been,
a person who had just moved in
and started a garden.

By June the bloomstalks rose
from two feet of straight leaves,
a dozen buds forming on each stem.
My mother sent me again
a list of descriptions:
    Cahokia—late apricot-pink
    Towhead—pale yellow with a green throat,
    blooms have eight petals instead of six.
And through this summer
corals and yellows open,
offering fresh each day
new aspects of the roots.*

And I am left remembering my mother's rock garden, which she dug on the slope of yard in front of our house. There was something austere and understated in the clusters of blossoms in among the rocks. She worked on her knees over her modest flowers, usually in the twilight. I would sit near her on the grass to watch. It seems to me now that there was an understanding between us in those hours, an intimacy we shared in silence.

Denise Low has made the choice to maintain this common interest with her mother. Her caring about her relatives and her need to be with them are among her strongest reasons for living here in the Midwest. She sees her parents regularly, and she cultivates the same close relationship with her husband's parents and his brothers.

"Don has a brother who lives on a farm outside of town—just an eleven-acre weekend farm," she explains, "and his other brother's in Kansas City. So I feel right in the middle of everybody.

---

* "Day Lilies," as yet unpublished, was displayed in a poetry/art exhibit at the Kansas City Jewish Community Center.

And there's space here. There aren't so many people. Sometimes I wonder if this is a weakness, and sometimes I say to myself, gee, why don't I go live in the *real world,* see if I could make it, you know, because things are fairly secure and familiar here."

The "real world." This expression makes me think of the choice I made so many years ago. I see that Denise's choice to stay here, near her family, has let her combine the sophisticated achievement of her psychic and literary work with the same stability, the consistency over time, that the farm women experience in the communities where they live. Like them, too, she is uneasy in big cities.

"When I go to a large city, I feel like an ant," she says. "I feel bombarded, forced to scatter and re-evaluate and to constantly shift my idea of myself. Even when I go into Kansas City I feel like I'm just one of millions of little organisms running around. Here there's more land to dilute it with, and my life matters more."

Her husband, also, grew up in Kansas, very near here, but his relationship to his environment was affected by his family's nationality. His father came over from China in his teens to work in a restaurant in Wichita. After serving in the army, he was discharged from Fort Riley and settled in Salina. There he joined with seven other Chinese men to run a restaurant, and later was able to bring his wife from China. When her husband was growing up in Salina, Denise tells me, the census showed something like two hundred people of Asian descent in all of Kansas.

Much of her writing explores the poignancy of a not-always-harmonious meeting of cultures in the society around her and within her extended family. Her tenderness toward her husband shines through the lines of her poem "Cousins."

> If they had dug deeper holes in their back yards
> they would have met:
> one digging through the clipped midwestern lawn,
> turning aside bluegrass and clay;
> the other spading near the fields
> through tired soil of the Middle Kingdom.

The young boys meet at the center.
The American has his Boy Scout knife
and maybe a tent.
The Cantonese has bowls and quilts
They sleep out summer nights,
fish with bamboo poles.

Except one will be missed;
night here is day there.

The Salina mother reads bedtime stories
as the sun rises in Canton;
the waking boy flexes thin legs,
leaves his wooden bed;
his double
folds in twin arms and legs.

The sleeper's imprint bulges into the other world;
he travels deep into the earth.*

The thin Kansas boy grew up to become a student with whom
Denise became involved during the last three months of their
senior year in college. They liked each other a lot but had to
separate when he went off to law school in Boston, and she went
to Irvine, California, where she expected to live with her older
sister and go to graduate school. But after that summer of separation, feeling their relationship was unresolved, Don Low arrived
in California. Denise had a "gut level feeling" that he was the
person with whom she was meant to be, so the two of them came
back together to Kansas.

She characterizes him as "totally stable, practical, and sane," a
good lawyer and a good husband.

Denise went to graduate school while beginning her family,
and earned her masters degree when she was eight months pregnant with her second son.

"For a year and a half after that I stayed home," she explains.
"Then we were in Manhattan at Kansas State and I started to
teach composition there as a part-time lecturer. Two years later

---

* Published in *Dragonkite* (Kansas City: Bookmark Press, 1981).

we moved here and I am continuing as a part-time lecturer-in-structor. When I first moved back from Manhattan, I sort of felt like I'd come out of the boonies, you know, out of a much more closed conservative place. Also, we moved in March and school didn't start until September. So for six months I did psychic classes and psychic readings on a very regular basis. It was really good. I got to thoroughly work through and explore some of the possibilities of psychic work as a profession and as a way of life."

Consistently she has maintained close ties with her Caucasian blood family and her Chinese-American inlaws. Her poetry reflects the particular richness and irony in the merging of these disparate people brought together in new circumstances, as in her description of a shopping expedition to the Chinese market in Kansas City.

Almost the whole family—
Cantonese parents,
three grown sons,
their white midwestern wives
and two of the grandchildren—

spread through aisles
of the remodeled A & P
late Sunday morning,

the five-year-old pushing
his sister—just balanced—
in the shopping cart
sideways into the *fun won* rolls,
fortune cookies, dried lychee fruit,
candies wrapped in edible rice paper

Past the candy section
they careen towards
garden seeds, Kung Fu dolls that punch,
frozen turkey egg rolls,
dried lotus leaves, banana leaves,
Coke, soybean sprouts, tiger balm.

The old-country mother
squints to read labels,

Japanese, Romanized Chinese, Thai, Vietnamese,
and questions the big, light-skinned
Mandarin-speaking stockboy;

the sons and wives wander
and joke about the funny labels:
"Jellied White Fungus,"
"Chinese-style Alimentary Paste,"
"Japanese-style Alimentary Paste,"
"Dried Silver Fish."

The old father
reads the walls.

He sees Buddhist annoucements,
Christian announcements,
New Years parties for the Thai community,
advertisements for home-made tofu,
no Cantonese message.

Past the check-out
with packages and children
we gather to leave,
blocking the glass doors
and two or three Vietnamese
dark-eyed, silent,
waiting to enter.*

In her own immediate family, Denise tells me, her two small
sons have inherited some measure of her psychic powers. But then
she believes that all children are psychic. "Each has a different
ability," she explains, "as we all have different mental abilities.
One of the kids is intuitive. We were taking a walk and he found
us when we were five blocks away in a totally different part of the
neighborhood than he had been in before. The other kid sees
auras. He says he sees 'angels,' and I'm not going to argue with
him."

Her husband does not share her interest in psychic phenome-

---

* "The Chinese Market in Kansas City," in *Dragonkite* (Kansas City: Bookmark Press, 1981).

na, although she trusts that he respects her psychic work. "He has a different path," she says, smiling. "He has been a really good stabilizer for me."

I ponder this last remark, wondering if she is sometimes afraid of her psychic gifts, of being so vulnerable to other-world influences that she may become disoriented in the everyday world.

She shakes her head, assuring me that she has no such anxieties. "I figure I'm a basically moral person who tries to do what's right," she tells me, "so I'm not afraid of being pulled off balance." She elaborates. "You know, I was very lucky. There was something inside me that kept saying, 'Do not experiment with drugs.' I have friends who were psychically inclined, who did experiment with drugs and who are crazy now, medicatedly crazy. It's very sad. But something inside of me, that little voice, did that. My psychic awareness is not a threat, it's a tool. I also have a lot of faith in will. I can say, Okay, psychic ability, let's go figure this out. You program it. It isn't just a randomly working mechanism."

Denise consciously labors to build a bridge between the rational and the nonrational sides of her nature. "At one point a couple of years ago," she says, "I made a decision that I'd really like to sharpen my rational mind. And I've been doing that. It's been very fulfilling to me. For instance, I say to myself, Okay, I'm going to learn all I can about Native American literature. So I read all the books, try to make notes, try to get an overview. My path definitely includes teaching. To me, to articulate things is really important; it helps me to understand it with both halves of my brain."

She considers herself a religious person, pointing out that people with psychic abilities recognize that their powers come not from themselves as individuals but from "somewhere else"; they know that their awareness connects them to the rest of the universe. But her relationship to institutionalized religion is not simple.

"When I was exploring different modes of thought I was very antagonistic towards Christianity because I see it really cutting people off from their own bodies, from their own consciousness. Now I'm starting to mellow, I suppose, and I think there are some very fine sects or groups of Christians that allow certain latitudes in belief. Such as the Unity Church. Their headquarters are in Kansas City. They've taught meditation and all these sorts of things for years and years. They have a very substantial organization. They have retreats, they sponsor psychic workshops on the grounds, have lecturers come through. A group of them is starting to establish a church in Lawrence. They've had women in the ministry for years."

Denise herself does not belong to any of the psychic or spiritual organizations in the Lawrence area. "I've never been very disciplined about things," she admits.

Soon she and I must finish our talk, for she has to pick up her younger son at kindergarten. As I prepare to enter the deluge once more, we conjecture about the people in little towns in Kansas: are they more "moral" than city people? Denise thinks small-town people have always done as they pleased, under cover. Eyes laughing, she mentions a nearby town in which there is an organized system of spouses exchanging partners. She tells about a woman friend who is an art teacher and a farmer, who defied her neighbors' mores to plow her fields in the shapes of female nudes.

Having said goodbye to Denise and stroked the basset hound once more, I drive off into the rainy streets, visualizing those gigantic earth-women reclining in their fenced enclosures. I remember Denise saying, "The earth is alive. It has its own rate of movement and its own consciousness." She has trained herself to listen, as she does to the earth, for the subtle communications of her deeper self. Perhaps it is because she is attending so closely that she betrays little of the intensity that motivates her. Placing herself in a situation in which a great range of her capacities is called upon, as teacher, wife, mother, psychic, poet, scholar, she has embarked on the first stages of an effort to integrate multiple facets of experience in herself, to transcend dualities in order to arrive at a more truly human or comprehensive way of being. I realize I have received a great deal more from Denise than the sheaf of poems I carry with me back to Bonnie's and Marty's house; she is someone who will stay in my mind, challenging me.

Clinging Vine

Barbara Grier has for twenty-five years been resource, model, and inspiration for lesbians throughout the country. A self-described zealot, she has labored on a schedule few people could sustain: writing, editing, publishing, speaking, to better the situation of lesbians. This effort has always occupied only her "spare" time, while she holds down full-time clerical jobs in order to make a living. At age forty-six, she still works at least an eighty-hour week. This way of life became a habit in the mid-fifties, when she began her work with the lesbian organization Daughters of Bilitis and started collecting books by, for, and about lesbians, a collection that has developed into perhaps the most extensive of its kind in existence. Throughout the fifties and sixties she wrote for *The Ladder,* the magazine published by Daughters of Bilitis, and eventually served as its editor. In 1973 she became a publisher when she founded Naiad Press, a company publishing only lesbian titles. About the same time, after many years of a reclusive and very private existence, she came out into the world as a lecturer and public person.

I have heard much about this woman since becoming a lesbian myself in the early seventies. To me, Barbara Grier represents the thousands of women living in midwestern cities and towns who have to hide their sexual preference, even from their families; who live in isolation from the surrounding society and from each other in fear of the negative, punitive attitudes of that society toward homosexuality. Barbara is the visible lesbian who stands for all those invisible women. Now I seek her out, to discover what it is like to live such an actively lesbian existence in the Midwest, far from the more liberal environments of east or west coasts.

The first thing I discover about Barbara Grier is that she has always had a great deal of fun. She and Donna McBride, with whom she has lived for eight years now, are clearly very much in love, their enthusiasm for each other seeming to bubble up from an inexhaustible spring. In their house on Weatherby Lake outside Kansas City, Missouri, the rooms are furnished in tones of deep brown, beige, and gold; the food is plentiful and well-prepared, and good wine is served with dinner. Barbara's gigantic collection of books lines the walls of their basement study, to which they descend on weekends and evenings to do the work of running Naiad Press.

Barbara loves to talk about her own history and that of the homosexual and lesbian movements. She can keep her thread of thought while chopping garlic, brushing stain onto the boards of the porch, or sorting laundry, all of which she does while talking nonstop to me in the days I visit in the house on the lake.

"I've been 'out' all my life," she tells me, "or at least since I told my mother, at age twelve, that I was a homosexual. I had been born in Cincinnati, but we were then living in Detroit, Michigan. I had fallen in love with a girlfriend and I recognized that, in addition to wanting to go to bed with her, in specific sexual terms, I knew I loved her. She was several years older than I. From about age eight on, I had formed a perfect repeating pattern, falling in love with older women. When you're eight, they're eleven; when you're ten, they're thirteen. I had done this, you see, and I went right on doing it. So there I was in love. But I had questions about all this."

She is a wiry woman, on the small side, dressed in striped T-shirt, and cut-offs. She has wavy brown hair cut short and brushed back above her ears, a sharp hook nose, and intense, prominent eyes behind dark-rimmed glasses. It is hard to imagine her as a child, she looks so stern and competent, but at rare moments a naughty twelve-year-old emerges to grin and joke.

"I was very bright and I read," she says of this child self, "so I went to the library with the object of my affections in tow. I went on the Woodward Avenue streetcar down to the Detroit public library, and I marched in and I remember telling the li-

brarian that I wanted to find out about people who liked people
who were the same sex as they were. I don't have any concept of
what the woman looked like, or how she reacted, but I often
wonder. I'll bet that was a pretty unusual request in Detroit at
that time. I'm surprised I didn't have to pick up a heart patient off
the floor! Whatever she sent me to, I remember being told that I
couldn't take away the books I was looking at and for years I
labored under the delusion of thinking that was because they had
to do with sexuality, when it was simply because they were reference books."

Barbara is loading the dishwasher, talking over her shoulder at
me. Obviously she takes great pleasure in her story but her face,
with its abrupt nose and straight mouth, maintains its intent, serious expression throughout. Her voice is brisk, clipped. When now
and then she does laugh, her eyes seem to jump at me from behind the lenses of her glasses.

"So I went home from the library and told my mother I was
that multisyllabic word, ho-mo-sex-u-al, and my mother quickly
responded that since I was a girl—woman—the term was lesbian.
I learned that word from my mother. When she got through
telling me it was all right to be a lesbian, she said that we should
wait six months before we notified the press, because I was too
young to make that kind of decision. My mother was a humorist."

Barbara tells this perfectly deadpan, in a swift rattle of words,
as if she has told it before.

"She was very supportive of me. Well, she came from an artistic background. Her family was primarily women and they were
all on the stage. Opera singers or musical comedy. All her aunts,
and great aunts, her grandmother, her mother. I was used to
living in a household of maniacs, most of them women, all artistic,
all temperamental. And nobody was very surprised that a few
people were queer, since half the people they worked with *were*
gay, both men and women. So my mother's attitude at discovering
that I was gay, was, Well, so you're probably gay, so what? I don't
know what she may have internalized, but what she said was very
reassuring and made me feel fine about being a lesbian."

Barbara was fortunate to have so liberal a family. Most lesbians of her generation in the Midwest encountered no such acceptance from their parents, and soon learned to keep their lesbianism secret, perhaps to be ashamed of it.

She stacks some more plates in the dishwasher and begins to shove bowls in around the edges, cramming the tray with a great bulging pile of dishware that grows more precarious with each saucer. I feel this as a physical demonstration of her ability to juggle, over the years, the mountain of tasks she has performed—when, while holding down a job, she worked for Daughters of Bilitis, wrote thousands of letters, hundreds of articles and reviews, and gave untold hours to the labor and endless detail of publishing.

But Barbara is methodical, and tells her story step by step, having progressed right now only as far as adolescence, some years before she saw her first copy of *The Ladder.*

"My teen years were like other teen years you've heard about," she says blithely, speaking over her shoulder at me. "I believe that teenagers act very similarly whether they are men or women, lesbians, male homosexuals, whatever. The teen years seem to be set aside for the purpose of being moderately unhappy. Now I could count more or less on the fingers of one hand . . . well, I've spent thirty days of my life being unhappy. I hit the floor every morning at 5 o'clock, happy. And run until I drop at midnight.

"But the teen years are meant for unrequited love and all that stuff. Naturally, because I was oversexed—Ha! there is no such word in today's canon—I was busy falling in love, and since we traveled a lot, everywhere I went, like sailors who are reputed to have girls in every port, I had to fall in love. I was all the things that you were not supposed to be: I was possessive, didactic, bossy, obnoxious, arrogant, and overbearing. And I always chose people to fall in love with that were probably beyond my reach, but when I really look back, that is not necessarily true, because out of the thirty or forty people I fancied myself in love with between the ages of twelve and seventeen, it was returned in probably half those cases, and that's pretty good. I don't believe that any of those women who did respond to me were harmed by the experience. Either they grew up to be gay, and it made no difference, or they did not grow up to be gay, and it still did not make any difference. I don't think people are born gay, but I do think that they're born with some strong predilection to be, and very little that you do to them, either supportive or negative, will change it."

Now, with great care, tucking in forks and cups as she does so, Barbara slowly closes the door of the dishwasher, turns to flash me a quick grin of triumph, and pushes a few buttons. Then she leans against the front of the machine, folding her arms across her chest and crossing her ankles, to tell me how she met the woman with whom she was to live for the next twenty years in a relationship she describes as a marriage. It was with this woman that she began her work in lesbian publishing and the collecting of books by and about lesbians.

At age eighteen, a year out of high school in Kansas City, where her family had moved, Barbara knew she was going to have to support her divorced mother and her two sisters. So she turned down a college scholarship she had won, went to work, and soon after she found her true love.

"I met Helen Bennett in the literature and popular section of the Kansas City, Missouri, public library. The year was 1951. She was married, unhappily. She had known for some years that she was a lesbian. Helen and I became lovers. She was thirty-four then, sixteen and a half years my senior.

"She was married to a man who was a pretty nice guy. They were very good friends and they liked each other very much, but Helen did not think and had never thought she was in love with him, not even slightly. When I came along, it was obvious that she was going to leave him and live with me.

"My mother helped us run away together. It was all plotted out. Helen was leaving her husband to go to Denver to library school. She got on the City of St. Louis, which was a famous train in those days, at nine o'clock one evening, to go from Kansas City to Denver. My mother and I at seven o'clock that same evening boarded a local train in Kansas City for Topeka. We got off the train in Topeka about 7:30 and went and had dinner together and went back to the station platform at about 10:15 that evening. She put me on the City of St. Louis when it made its stop in Topeka, and Helen and I ran off together for Denver."

Barbara is walking back and forth from kitchen to dining area now, putting place mats and silverware on the large table.

"We stayed there for about two and a half years. It was there I began to write, and began to collect lesbian literature. As it later turned out, that's what I was to spend my life doing. In 1954 we moved back to Kansas City, Kansas, and Helen became a librarian in the Kansas City public library. Soon after that I got a clerical position in the library. That's where I was when I started working with Daughters of Bilitis and *The Ladder*."

Daughters of Bilitis, the first American organization for lesbians, was founded in 1955 in San Francisco by Del Martin and Phyllis Lyon. The organization, which was at first a social club and later engaged in some political activity, took its name from the heroine of a late nineteenth century French literary hoax consisting of supposed translations of newly discovered work by a female poet of the ancient Greek world, a contemporary of Sappho. The poems turned out to be male erotic fantasies. Daughters of Bilitis was chosen as the name for the organization because it was felt that the reference was so obscure it would not be generally recognized as designating a lesbian group.*

In 1956, Daughters of Bilitis published a bulletin out of San Francisco consisting of ten mimeographed sheets, which it called *The Ladder*. Presumably, the ladder symbolism derived from the idea of lesbians climbing a ladder up out of the "well of loneliness" described in Radcliffe Hall's book by the same name, the most famous lesbian book then available. On the cover of the fledgling publication appeared stick figures of women climbing a ladder up into the sky.

"I took one look at *The Ladder*," says Barbara, "and fell in love. I remember thinking that this was what I was going to spend the rest of my life doing."

---

*A capsule history of Daughters of Bilitis can be found in Del Martin and Phyllis Lyon, *Lesbian/Woman* (San Francisco: Glide Publications, 1972), Chapter 8, "Lesbians United."

After the founding of Daughters of Bilitis in San Francisco, chapters sprang up in Philadelphia, New York, and other parts of the country. But Barbara, who was always living in the Kansas City area, was not near any groups. In this heartland isolation, without the physical proximity to other lesbians, she had to depend largely upon the mails to connect her with other women like herself.

In those years, Barbara and Helen lived a secluded existence, never going out or receiving guests. Helen was interested in Barbara's work, but she did not participate in it, only now and then doing research for a bibliography or article. Most of her contribution to Barbara's work during the succeeding twenty years was to help create the atmosphere in which that exclusive devotion to duty could take place.

Only since living with Donna has Barbara learned to tolerate and even enjoy visitors in the house. When I arrived, she was engaged in a flurry of last-minute cleaning, looking harried and even a little annoyed at my presence. Donna stood by, smiling, to explain, "Barbara didn't have any guests for twenty years. Be patient. She'll calm down in a little while."

It is time for lunch now, Donna handing us the sandwich makings over the counter from the kitchen. As we sit to eat, I can hear the wistful tinkling of wind chimes in the steady breeze outside.

Donna, a few years younger than Barbara, is a librarian. She met Barbara when she began doing work on *The Ladder.* The two women's appreciation for each other is obvious. They touch each other often, look each other full in the eyes, and especially they laugh together. Barbara likes to talk about Donna's virtues.

"She's solid as a rock. Solid, midwestern. Honest, flatfooted. And she can do anything, make anything, fix anything!"

Donna seems unembarrassed by this praise. She puts another slice of lunchmeat on her sandwich and hands me the mustard jar. She and I established an easy rapport soon after my arrival, discovering that we both belong to the sign of Cancer, recognizing our slower pace in contrast to Barbara's headlong race to the next task. Donna is physically broader and heavier than Barbara, her energy more even.

Now she tells me a story of that time eight years ago when she was first getting to know Barbara.

"I used to go to Barbara's and Helen's house to work on *The Ladder*. They were *so* organized, so regimented! Someone at the library told me that on Sunday night Barbara made their lunches for most of the week and packaged them up individually and put them in the fridge, so that they could get them out each morning."

Barbara begins to look uncomfortable.

"I didn't believe it," Donna continues. "Can you imagine what a baloney sandwich would be like by Friday? But then one Sunday I was over there and I happened to go in the kitchen and there was Barbara making the sandwiches and cutting up the carrot sticks and marking the bags. I thought it was hilarious. I went and told my friend, 'It's true! They really do it!'"

For the first time since I arrived here, Barbara can find nothing to say. She looks stern and elderly, living up to her nickname "Granny Grier," perhaps in the hope of intimidating Donna and me as we giggle.

They tell about their falling in love, a wonderful and difficult time for Barbara. She had imagined she would be "married" forever to Helen: how could she be in love with someone else?

"Those were some of the thirty unhappy days I mentioned before," she tells me, and describes a painful time of transition from that first, very longstanding relationship to this new one with Donna. When the break was made, Donna and Barbara went to live for a few years in the country near Bates City, Missouri. They left that place when Donna started travelling four days out of seven selling computer systems to libraries, and the country place was too far from any airport to be practical.

"And Helen?" I ask.

The subject is obviously a difficult one, I can tell by Barbara's uncharacteristic hesitation before she speaks. "I am still in touch with her, but it's a very distant and stilted relationship. A matter of her choice. She *does*, after all, have a right to make that choice."

Barbara goes on. "My life since Donna is really completely different. We move about a great deal. I make speeches on campuses such as Missouri Western State College, where lesbians have been able to make their presence felt. I have had a great deal written about me, about us, about Naiad Press, about the lifelong commitment to lesbian/feminist work, about *The Ladder* years, about book collecting. I believe it's safe to say that if I had not lived with Helen I would not have collected the books and done *The Lesbian in Literature* bibliography in 1967, which also means I would not have spent as much time with *The Ladder* or its work. I probably would have been a very different person. I am much much much happier with Donna than I even guessed might be possible for a human being, but I was never unhappy while I was with Helen."

Part of Barbara's happiness derives from her living in the Midwest, she tells me. "I love this part of the country. Statistically it can be shown that more people live better for less between the Appalachians and the Rockies. I was born in Ohio and by the time I was five I had lived in every state in the union and Canada and Mexico. My parents were cosmopolitan. My mother believed that New York City was heaven on earth, and always dreamed of going back to it. She specifically requested that her ashes be scattered in Central Park. So I did not have middlewestern things beaten into me. My mother also had some of what I consider the normal Eastern arrogance about the Midwest.

"But I grew up believing that the Middlewest was the place to be, despite my mother's ideas. And I've done a great deal of traveling. In other words, I didn't form this provincialism by being provincial. One reason I like the Midwest is there's a great deal of space left. Privacy. Still room to have adequate property. I have very strong ideas about privacy and being alone. Crime certainly is everywhere in the country, and the midwest is no exception to that. But the midwest is still physically beautiful, and there is a lot of outdoor physical activity still available that is a little less readily available on the coasts. I like small towns. And I like middlewestern people. They're very honest and candid, straightforward, pragmatic."

"How about their attitudes about homosexuals?" I ask.

"There is not the harrassment in the bars that occasionally happens elsewhere," she tells me. "Middlewestern policemen have long since determined that the way you enforce a ghetto is not to disturb it, and of course the gay bars are, to some extent, a ghetto. Oh, there's an occasional battery or mistreatment, but for the most part it's pretty mild. Most people, though, are afraid to come out. I know so many women in Kansas City who are closet lesbians. The gay community here is enormous, but like a lot of gay communities in the Midwest it is not power-oriented; they don't have a lot of formal meetings. Organizations start and die here all the time. Nobody's even remotely interested in them.

"A man who was doing a feature on the homosexual community for the *Kansas City Star* came here to see me," she says. "And in the course of interviewing me and looking around this house, he made it clear that he would not take any photographs here, because, he said, 'I know I can't get by in the *Kansas City Star* magazine with presenting a house like this and people like you in an article on gay people. They'd never accept that.' Because, you see, we're too respectable, not at all the midwestern public's view of what lesbians are."

When we have finished lunch and cleared the table, Barbara announces it is time to stain the deck on the front of the house. I offer to help, and we go outside where the lake is beautiful in the bright sunshine, its surface rippled by a strong, steady wind. Leaves drift out from the trees on its banks, speedboats bob at the docks. All is in motion. Everywhere around us are more houses like this one, some done in dark wood with decks and large windows fronting the lake, others in more traditional styles, all immaculately kept.

As we brush the foul-smelling dark stain on the floorboards, Barbara tells me about her work with *The Ladder*. She leans to dip her brush in the can of stain and looks up at me. "I was convinced we were not only going to take over the world, we were going to *improve* it!" Her face opens in a cheery smile that dissolves the stiff Granny Grier sobriety into an aura of pure, almost childish, delight.

"Remember, I'm a light-eyed maniac," she says, her eyes jumping.

From her home in the heart of the country, she wrote book reviews for *The Ladder* in a column called "Lesbiana," and it was here that her pseudonym "Gene Damon" was born. Most people who know of Barbara from the early years recognize her by this name. "I was fifteen different names in the pages of *The Ladder*," she explains. "Gene Damon was only one, but it's the one I'm well-known by, because she became the editor. What it actually means is, I have a middle initial, G, for Glycine, which is the botanical name for the wisteria flower, and that's clinging vine. Incidentally, I've always enjoyed being named after a clinging vine. But when I was a kid I loathed that name because it's the kind of name that makes other children call you things like glycerine and lysol, so I determined that when I grew up I would change my name from Glycine to Gene. Since I was smart enough to realize that for legal reasons I should keep the same initials, I was going to make it Gene, spelled with a G, not thinking of it in terms of gender identification but simply in terms of keeping the initial the same. So . . . what we dream of doing at thirteen we don't do when we're grown, and I didn't do that, but instead when it came time to choose a pseudonym for the pages of *The Ladder*, I chose Gene because I liked it and Damon—remember, I was twenty-two or twenty-three years old, a romantic age—I chose Damon because it's German for demon or devil and I fancied myself as quite a dashing figure at that age."

Most of the women who wrote for *The Ladder* used pseudonyms, out of fear, for their identification as lesbians could have caused them to lose their jobs, their standing in the community, their relationships with friends, coworkers, or even family members. Unarguably, times have changed since the 1950s; but as Barbara has pointed out, there are still many lesbians who must hide their sexual identity in order to protect job or social situations. Our society's homophobia reaches deep.

Barbara staightens up to ease her back and looks out over the lake, the wind rearranging her neatly brushed-back hair.

"I did an awful lot of writing for *The Ladder*. In one instance, Phyllis Lyon got in touch with me and told me they had two weeks to produce an issue of the magazine and they'd been busy with other things, and what could I send them. That issue of *The Ladder* has a story by me, two articles by me, my 'Lesbiana' column, and two letters, also written by me."

Because there was no Daughters of Bilitis chapter in Barbara's area, she ended up answering a lot of correspondence, in addition to her writing chores. "And because I was collecting the books and dealing with people who were interested in books, I started building up an enormous correspondence. I believed it was terribly important to answer all the outlying mail—to communicate with those women who felt isolated. We built up an enormous network, which many thousands more women have joined since the death of *The Ladder*."

Barbara's having written those letters arouses my affection, for such individual human connections sometimes made the difference between life and death for women in the fifties and sixties. When I became a lesbian in 1971, the situation was much different. There was a great surge of identification with and love for women in the most recent women's liberation movement, and included in this was the embracing of lesbianism as a wholesome and even progressive lifestyle. Furthermore, I was in San Francisco, the American city most tolerant of homosexuality, a very different environment from the cities of the interior. Here in the heartland, in small towns, farm kitchens, motels, diners, I experience the isolation, the sense that one's self and one's deepest allegiances will not be acknowledged by others; or, worse, that one will be despised, verbally or physically attacked. This constriction, the sorrow and rage that accompany it, help me to understand the value of Barbara's early work. The letters she took time to write were a lifeline to women who knew no other lesbians in their town or city; women who lived furtive, frightened lives; some who were filled with rage at the world's treatment of them. Her letters to them were food for survival, validations of self, offering the possibility of acceptance and even pride in one's sexual identity; for Barbara has always been proud of herself as a lesbian. She made connections between people, and she became a model for these women, especially young women, one or two of whom may have worked in the drugstore in Concordia, gone to high school in Clyde.

By now we have finished staining the deck and are sitting on the steps, enjoying the sunshine and the fresh wind. I realize that this correspondence work of Barbara's was done in the evenings and on the weekends, sandwiched between her publishing chores and book collecting, the work on the bibliography, and the business of making a living. I ask how she managed this latter during all those years.

"I've done all kinds of jobs," she answers. "I was a nonprofessional worker in the Kansas City public library, I was a correspondent for a mutual fund, and I did all kinds of what the kids call 'shit jobs'—just jobs, you know, clerical jobs. In a sense I object to that phrase 'shit jobs.' I've got the old puritan mentality: any job worth doing is worth doing well. But I'm lucky now. I have a very good job. I work counseling people who get into financial difficulty. I've worked in the credit field off and on much of my working life. I'm an excellent collector. I always want to see people get out of trouble, and I figured the ones who responded to my collection efforts were getting into less trouble than if they went beyond me, because where they go after me is into court, and being sued is not pleasant."

Gathering up the can of stain and the brushes, Barbara chortles naughtily.

"I like counseling," she says, "because I like to tell people what to do."

I follow her across the newly darkened boards of the deck to the front door. In the entranceway we step carefully around the large delicately colored conch shells drying on newspapers on the floor. The shells are souvenirs of Donna's and Barbara's recent vacation trip to the Bahamas. The beautifully furnished living room opens to our right. Donna has told me that when they moved into this new house they bought all new furnishings. I remember thinking, when I first entered it, that this is the most luxurious house I have been in so far on my journey. This lifestyle clearly requires that both women maintain full-time jobs, yet, as do many people who have worked full-time all their adult lives, Donna dreams of a time when she might devote more of her effort to the crafts she does now as a hobby, hoping eventually to live off the proceeds of her silverwork and woodworking. "But having the nerve to do it is a different story," she admits.

Later that afternoon Barbara and I work in the kitchen, adding spices to the spaghetti sauce, preparing the garlic bread, and Barbara tells me how *The Ladder* ended and Naiad Press began.

"In 1968, when I became editor of *The Ladder* and brought it here to the Midwest, there were a great many people in Daughters of Bilitis who felt that lesbians were in one cage and women were in another, and never the twain should meet, and that therefore the magazine should not be concerned with feminist issues. I felt differently, and as the new wave of the feminist movement became a powerful force it seemed obvious to me that that's where the magazine had to go. For the last two years of *The Ladder's* life we had an awful lot of very fine young writers whose early works all appeared in our pages. Jane Rule, the Canadian novelist, Rita Mae Brown, Judy Grahn, Helene Rosenthal who's a Canadian poet of some note, Isabel Miller, Martha Shelley, and a lot of other very good poets and short story writers.* So it became a good magazine. We were very pleased."

But economics do not always cooperate with other kinds of success and, as has been the case with many other magazines, *The Ladder's* circulation grew faster than its operating budget and it had to cease publication in 1972. Its legacy, however, led to the establishment of Naiad Press.

"In 1973, two women who had helped put out *The Ladder,*

---

* For a listing of works by these authors, see Barbara Grier, *The Lesbian in Literature,* 3rd ed. (Tallahassee, Fl.: Naiad Press, 1981).

much older women who had always had the idea of having a lesbian-feminist publishing company, put this to me as a proposition: 'We are in retirement and physically are not up to this work. If you will do the work we will give you some of our retirement income to get started and we will publish books.' So we founded Naiad Press. In '74 we brought out our first book, and now five years later we've brought out thirteen books."

Barbara talks about the authors published by Naiad, discussing specific titles, admitting that many of the novels are light, happy-ending kinds of stories rather than attempts at serious literature.

Donna, who is passing through the kitchen at that moment, comments, "You know what it is? It's that lesbians, as well as housewives, like mindless romances."

Barbara blinks up at her, and hastens to point out that Naiad, in addition to such light works, has published translations of the writings of the Parisian literary figure Renee Vivien, a bibliography of lesbian titles, a book on lesbian sexuality, a collection of early German lesbian-feminist material, and other serious titles.

Naiad Press brings in enough money from sales of its books to keep publishing more, but there is no money for salaries. I think of so many of the publishing ventures of the feminist movement, including a newspaper on which I worked for three years. Working without pay requires extraordinary dedication and perseverance, it seems, and generally means that the participants cannot sustain their commitment over time. I wonder how Barbara and Donna manage the Naiad Press work.

"I do fifty to sixty percent of the editorial work and all of the correspondence," Barbara says. "A woman in Denver does the billing. There is a woman here who does our early readings and she and her lover come here to the house once or twice a month in the evening to just help with all the things like filing, entering orders on cards. Donna does a lot of packing for me because I am hopeless, I can't even wrap Christmas presents so that anyone would accept them, and she does some of the accounting, because even though I've worked with figures off and on most of my life, I loathe math."

"How do you manage all this while working a full-time job?"
I ask.

"Well, we get up in the morning about a quarter to six, and
we jog. Then I go to work. When I come home at night, if
Donna's home and the amount of work warrants it, I may go
downstairs to do Naiad Press work for two or three hours. She
may or may not be working with me. Then we have dinner, relax
a little, and go to bed. That's the day.

"When Donna's gone, it's an entirely different thing. I get up
at five A.M. and I work until seven o'clock on Naiad Press stuff,
than I scurry around and get ready to go to my job. When I come
home at night, I go downstairs and I work, from, say, six o'clock
until ten o'clock. Then I eat and go to bed. Or sometimes I work
until eleven or twelve, and then eat and go to bed.

"I work at least eighty hours a week—forty at my job and
forty for Naiad Press—pretty much every week. And Donna and
I have millions of interests. On weekends we work outside in the
yard. When we lived out in the country we had five acres and we
planted fourteen hundred trees. Although we only have a third of
an acre of land here, we've started to do a lot of planting. We also
maintain a garden, and strawberries and asparagus and tons of
flowers. Donna wants to do framing and photography and silverwork and leatherwork. We brought back these shells from the
Bahamas and now Donna's going to build a table with a glass top,
and put the shells under it in sand. And that's just project number
nine thousand two hundred and twelve and a half. There isn't
really time enough. But I don't know anyone who's happy who
has enough time to do what they want to do."

Over an excellent dinner of spaghetti and red wine, we talk
about the process of "coming out." Barbara is adamant on this
subject, her delivery clipped and didactic. Indeed, she gives
speeches at universities and women's groups on the necessity, if
you are a lesbian, of letting people know your sexual orientation.

"I believe in coming out, to the extent that I have perfected it
to a fine art. I don't consider it particularly brave to come out in
a community that's made up primarily of 'liberals,' " she empha-

sizes the word, loading it with irony, "for instance, a college community. But in the real world, where people are waitresses and cab
drivers and office workers in banks and department stores and
places like that, it's different. At the bank where I worked just
before getting my last job, I had a whole roomful of women
working with me, and a few men, who were collectors; they all
knew I was a lesbian. I was called Granny Grier, Head Queer,
and the term was no insult. I've never in my life been forced to
walk up to people and announce that I'm a lesbian, but I make
sure that they finally get the drift. The way I do it is simply to act
like I am. I do not dissemble, pretend, disclaim, or skirt issues. I
treat our life the way it is. Donna is clearly my lover. If you're
around married women who talk about Don and Bob and Bill
and Harry, and you talk about Donna is the same way, even the
most dense among them will pick up on it."

In her speaking engagements at universities, she sometimes
lectures on early gay activism, which she feels competent to talk
about because there were so few participants in the early days of
the gay movement that they all knew one another. In her talk on
coming out, she says there is really no need for a gay movement in
this country, no need for marches or demonstrations, that if every
one of those people who marched or demonstrated would be
openly gay in their lives, there would be no more oppression of
gay people.

"They may not like us," she says, referring to heterosexuals,
"but they'd have to get used to us if they knew who we were.

"Practically every time I get up and talk," she continues, "particularly in the Midwest and particularly if the audience is a
straight middle-class, middle-aged group, they ask this question:
'If you had a daughter, would you want her to be a lesbian?' This
is a ridiculous question! I would be heartbroken if she *wasn't* a
lesbian. And of course lurking behind that question is the belief:
that's the reason we heterosexual people don't want you nasty
lesbian people teaching in our schools, for fear you'll teach this to
our children. Which is ridiculous. I don't think it's possible. The
seed is there: I really think it's just a matter of getting to that

level. I have no solutions for the social problems that some of this creates, but I also refuse to lie about it.

"The one thing I think the heterosexual world is scared to death to find out is the number of prominent, wealthy, important people who are homosexual. People they can't afford to do without. I want those people to come out. The ones I really resent are the well-established, the tenured of the world: I am talking now about university teachers, I'm talking about people whose positions are so sacred they can't be fired no matter what they do, short of murdering their grandmothers. Those people can't be hurt, and therefore when they don't come out, it's an act of cruelty to the world. They're literally not living up to their responsibility as human beings."

Barbara, in a much less secure position, has certainly adhered to her principles in a life that might be considered quite extraordinary, yet her values are in many ways the same as her neighbors'. A midwesterner by birth, she personifies the oldfashioned virtues of hard work and respectability. She is a solid materialist dedicated to the improvement and maintenance of her immediate environment; a true American consumer who bought all new furniture for her new house; a traditionalist in love who believes in and practices fidelity in marriage. All these she is; but, at the same time, she is an intellectual, a bibliophile, a writer, an editor and publisher, and—in a category surely discordant with her neighbors' mores—an aggressive lesbian bent upon publicizing her sexual orientation.

All this might be more easily reconcilable if Barbara Grier went to work at the credit company, paid the bills, and mowed the lawn, while "Gene Damon" did the publishing and public speaking. But Barbara Grier now does all these things, talks about them with her friends and acquaintances, and by so doing brings to her neighbors and coworkers the challenge of relating to a whole, healthy human being who openly declares herself to be a lesbian.

"I've always considered myself a garden variety lesbian, resistant to blight and guaranteed to grow." With these words, Barbara begins her "coming out" speech. Indeed, I can't imagine what could blight her, and I know she'll go on growing, a twining wisteria in the rich Missouri soil.

Black and Proud

The university is the heart of Lawrence. On its campus sit old ivy-covered buildings; lawns stretch softly in the sunlight; students hurry under graceful arches. Searching for the way back to Bonnie's and Marty's, where I'm staying, I drive through sections of elegant old Victorian houses, into newer middle class tracts, then into the outskirts of town, where the houses are small with paint worn thin and porches sagging.

The weather has turned raw, a damp cold wind whipping the trees, sending dry leaves out in erratic swirls. At the house on 13th Street, I hear a train clacking by on the track a block away. Its sound sends a ripple of loneliness through my body. The dog cringes as I near the porch, her chain rattling on the floorboards. Having taken the key from under the flowerpot, I let her in the house with me, and go to make tea in the kitchen, waiting for Bonnie and Marty to come home from work.

Their friend Barbara Barfield had agreed to talk with me tomorrow, but she'd said she'd like to meet me tonight and would stop in on her way home from her job as an attendant in a rest home. I understand her being more cautious than are most of the women with whom I have been spending my time. In important ways, she would seem to be very different from them. She is not only black, but has engaged in direct political action and has lived all her life in cities. She is painfully conscious of that remote, larger world which to white small town and farm women appears to have so little effect on their lives. Her identification with place is not as strong as theirs; she can never feel she owns her world, she will never be as firmly a part of it. As with Richae Colby in Concordia, Barbara Barfield's life, her struggle to survive and raise her family, says a great deal about the city in which she lives. It speaks for the lives of many women of color in the Midwest.

Despite the obvious differences between Barbara's life and those of the more rural white women, there are similarities too. Although women on small farms may not technically fit the model of the working class as it developed in industrial situations, the basic assumption in these women's lives from a very early age is that they must work. This acceptance of necessity, this capacity and willingness to labor, cuts across lines of race and blurs the urban/rural demarcation. That Barbara Barfield in many respects lives a life vastly different from the farm and small town women's existence only brings the similarities between their lives into sharper focus.

This evening, when Bonnie and Marty have come home from work and we have eaten dinner, we sit in the living room listening to music. Hearing footsteps on the porch, I look up to see a woman in a nurse's white top and pants come in. She is sturdy, square-shouldered, in her mid-twenties, her skin very dark brown, her eyes intelligent and a little wary.

I am introduced, and Barbara Barfield gives me a quick, appraising look. Then she lowers herself into a chair with the slow carefulness of someone who is very tired.

Marty goes to turn off the phonograph and offers Barbara a beer. Barbara hesitates, then agrees, "Well, maybe one." When she receives it she drinks it in sips, as though she does not like the taste.

Oh, her children are fine, she says; her husband is with them tonight. But it is understood by all that the purpose of this visit is Barbara's and my getting to know one another. Marty and Bonnie say little, leaving a space for us to fill.

Tentatively, we begin a conversation. At moments Barbara watches me, then her gaze shifts to rest tiredly somewhere else in the room. We talk about her job at Wakaroosa Manor, and she tells about the old woman who walked off after bed check last night. The police had to be called to find her wandering out in the streets. She tells about the two old men who fight each other. One is named Shotwell. The other calls him "Shitwell," and the fight starts.

I am amused by this, and Barbara laughs with me, but pain shows in her eyes and the curve of her lip as she tells about the man who went crazy that evening and began to attack the other patients. It took six nurses to hold him down while they gave him a shot of thorazine. "I don't like to do that," Barbara says. "It has such a big effect on those old people. They're like zombies for a week afterwards. There was one man who wound up in the insane asylum and it was because of the drugs they gave him. That combination of drugs over time just drove him crazy."

She says many of the families want nothing to do with the old people and never come to see them. "That's the hurting part." I see how deeply she cares about her work.

"That's why that lady ran away tonight. Her sister won't have anything to do with her, and she just felt so bad she wanted to get away."

Barbara takes one last sip of her beer and sits gazing down at the empty can. She squeezes it, bending the metal in her square, dark hands. I wonder if she is worrying about her children, wanting to be home with them. In a few minutes she says she has to leave and gets up to go.

I walk with her to the door, and we renew our plans to meet at her house in the morning.

Later, Marty tells of going out to the rest home with Barbara to see about getting a job there.

"I couldn't do it," she says. "It was too sad. But I saw how Barbara is with the people there. She's wonderful. One old woman thought Barbara was her mother, and Barbara just let her think that. She was so *regular* with them."

When a woman has a job and four children to care for, life does not always go as planned. Barbara calls me the next morning to say that her four-year-old boy is sick and she has to take him to the doctor. He has been vomiting, she says. "He has arthritis and he's already too thin." We make another date.

The second time I come in driving rain to an apartment complex off Route 40 outside of town. Two-story brick and shingle, the buildings stand on curving drives behind narrow plots of grass. Barbara's apartment opens onto a concrete walkway. Through the sliding glass doors I see a neat couch on a cocoa-brown rug, a studio portrait of Barbara and her children on the side table. The place looks pleasant and comfortable. Barbara is not there.

Back at Marty's and Bonnie's, I begin to wonder if I am going to have to give up on Barbara. Just then she arrives, carrying her youngest child, her hair twisted tight against her head in curlers. Another crisis with the little boy, she tells me, had taken her away from her house. She had arrived back there just a few minutes after I left.

We sit down on the couch, and Barbara lets herself take a long breath. Harried as she is, still she looks composed and solid in her jogging suit with white stripe down the side. She has a large face, a strong jaw, and ample mouth. She does not smile often, but when she does the smile is generous.

We settle her little daughter Tory on the floor with some magazines. The child picks up a magazine and glances over the top of it at us.

Barbara begins to tell me about her growing up. "I was born here in Lawrence. About the same time, my mother's sister had a baby and her baby died. So since my mother had seven kids anyway at the time, she let Monty keep me, supposedly for a week in Kansas City. She kept me for ten years. I came back and forth on weekends, different things like that. Then when I was eleven I came back to Lawrence to live. My mother had fourteen kids in all."

"How was it for your parents, raising all those children?" I ask.

"My mom had a hard time," Barbara says. "My dad was working construction, so in the wintertime when he couldn't work it was pretty rough. My mom was a cook up on the hill—up on campus. She'd go in at six in the morning, at one of the fraternities, get off around 12:30, have to go back around 1:00, and then get off at seven. She did this for years, taking care of all us children at the same time."

For a moment I try to remember the woman who cooked at my sorority house at Ohio State University, and I can see no picture, hear no voice. I lived in town and rarely ate at "the house," but I was often there and must have seen that woman.

"At home, the older kids helped with the younger," Barbara says. "Yeah, we had to. We're all one year apart and everybody had to pitch in and do their share."

Her words shift my point of view, as if I were picked up and moved a few inches to the side, where I see a house full of children taking care of each other while their mother works in a kitchen "up on the hill." As she begins to tell me about her own children, I feel shifted even farther from my usual perspective, for Barbara became pregnant with the first of her four children when she was thirteen years old.

"The boy that I was dating had a football game, and his brother was supposed to give me a ride out to the game. Instead he went out on a road someplace, and he took it. And at that age, I was just . . . I was in a daze. I was afraid to tell my mother and father and . . . before my mother knew I was pregnant I was eight months. I was ready to have it before she knew about it.

"I was just very afraid. I would try even to wear a girdle to, you know, keep it hidden. But I've got one big-mouth brother who tells everything. And that eight-month stage, there's just no way you're going to hide it. I just started popping out, getting kinda plump, and my mother said, 'Okay, Barb, sit down,' you know. My brother had already ran his mouth. 'Mom, Barbara's pregnant!' And she says, 'Well, why didn't you tell me?' 'Well, Mom, I was just scared.' She says, 'Let's go to the doctor'—Doctor Margaret—she's dead now. But she says, 'Why, *you?*' I said, 'Yeah, eight months.' 'And you haven't been to see me!' She really laid me out. She was our family doctor and she just laid me out royally. And at that time I didn't know anything about abortions, where to get them, you know, and it was too late then."

Tory begins complaining loudly from her place on the floor, and Barbara takes her up into her lap. The little girl lies back and begins to pat my hand, looking up at me with big curious eyes. Gazing across the room, Barbara remembers.

"My mom said, 'Well, do you want to press charges?' I said 'No, it's not going to do any good now. The damage is done.' And the things you had to go through to press charges, I didn't want to do it. How in the devil would I have proved it anyway!

"I was just in ninth grade then. I was getting ready to start high school. And after I had Ronnie I think I was home for maybe six months and then I moved out. I seen what my mother went through taking care of us. I mean it's just a tremendous strain, you know, one kid after another. One in diapers, one just coming out of diapers, and I just said, this is *my* responsibility— I'm leaving. I'm going to take care of it. She didn't want me to go, but I did. I got out, found myself a little two-bedroom house. I paid ninety dollars a month, and I knew the lady so she paid the utilities, and I had a part-time job at a camp for handicapped children. I been out scuffling on my own ever since."

I realize that at the time of her life Barbara is describing, I was winning spelling contests, practicing for the marching band, trying to adjust to the changes in my body. I was sullen in my flesh, resentful at having to leave the freedom of childhood. If I had given birth to a baby then, how irrevocably would my adulthood have been stamped upon me.

"I went on to high school," Barbara continues. "I had my son to take care of. I had my part-time job and I drawed an ADC check at that time.* It was $183. So I managed between the job and the check. When I graduated from high school, I went to K.U. for about a year and a half, maybe two, but I had had my daughter, my second child, about that time and it was just kinda hard. I wanted to be a physical ed. teacher, but after I found out what all it takes to do it, I just didn't have the time, what with having the kids, so I just dropped out.

---

* AFDC—Aid to Families with Dependent Children (i.e., Welfare).

"If I went back to school, I don't think I'd study nursing. I mean, it takes a lot out of you. I still would love to be a phys. ed. teacher, and I think if I could keep my body in shape I could do it . . . even when I hit my thirties. . . . That's something I'd really love to do." Listening, my mind turns to Bessie Caldwell, who was able to realize the dream that seems now so far beyond Barbara's reach.

Barbara describes her children. Ronnie, at age eleven, is the oldest; then there are eight-year-old Michelle and four-year-old Henry, and finally Tory, who is one-and-a-half years old. When Barbara met her husband, she was pregnant with Michelle.

"We've lived together for five years," she says, "and we got married after the first year. We went through adoption procedures for my first two, and he even had to adopt his own 'cause at the time when I had him we weren't married. That was pretty shocking to both of us, that he would have to adopt his own son.

"My husband makes about $600 every two weeks. I make about $250 every two weeks. So our income is halfway decent. We live together but I guess when we get where we can't tolerate each other any more, he just goes his way and I go my way. It's fairly loose, but he can be very jealous at times. He wants to go where he wants to, but the minute I can find a time to go someplace, he doesn't want me to. 'Well, you've got the kids to take care of.' I say, 'Hey, they're yours too! You take care of them.' And sometimes I'll just get mad and say, 'You can take care of them for this evening, I'm going.' It's not very often I do that but there are times when I just can't take it anymore, the stress and strain I have at work, the kids, they always need this, they always need that, something's wrong here or, you know, the build-up is tremendous. And sometimes I feel like I don't have any time for me, just me alone. I haven't had an evening to myself in so long I've forgot what it is, I honestly have.

"My husband and I had a very rough time when I was carrying Tory. He was running around on me. Then he moved out. I wouldn't see him for weeks on end, and I had the total responsibility of the kids, the bills. When he would get paid, if I wasn't there, he'd lay the money on the table and then leave. I had to make ends do, because I had to quit work when I was four months pregnant because I was so big! I just got tremendous with her, I couldn't even bend over and help make up a bed.

"I had some maternity leave from work, but it wasn't enough to take care of everything. So I was out of work from the time I was in my fourth month. I went back to work when she was about two-and-a-half months. The doctor said, 'Barb, that's too early,' and I said, 'Well, I've got to do it, regardless.' And about eight months after that I had to have my appendix and gall bladder taken out. The doctor said I was just pushing too hard, too soon. But I had to do it to make it."

She has never been very close to her parents and brothers and sisters, Barbara tells me, and I wonder if that may be because of those early years living with her aunt in another city. She visits her mother occasionally, but she rarely sees her eight siblings who live in Lawrence. Their lives are very different from hers. They like to party, and talk about partying, while she has never had a chance to lead a carefree existence. Her childhood ended abruptly with Ronnie's birth, her adolescence was spent working, studying, raising a child. Now she is twenty-six years old. Her more playful brothers and sisters, she says, do not understand her interest in her work.

She likes to talk about her job, acknowledging the very large place it occupies in her life. She has worked at Wakaroosa Manor for three years now, and is assistant to the director of nursing. "Wakaroosa is supposedly a nursing home for the elderly," she explains to me, "but the majority of our residents are either schizophrenics or mentally retarded, so I really, myself, don't classify it as a nursing home.

"I had been working there for a while before I was Betty's assistant. At the time she says, 'Well Barbara, would you be interested in being my assistant?' And I said 'Yeah.' She says, 'Well I see that you're not afraid to go out and tell the girls "This has to be done, do it"—and not pile all the work onto them and do your fair share at the same time.' That's what she needed on the night shift because she's there during the day. And so I've been her assistant for about a year.

"On a good night, we have six of us on. A bad night, I've seen us with just three and trying to take care of eighty people. It's very very tough, and especially if you're way down the hall changing somebody. Some of the ladies that we have are paralyzed waist down and it takes three of us to move them around, to do things right—the phone rings, we have to run up the hall to get the phone. Then we have the wanderers that go off ... outside....
We're trying to keep an eye out the window while we take care of somebody, to make sure a person doesn't go off.

"I mean, it's just.... We have a lady out there that is 104, and she's nothing but bone and skin. She's still fighting to live on, but if you look at her, you're just literally in tears. You have to have a real strong mind to work in that type of situation.

"I found it very hard at first. The very first person that died on the shift that I was working on was a black lady that used to live across the street from me. And every morning at six o'clock she was up jogging, and she was seventy-eight. Yeah. I couldn't believe when she came in, the shape she was in. She had had a stroke. She was there for about a week, and I had went in to feed her breakfast, and I said, 'Mrs. Black, I'll be back in about ten minutes, to wash you up.' She nodded her head, she understood. About fifteen minutes later when I went back in, her face was pale, her eyes were wide open, and I just knew then that, oh my God, she was dead. I had to check her pulse, take her blood pressure, and then I could get no vital signs. I knew she was dead.

"I was in tears for about half an hour, I honestly was. I had never been around a person that had just died. Then I had to help clean the body up and I was in tears all the time I was doing it, 'cause I knew the woman. I was just crying so hard—the girls was saying, Barbara, just go out, we'll do it, we'll do it, you know. That was my first experience. With death. And she went quickly. The thing that hurts is when you see them go for days and you know they're dying."

Barbara shakes her head, rocks Tory gently in her lap.

"There's something you never get used to in death," she says. "I've been around it so many times, but you never get used to it.

I always say it takes a little bit out of you because when you're out there and you know these people, after being there for so long, and you just see them die, and your hands are tied, you're helpless, then you get mad. All this help I've done and this person still dies! It's really ... it really hurts, is all I can say."

In the silence that follows, we both look down at Tory, asleep now in Barbara's lap, her limp hand still resting in my palm. I understand how consistently, both at her job and at home, Barbara is taking care of other people. I too have worked in hospitals, in situations where people were vulnerable and needy, and very ill. I have lived with children, taking responsibility for their mainte-nance and safety and peace of mind. These experiences help me to understand the richness of Barbara's existence as well as the all-consuming demands on her body and spirit.

"That job really puts you on our P's and Q's, it honestly does," she says.

We relax for a few moments, hearing the rain steady outside the window. I am aware that this talk with Barbara is using up her precious morning when she must have a hundred things to do. But she is strongly here with me, glad to tell me about herself.

In the city of Lawrence, she says, changing the subject, black people face prejudice in several important areas. It is as if, while allowing the ways in which I can know her life, she moves to fill in this aspect of her experience which is necessarily different from mine. She describes the race riot that happened in 1970. She was a sophomore in high school then, and she became one of the "ringleaders."

"It started in the high school," she explains, "because the black girls would go out for cheerleader or queen but they never would get it. This was true even years before I grew up to the high school. And my generation just was not going to put up with it. Yeah. We went in, we talked, we talked, we talked. We said, 'This has got to change! Fifty percent of the football team is black, they're making your team what it is. Fifty percent of the basket-ball team is black, they're making it what it is. And yet when the black girl goes up for queen, bam, she doesn't get it. And some of the girls are just as pretty as the white ones are.' 'Well, we can't change the system of doing this,' they said. 'It's fair the way it's been done.' The hell! It wasn't being done fairly! So we got together at the school. We said, 'Hey, are we going to keep putting up with this shit?' The boys on the basketball team and football team, we asked them kindly, said, 'Hey, drop out, just don't go to practice.' They didn't. The school got in a rage. You know, 'If you don't do this, we're going to kick you out!' 'Kick em out 'cause they're not going to go to practice anyway.' Then the school said, 'We want to talk again.' We go in, we say, 'Okay then, what are you going to do?' They say, 'What *can* we do?' We said, 'We've been giving a list of what you can do for the last six weeks and you have done practically nothing.'

"So they said, 'Well, we'll see what we can do about the system of the cheerleading.' So it was time to pick the cheerleaders, and no black girl got on it, and we said, okay, the hell with it. So we had a meeting and we said, 'Okay, at lunchtime tomorrow every black meet in the lunchroom.' All the teachers, the principal are usually there at that time. We all came in at the same time—there was about four hundred of us—and we said, 'Since you can't meet our needs, we're walking out and we will stay out!' "

Barbara's eyes shine with the intensity of her feeling, and she holds Tory more tightly.

"We had a jukebox in the cafeteria. There was a record by, I can't remember who it was by, but it was called 'I'm Black and I'm Proud.' I had played it and one of the white boys went over and rejected it. And I just kindly punched him in his mouth! That was the start, I guess, of everybody's anger getting out. There was just literally fighting and throwing all over the cafeteria! By this time there was police coming from all ends. Then, you know, they put a curfew on Lawrence. Then the campus got into it, and then they had the national guard out and there was a couple kids from the campus got killed during this time—yeah—black and white, by snipers, people shooting."

She looks intently at me, letting me see how harrowing those times were for her. Gradually her expression changes, her upper lip curling in disgust.

"So now they have Mexican-American, black, white and Indian queens. I mean here you are, still separating all these groups. And even with the cheerleader squad. I mean it's just a different slap in the face. Yeah, just another kind of segregation."

Barbara shakes her head. She is discouraged about the events surrounding the riot, and says that recent difficulties at the high school make her think that those violent days have been too easily forgotten. In the town itself, she tells me, she has experienced obvious prejudice.

"I have literally been turned down from houses here in town because I'm black, and I've proven it because I've had some black girlfriends go up. 'Oh, you're not going to rent it?' 'No, it needs some work done to it.' And I have some of my white girlfriends go up and—'Well, you can have it such and such a date. Come in for your deposit.' So I have very strong feelings about this town. I know you find prejudice everywhere in the Midwest, but Lawrence is just. . . . Where my husband works—at a chemical plant in the nitrate department—up to about six years ago there was one black working out there. But I don't like this thing that they have going, you know, I've got to hire you 'cause I've got to have my quota for my money from the government. Hey, you hire me for *me*. Or I don't want your job. That's just the way I feel. Yeah, it's a way to get in and some people use it to get in. And then you have people like me, resents it. Don't hire me because I'm black and you've got to have me in there to get so much of a grant or to keep you from getting closed up. Don't use me! That's the way I feel about it.

"All this kinda stuff's been going on for years and it's still going on. Why there's so much trouble, racial-wise, at the high school, is because you got three junior high schools, and you can define them. You got Central on this side of town with low-income children, you got South junior high school with middle-class kids, you got West with rich kids going there. Then you put them all in one high school!? I mean you got instant no-com-munication whatsoever.

"The people that run Lawrence, I mean there's basically about six families that has this town sewed up. They say what can come in, what can't come in. Like K-Mart. They don't want K-Mart coming into the Lawrence area. K-Mart is actually about half an inch out of the city limits because they did not want the store coming in here taking away Gibson's little business and all the downtown. . . . You go downtown, you have to have about a hun-dred dollars to go in one of those places. You spend between thirty and forty dollars for one blouse. A poor person can't afford that; even some middle-class people can't afford that. And they didn't want K-Mart coming in here, I guess, because of the sales that K-Mart has.

"The early families that's been here and have businesses here, their sons or their daughter or whatever has taken over. They don't want competition, and they will not have competition. The needs of low-income people are not taken into account, they're canceled out completely.

"We have a human relations service here in town, which is trying. . . . yet you still have these families has got all the pull. You've got all the lawyers working together here in town, and I just don't see any hope around this, around Lawrence, myself."

Barbara's face has become heavier, darker, as she talked. Her large jaw is set, the expanse of her cheek gleams in the dim light from the window. I noticed that her part in the riots was told not as a prideful account of her exploits but as a grim recital of events. Still I could feel her energy and her determination as she told it, and her anger as she spoke of the class as well as the racial aspects of the situation here in town.

I wonder, then, about her personal life, whether she has any time in it for recreation or going out with friends. After a few minutes have passed, I ask her about this.

"I really don't," she admits, "and I want to change it. I'm feeling this change that I'm going through, you know, I do want to go out and have fun at different things, 'cause I never had a chance to do it. I've always had my son to take care of, and then my family to take care of. I've never been able to be, I guess, foot free and just run a little bit.

"I made up my mind I didn't want any more children. After I had Tory, I had a tubal ligation. I just figured that was the safe thing. Yeah, I had made up my mind.

"One problem is with my youngest son's arthritis. Like when it's raining, now, and it gets a little cold, he has pain in his knees and he can barely walk sometimes. He takes two aspirins every four hours, it's a constant thing, and if I miss a day or take him to a babysitter or miss a couple of days just working, it tells on him when he runs. . . . 'Mom, my knees are hurting!' He's in a lot of pain."

Barbara mentions again that period in which, in order to support her children, she had to live on welfare payments. Her feeling about this, I find, is different from the attitudes of young mothers in the large coastal urban centers.

"I would not go on welfare again to save my soul. No. I'd work washing dishes twenty-four hours a day if I had to, to take care of my kids. I would never get back on welfare because of the things they make you go through. It makes you feel less than a person. I mean, they give you forms this thick, and they're making unexpected calls at your house to see if you've got someone living there. If you've got any halfway decent furniture, they want to know how you got it, making it on a welfare check. I mean, just the tremendous things they take out of you. I would not go through that again for nothing."

Women elsewhere often see welfare as providing a legitimate way to survive while looking for a job or going to school, and simply tolerate the indignities inherent in the process. Barbara's pride and independence are much like the determined self-reliance of the more rural midwestern women I have talked to. I remember Ruth Chaplin's speaking of having been forced to apply for welfare to support her children, a situation that "nearly killed me," she said.

"If I was to go back to school," Barbara continues, "I'd get

some grants. I can get minority grants and different things like
that. But I wouldn't be able to quit work, and between getting the
kids ready at eight in the morning and taking them to school, and
getting Tory off to a babysitter, and then having to get done with
classes before three o'clock—well, it can be done, but it would
take a lot out of me to do it.*

She looks wistful. "There's just not enough time. I'd love to do
sports. A lot of nights, if I'm not too tired, I like to jog, I like to
just run. I get some of my anger out that way. And I like to play
basketball, and get out and play football with my son."

Barbara grins. "Me and Ronnie, it's just like we grew up together. I mean, last night I was sitting there watching TV. I was
drinking my pop and he came up, pulled my legs way up in the
air, and said, 'Mom, this is good exercise. Come on, do my exercise.' He was doing his football exercise and he expected me to get
down on the floor and do it with him. And then he just hit my
thigh and we start wrassling around and then all the kids came
bouncing in and we just start wrassling on the floor. It's just like
he and I grew up together. We have the same interests. We're
both crazy about football. We were sitting arguing one day about
the call that the referee made. I mean, nothing like a mother and
a son situation. It was just like we were brother and sister, sitting
there arguing about something."

Her laughter is warm, now, her affection for her son relaxing
her, making her seem younger, for the first time lighthearted.

"Yeah. And our interest in music is about the same. He works
in a cafeteria. He gets about twenty dollars every two weeks, and
he'll say 'Okay, Mom, did you hear the record by the Jackson
Five? Do you like it?' and I'll say, 'Yeah, I like it.' And he'll go
down and buy it. 'Well, look what I bought for us.' It's always
'us.'

"He wanted a stereo for Christmas last year, and I busted my

---

* In a recent phonecall, Barbara told me that she had re-enrolled at the university. Now
that her older children are in school and Tory is in daycare, she is beginning studies for a
degree in physical education.

butt working to get it for him. It was one in particular that he seen which cost about $180, and I said, Here's an eleven-year-old, and here I am busting my butt trying to get him that stereo! But he wanted it so bad and I guess just the relationship that he and I have . . . I went out and bought it for him and said, 'Now you're going to have to take care of it.' You know, right now, his works and mine don't!"

We chuckle together at this irony. Then Barbara turns to look out the window at the rain, a grey curtain blurring the trees.

"Guess I ought to go," she murmurs, and I feel her reluctance. Tory lies asleep in her arms, one limp hand flung out in my direction. We sit for a while longer, and I feel how much our meeting has been a break in Barbara's routine, a time to be listened to, to talk with someone outside her life. She has communicated a great deal in our few hours together. I believe that sometime in the future she will be able to transform her circumstances into a situation in which she can do more of what she wants to do. She seems a very large person, one who will retain her dignity, develop her capacity and wisdom in whatever circumstances may befall her.

Tory frowns and stirs but does not wake as Barbara gets up. "You take care on the highway now," Barbara urges. In her life that is so consumed with caring for others, she has the generosity to be concerned about my welfare. As she prepares to step out into the weather, I wonder whether there is anyplace in Barbara's life where *she* is nurtured, if there is anyone who takes care of *her*. I hold open the door for the two of them, watching her make her way out to her car, turn to lift her head in a gesture of farewell, her arms too full of Tory to wave.

Making Magic

In Omaha, Nebraska, better known for its stockyards than its culture, two women operate a most unusual theater. Megan Terry, an experimental playwright who is much produced and much celebrated on both coasts, writes plays for the theater troupe; Jo

Ann Schmidman—who, at age thirty-one, has worked with the famed Open Theater in New York and toured with them all over the world—produces, directs, and acts in the plays.

Jo Ann was born and raised in Omaha, and she devotes all of her talent and energy to the Omaha Magic Theater. The group's first playhouse was in the "old market," a fruit and vegetable warehouse area of Omaha. The theater troupe was given a whole building rent-free while they cleaned it out and built a theater in it; later they rented the building for a nominal sum. Eventually, the area was upgraded and a collection of little shops, restaurants, and a dinner theater were opened, causing the rents to rise so astronomically that the Magic Theater had to move uptown to its present location. Jo Ann chuckles. "It's just a riot to think that the nicest restaurant in town is in our former basement!"

It was Jo Ann Schmidman who founded the theater eleven years ago. She was studying at Boston University and was becoming more and more disgruntled. "In those days, you had to be blond, blue-eyed, and very pretty to make it in the theater," she says. Jo Ann is a dark-eyed, dark-haired, slender woman whose extraordinary intensity seems to hover around her like a flame. "The director would choose two or three good-looking people and give them all the best parts. The rest of the people were slaves. We carried swords and sewed and were constantly busy, but there was nothing really to take up your mind. I think I played every Irish maid possible." She makes a comically sour face, only one in her repertoire of expressions. This elastic face, in conjunction with her wonderfully supple body and commanding voice, makes her the center of attention in any scene she plays.

The extremely competitive situation Jo Ann found in Boston was typical of the great coastal urban centers, where much talent goes to waste. She tells me that, to keep herself interested while at Boston University, she began making long distance calls back to her midwestern hometown, proposing the start of a theater group. Two women raised some funds for her, she gathered actors in Boston and found a director (she was not directing at that time), and brought them all to Omaha in the summer to produce plays. That first summer the troupe presented eight plays, most of them

avant-garde pieces from Europe, a few American plays and one
original theater piece. The audience response to the American
playwrights was so much more enthusiastic than to the Europeans,
that the troupe decided to produce only new works by American
authors.

Soon after the establishment of the Magic Theater, Megan
Terry saw the company's production of one of her plays, liked it,
and came to work with the theater, at first spending half time in
Omaha and half time in New York, then eventually moving to
Omaha to become involved year-round. Megan was already well
known, her play *Viet Rock* having been in the vanguard of opposi-
tion to the Vietnam war, her brilliantly innovative dramatizations
having earned a reputation for her in the world of experimental
theater. She brought to Omaha a definite view of the function of
theater. This she expressed in a speech given at the Southeast
Theater Conference in 1977. "Many of us are convinced that spiritual truth touches and heals and we can find spiritual truth in
theater experiences.... All around us we are bombarded with
human beliefs that argue for loss, lack, separation, loneliness, violence, incompleteness.... Theater has the property to turn these
negatives into positives through catharsis and transcendence to
give confidence, to hearten, to restore, and recreate a sense of
community, by calling the community together to be present as
active witness to a creative act."

For one show, entitled *100,001 Horror Stories of the Plains,* Jo
Ann and Megan solicited stories from old timers in senior citizen
and community centers, from children in schools, and from anyone who cared to participate in story-telling sessions at the Omaha
Magic Theater. From this raw material they put together a
"crazy-quilt of first-hand accounts, family histories, genuine midwestern tall tales, poems, and horror stories from the people of
Iowa, Kansas, Nebraska, and South Dakota," chiefly about the
pioneer experience. The show was staged as a potluck supper, and
audience members brought dishes to share.

"They would bring in marvelous food," Jo Ann says. "If they
didn't bring food they'd have to pay for their ticket, but they got
to eat with the rest. There'd be homemade wines, incredible

dishes that we couldn't eat because we would've been too stuffed
to play. We always prepared a big pot of soup, carrots and celery
sticks, and popcorn, in case there wasn't enough food. Munchies.
And we would start the show from around the tables with the
audience. It started off with a song about all the people who came
from Nebraska: Dorothy Maguire and Johnny Carson, Dick Ca-
vett, Fred and Adelle Astaire, Henry Fonda, Marlon Brando,
Sandy Dennis, you know, and then we went on from there."

In the Magic Theater, where audience size is about one hundred maximum, Jo Ann Schmidman produces eight shows a year.
Each new piece plays at the theater on weekends for a month or
so, and then is taken on a tour of high schools and universities
throughout the Midwest. Of their more topical plays, she says,
"When an issue needs support and focus, and it's time to get
people to do something about it, then we focus on it." She speaks
of how, in 1974 and 1975, they did only feminist pieces, and frequently made the theater's space available for concerts of women's
music and the showing of women's films.

"Have you ever done a play with all women in the cast?" I
want to know.

"Yep. Well, wait a minute, no. Within those two years, we did
an extraordinary play by Rochelle Holt, called *Walking into the
Dawn: A Celebration.* It was about when the goddesses were here
again and talking to each other. It was a celebration for women. It
was lyric verse, and beautiful. We had men in the company
though. They dressed as women, tried to get into that sensibility.
We also did a marvelous play of Megan's called *Babes in the Big-
house,* a play about women's prisons, life inside a women's prison.
In that also there were men in the company. We did another play,
by Judith Katz, called *Temporary Insanity.* It was a game show
about achieving intimacy with your opponent, and all the contest-
ants were women, which was very interesting. Especially since I
was raised with the idea that you certainly don't trust a woman,
that she's the first to do you wrong, steal your man away, all that
stuff. So ... this play was about friendship and just woman-con-
nection."

41

On a downtown Omaha street, amid giant old brick buildings, vacant lots filled with the rubble of redevelopment, dimestores, and seedy eating establishments, in an area where businessmen from the newer buildings rub shoulders with bums and aged eccentrics, where working people wait for buses and crowd into the big dark restaurants at noon—here behind a storefront facade is the Omaha Magic Theater.

On its windows hang copies of recent reviews of its productions. I stop to read one about *Running Gag,* a musical play about jogging, written and directed by Jo Ann Schmidman. The cast of seven ran in place for sixty-five minutes, says the review, and in the process entertained the audience with insights into running as well as many other aspects of contemporary society. The play was such a success that it is to be performed at the Winter Olympics.

Entering the small lobby, I hear a rhythmic grunting coming from the performance area just beyond the scaffolding that holds the seats. There, in a circle, six people labor through strenuous exercises. Jo Ann, dressed in T-shirt and slacks, her long dark hair streaming down her back, is leading them. Her energy dominates the space, her body twisting into extravagant postures while she barks at the other people to follow her lead. Noticing my presence, she bounces up from her latest contortion to greet me. "You can join us if you like," she offers.

The actors, who range in age, seemingly, from the twenties up into the forties, regard me expectantly. Around them, in a set painted in brilliant basic colors, a giant Raggedy Ann doll hangs from a platform, a mock cabinet displays soft-sculpture boxes and bottles.

I go out into the playing area to join the actors in their exertions, just as Jo Ann calls, "All right, let's go!"

When the warm-up exercises are over, rehearsal begins, and I am relegated to the audience side of the lights, where I sit catching my breath.

The actors pair off to do the title song of the show, *Goona-Goona,* a musical comedy written by Megan Terry. They swing at each other, in tightly choreographed movements, pantomiming the physical abuse that is the play's subject matter. This is a rough play, about the cruelties and violence enacted by members of a family upon each other.

When Jo Ann joins me, I ask her why the company is producing a play about such a subject. She explains her philosophy that part of the job of the theater is to let people know what's happening. "It's a more viable form than the news media, or the newspapers or the pulpit," she says. "This play is about abuse. It's to say that we all have these feelings. I mean it's normal that two people be in the same family and my rhythm be real slow and laid back and yours be quick, like that . . . and we're married to each other and I'm gonna want to haul off and sock you because you get on my nerves! And it's especially normal if you have adults going about their own world and all the trips they have to deal with, and kids in *their* own world. And one has nothing to do with the other, so why *wouldn't* they want to kill each other! So people that are beating their kids, they can say, oh, okay, that's what's happening. And neighbors who are living next door can take a look at what the neighbors in the play did and they can call the visiting nurses, call the police, *do* something about it. You know, you get them in here for a nice evening, a musical comedy, which is what it is, and then you say, this is what's really happening."

While this play is about abuse within the family, both Megan and Jo Ann are careful to avoid propaganda. Their intention is not to arouse easy judgments, but to create a portrait of the situation that will lead the spectator to see into it as deeply as possible. This is a difficult task, especially with contemporary events about which there can be no benefit of hindsight. Plays of this type require risk-taking, but the Magic Theater has never shied away from risk. Megan Terry, as Jo Ann points out, "is always ahead of events. She reads everything and knows what's going to happen before it happens."

Out in the playing area again, Jo Ann transforms herself into Dr. Goon, the play's principal villain, who delivers a soliloquy on his career as a physician. Jo Ann grows very large under the lights, her eyes insanely gleaming and her words ringing out with a mad poignancy that is funny and excruciating at the same time. The language of this rant whips through cliches and poetry and spurts of mordant self-perception to show us the dashed hopes, the cynicism, the anguish of a man stripped bare.

This monologue is Megan Terry's work. From the platform above the audience seats her voice issues at intervals, making suggestions, giving orders. "You've got the dark values," she'll say, "now try for the light." Or, "More authority!" Now and then she comes down from her perch to pace through the action, a short woman whose thick curly brown hair bushes out around a classically pretty face. She moves and speaks with authority. This is the product, no doubt, of a lifetime spent in the theater, and also of the sense of her own accomplishment—for she is the author of over forty-five published plays, and many unpublished, a playwright who may in a single month open a play in New York City, another in San Francisco, another at Omaha's Magic Theater. I find myself a trifle intimidated by Megan, not only because of her remoteness and her air of command, but the awareness of how fully she has developed her creative gift.

Now she brandishes the newspaper she has been reading, giving me a significant look and announcing, "If the Democrats don't pull up their socks and get busy, we're liable to have a rightwing takeover in this country next year!"

And with that she disappears up the stairs to her shadowy platform. At that moment, Jo Ann Schmidman leaves the play's action to come sit with me.

I ask her about the early days of the Magic Theater, over ten years ago, and she tells me that at first the members of the troupe lived collectively, twelve people in two houses. "So you got into the whole lifestyle thing too, besides the theater work—who would fix the meals, who would clean up, laundry day. I mean it was unbelievable. Meetings! But that was okay. It was the late sixties, when people were doing that. One thing though, we were never quite crazy enough to think that everybody could do everything, like collectives now. They have no director, everybody tries to direct. It always, well, at least in my experience, things always end up to be kind of a mess. Or take a very very *very* long time to make happen.

"We had two weeks to put together a show in those days, so we had to have a director. But people are always interested in running things, so they wanted to take turns at producing. It boggles my mind to think that we did this. One member of the company would be the producer for a month and then we'd shift and then ... and it did *not* work. At all. You know, I think theatre has to be a benevolent dictatorship. The way we work now, there are specialists in each department. I'm not going to tell Lynn how to compose her music. If it doesn't work with the show, I'll say something and Megan will say something and she'll rework it, but I'm not gonna say, 'That note doesn't go with that note.' That's her field. I'm not going to tell Colbert, 'Focus the lights this way.' I'll say, 'I want to see this, can you do that for me?' And it happens. People all have their specialties."

I ascend briefly now to the shadowy platform. Megan Terry has read through the daily papers and is applying mascara to her long eyelashes. "I love makeup," she admits, peering intently into her mirror. "When I was first in the theatre, I used to go early just to play with the makeup."

Down in the playing area, actors and actresses run through a song. Everything is done with great verve and concentration, the woman at the piano pounding the keys, looking over her shoulder to catch the action. This is a fast-paced style of theater, bodies in motion at all times, capturing the eye. Drawing on the work of Michael Chekhov and Viola Spolin among others, Jo Ann leads people to rehearse very physically. "I work with throwing the body into a shape and then justifying it," she says, "discovering what it feels like from the inside and also what it looks like, how you perceive yourself from the outside. An actor has to be aware of the body as well as the emotions and the thoughts. As an actor, I have to have a real specific thing in my head to work with, I have to make a real specific choice. But you as audience can read anything you want into it. It's not that I have to second-guess the audience. That's why theater's so fascinating. It's you see one thing, the person next to you sees something else, and that's all right!"

One by one, as the players leave the action, they go to work at the long table between the stage area and the seats, where great stacks of leaflets wait to be stamped for mailing. Here I take the opportunity to talk with them, discovering who they are. For the most part, they have scant theater experience, some of them acting for the first time here at the Magic Theater. Jo Ann Schmidman who, in Megan's words, is "one of the greatest warm-up coaches in the theater today," prefers working with actors who have had little or no training. "Universities and theater schools tend to really fuck people up a lot," Jo Ann told me. "I don't know why or how, but they do." She explained how she trains people to act. "When I set up a workshop, I kind of give a structure to people. Say, with one scene from this show, I ask them to come in with as many different ways of protecting themselves from blows, or from life in some way, for those isolations they're working with in that first song. So it's up to them. If Craig lives in a black community and deals with those kinds of prejudicial blows, his movements are going to look different than Lynn, who's swatting at cockroaches in her apartment, let's say. Or Eve, who's avoiding men on the street. Everybody brings their own. It's a lot healthier."

The work begins again. Dr. Goon rants, the children frolic on the teeter-totter, Mrs. Goon wanders about in a daze, passively enduring the brutality of her husband. For the fifteenth time, the actors run through the precisely choreographed movements of the title number.

The house Jo Ann and Megan share is large, its interior casually furnished and cluttered with fascinating junk, a place where traveling theater people are welcome, where the atmosphere is rich with humor and possibility. This evening I am met at its door by several dogs, one of whom hops about on three legs. The rooms are filled with a jungle of plants. Cats steal about on ledges up near the ceiling. The coatrack bulges with hats (and I remember Megan crossing the rainy street at noon, in a satiny blue Chinese jacket and large floppy hat). While a friend named Tim starts cooking the steaks for dinner, Megan decides to change the sheets on the king-size bed in the living room. Jo Ann and I cut up oranges and bananas for fruit salad.

Soon we are seated on creaking wicker furniture in the middle room, holding our dinners on our knees while the dogs beg for scraps. Somewhere in the house chimes tinkle faintly.

We eat, Tim and Jo Ann saying little, while Megan and I talk about New York City. Even in this casual conversation, I am not at ease with Megan, whose manner is scrupulously neutral. Suddenly, I realize why I am so flummoxed by her! It is because I too maintain this impassivity, this air of lofty indifference, when I am talking with people I have just met and am not sure I like. When I do it, I am watching the person, assessing, investigating. It is this I feel from Megan now. I am kept off balance by her, and my awareness that I do this to others helps not at all.

Jo Ann rescues me, taking me up to a second floor room where we can talk in privacy. Here we flop down on either side of a big, heavy table. She looks tired now, her face a little sallow, her great dark eyes shiny with fatigue, but it is clear that the energy coursing in her could keep her going for many more hours if necessary. "I'm an Aries," she has told me, "an intensity junkie." She is a singularly dedicated person; ever since childhood she has put all her thought and effort into only one endeavor at a time. At first she was religious, attended Hebrew school, had a bas mitzvah ceremony, learned to read Hebrew well, and was very scholarly. She would have made religious study her life if another and ultimately more compelling passion had not presented itself.

"When I was twelve years old," she relates, "I saw this colt in a field and asked who owned it. They told me who and I asked the man if I took care of the horse and raised the horse, could I have it? It's one of those great incredible dreams that came true. So I raised this horse. I was there constantly. I didn't talk to people, I didn't see people, I just dealt with that horse. For all those years, junior high and high school. I took all my books down to the barn, shoveled shit, just spent my life down there! And that actually led to my disillusionment. I was, as I said, very into religion. They were going to give me this scholarship to go to a Hebrew camp. And I said to the rabbi, 'I can't possibly take it because my horse is at a very formative age and I *must* feed him and take care of him and nurture him this year.' The rabbi blew up, went crazy, you know, 'How *dare you* think about staying and taking care of this horse and foregoing this religious education! You're a fool!' And that did it for religion. From then on, it was just the horse."

Jo Ann brought to her interest in theater all the fervor of these previous involvements. Theater, she believes, requires "incredible discipline—the same kind of focused attention as a professional athlete, a religious master, or a nuclear scientist at the height of investigation."

Why, I ask her, after all her experience in New York, does she choose to run a one-hundred-seat theater here in her home town?

Jo Ann leans toward me over the table and rambles around the question, her eyes intent. "I'm interested in being very good at what I do. I want to be terrific! I want to learn as much as I can possibly learn about acting, about directing, about writing, and about making theater exciting again for an audience. I stay away from the theater a lot usually. I mean, I keep going hoping something will turn me on but I'm not real turned on by most of what I see. You must have experienced shows where there are little instances that make it worth it, but the whole thing doesn't flow and isn't exciting and doesn't fly by. You know, there's so many things about the theater, it's so much like religion, it's so much like a family, and the interrelating of people is fascinating. In the growth of our theater, we've gone through all this psychoanalytical stuff that I think is part of the growing pains of a small theatre company. Now it really is focused on the art and the work and the quality of it, the flow of it, and theatre time and spectacle."

"But why is it easier to do this sort of thing here in Omaha than in New York or on the West Coast?" I persist.

"Well, the people in the midwest are open. In our location here, because we're right on the bus route, we get a lot of blue collar workers. We are shunned by theater goers in this town, which hurts me a little. I mean I'm sorry that they don't come, but they don't. They go to the Playhouse and they go to the dinner theatres, but they don't come to our theatre. But the blue collar workers do. The ones going to the factories who have never been to a live performance before, they walk in and for the first time, you know, some sit there in awe! But they come back again and the next time they can relate. They weren't bored and things were happening and thoughts were, you know, people were really relating to them. That's the other thing about the kind of theatre that we do. We can relate to our audience. You're two feet away. I could look in your eyes when you were sitting out there this afternoon. And I could see when you were getting off on it, when you weren't getting off on it, you know, and deal with that. Or people come in off the street and see a show for the first time and they're totally beside themselves. They can't believe that it's something so topical and so new, something that happened yesterday at dinner and now it's onstage. Especially high school kids. Audiences here are not as sophisticated as on the coasts, I think. They don't have preconceptions that theatre has got to be a particular thing and if it's not this, I don't want to see it. They're real open and if they don't like something, they come afterwards and they say 'I hated that part!' "

Jo Ann maintains close ties with her family, she has told me. I ask how her family feels about her chosen profession.

"They wanted me to get married and settle down and then I could do this as a hobby," she says, "or teach. My grandfather is still heavy into the teaching idea. He ran a grocery store, and my dad has a clothing store. It's the insecurity of the theater that bothers them. And they see me working very very hard. My grandfather couldn't believe *Running Gag* when he saw it. 'Just why?' he asked, 'Why?' 'Cause we run in place, or nearly in place, for sixty-five minutes in that show. The sweat just pours off. I'm just soaked."

Has her age been a problem? I ask, realizing that she must have been only twenty-one or so when she began the Magic Theater.

"Oh yes," she says, "it meant people's not having to take me terribly seriously. It was especially true working with men in the company, and certainly men older than I was. That has changed. But as far as the community goes, because it's new theater, because it isn't established, I still run up against the same thing, which makes it real painful for me. They still treat me like a hippie, or something. Which is ridiculous!"

Of the men in the company, especially those who have played women's parts, she says, "We've been very lucky. The men that work with us, that stay and work with us, are very sensitive. In the play *Walking into the Dawn,* the men decided they wanted to play women's parts. A lot of men freaked out, refused to put on dresses. If they aren't sure of their balls, they're not about to set foot in a dress. The most macho of the men usually would do it and would try to feel what it was like to be their wives or their girlfriends or whatever, but if there was any question about not wanting anybody to think of them as a little fey, whew! they left the company in a big hurry."

Jo Ann is tiring now, I can tell, her body relaxed in the chair, her eyes not quite so bright. But she tells about the development of a play by an Omaha woman, an instance of the Magic Theater's responsiveness to the community and to current events. This woman, whose name is Mimi Loring, had lost her three daughters to a religious sect in the area. One of the vows of the sect was to cut all ties with family and friends, so she was not able to see her daughters. In addition, her husband had just died, so she was alone. Extremely upset, she went to the FBI to investigate the religious group and discovered many extraordinary things. She wrote a play based on this information, called it *Astral White,* and brought it to the Magic Theater. Jo Ann and Megan at first were not interested.

"It was not as in-depth when she sent it to us as it could have been," Jo Ann explains. "She was a writer-type writer, not a playwright. This was her first play. But then suddenly all this stuff with Reverend Moon and all this crap just burst onto the airways. She'd been coming around for a year with this play and we said, 'Oh, it's time! Let's do it. We'll develop it with you.' And we worked like hell. She learned a lot. I *hope* she learned a lot. We learned a lot too, just tearing it apart and redoing it, trying to get her to ... you know, to get to the real truth."

"Why did she choose the play form?"

"I think she goes to a lot of theater and I think it was the form that made most sense because of all these characters and events— the head of the organization and fucking at Equinox and all that stuff, weird rituals. I think it had to come out as a play. Also it would remove it so it wouldn't be so personal when her daughters did come back—which two of them did. . . . After a certain amount of time the order let them reconnect with their family and two of them dropped out. . . . I think she didn't want a factual thing. This is somewhat removed and in fact all the members of the order came to see the show, and got off on it! Our seamstress, the woman who sews all our stuff, is an ex-member of the order. She actually joined the company."

Once again this play is an instance of the Magic Theater's not being dogmatically critical of its subject matter. *Astral White* was, Jo Ann says, an "expose," in that it showed the inner workings of a religious cult, but it did not put down the participants in any obvious way.

Jo Ann is still speaking energetically, but I realize now I too am tired, my day having started with those strenuous exercises at an early hour. We get up to leave the second floor room with its large table and family photographs, and go out onto the landing.

From below comes the garbled noise of a television set. We make our way down the stairs, past that extravagantly decked hat stand. I glance into the living room. A large color television set is alive at the entrance to the darkened middle room, throwing ghosts across the giant bed in which Megan Terry is fast asleep. She lies on her back, thick hair spread out on the pillow around

her face, mouth agape, the covers pulled to her chest. She looks
like a deposed Irish queen adrift in her regal bed.

Jo Ann and I tiptoe past the doorway, brushing ferns, stepping
over sleeping dogs to reach the front door. When I come out into
the cold wet midnight, I stand on the sidewalk looking back at
this large, blocky, deceptively ordinary house on a street of similar
houses. It is dark, all occupants tucked in, now, at the witching
hour.

Next morning at the Magic Theater, the cast gathers. They
have labored through their exercises and gone to their places for
another run-through. Dyan coaxes wild harmonies from the
piano, then slumps on the teeter-totter as the dazed and mistreat-
ed wife. Lynn and Craig, wearing their floppy baby bonnets, hear
their father Dr. Goon rave, and later they watch as he is carried
from the stage by a policeman. The other actors and actresses
paint, hammer, seal envelopes, stamp return addresses, do all the
work that will bring *Goona-Goona* to completion in time for opening night.

This morning Megan seems benevolent, stopping to give me
instructions on photographing in this theatrical lighting. I feel less
of the tension I experienced before in her presence, for the picture
is still there in my mind of her asleep in the massive bed, buoyed
up like a dumpling in a stew—even as she talks to me of camera
settings.

As the rehearsal swings into high gear, I settle back to watch.
Jo Ann Schmidman, her slender body lithe, her hair in a dark
horsetail down her back, her face radiant with determination as
she attends to a hundred details, gives herself totally to each facet
of the production. I am glad she has chosen to do her own work
here in her hometown in the Midwest. She has said of the Magic
Theater, "We have a commitment to this community's people and
to their roots—to the land. We love the people here." The community responds in kind, Omahans coming to the Magic Theater
to watch some extraordinarily imaginative productions, to take

part in the discussion often held after performances, and to carry home with them some critical questions provocatively raised.

When I arrived in the Midwest this time, I thought I would feel alienated. Instead, I have begun to understand how everything, including parts of myself, is interconnected and has its function. Soil, weather, animal life: there is not much here that is gratuitous. The people themselves move in a meshing of concerns, the town and city dwellers offering their services to the farmers, the farmers serving the land. I have come to perceive the particular place of the artist here. Driving down from Omaha, Nebraska, into Kansas several days ago, lifted by that vast sky studded with clouds, I had almost the sense of flying through open space. I thought back to the farm and small town women with whom I spent so much good time. They do not record their lives. They work, they live fully and long, but their habits and opinions, their particular experience will be kept alive in their families after they die for only a generation or so, and then will fade to nothing more than the images in old photographs.

In my contact with Jo Ann Schmidman, Megan Terry, Denise Low, I recognized the role a woman artist can play in articulating the concerns and aspirations of such women. These artists may have perfected their craft elsewhere, but they returned to practice it in the area of their first growth. Denise Low makes the connections between the natural world, the psychic or spiritual, and the intellectual, attempting a crucial integration, while she lives among the people she loves best, valuing her family's closeness. Jo Ann Schmidman and Megan Terry have achieved an ideal of creative work and development in a sprawling, stock-butchering city on the prairie. Denise and Jo Ann show me the choices I might have made, to return and become a part, once again, of what bore me, and to use my capacities to the fullest here, as they do. Like the pioneer women, they risk and they improvise, making their lives in the setting they have chosen.

Barbara Barfield is different from the others, in that she has had fewer choices, fewer paths open to her. But she is a model of integrity for me as much as is Barbara Grier; and while Grier's life epitomizes a particular political stand unusual to the Midwest, Barfield's existence and awareness illuminate the race and class realities of her heartland environment.

My journey to the farms and small towns of this region led me back into the world of my childhood, the women arousing my consciousness of myself as a child living each day close to the soil and the earth's pulse, responding to the seasons and weather. The four women I sought out in midwestern cities confronted me with aspects of my adult self: the spiritual dimension that I am only now beginning to develop, my love for women, my consciousness of power relationships in this society, my relationship to art. But these seeds were planted long before my adult life began, in the earliest years, so that my encounters with Denise Low and Barbara Grier, Barbara Barfield, Megan Terry, and Jo Ann Schmidman seemed a rounding out, as if I had come full circle back to the land that nurtured me, bringing with me all I have learned in the "larger" world. While the choice to live in the heartland still is not mine, my cognizance that these women live and work where they do is a powerful affirmation of the possibilities of growth in the environment that gave me my beginning. I know now that I *could* go back if I wished, and be who I now am.

*Barbara Grier and
Donna McBride*

Barbara Barfield and Tory

Jo Ann Schmidman

Megan Terry

Toward the Future

In the echoey cavern of the basketball court in the O Ketche Show
O Now center, I sat with Margret Mahkuc—she kindly tolerating
my presence, I hesitant within a maze of unfamiliar social signals
—and I asked her about Native American concern for ecology.

Margret took her time, gazing out at a net that hung immobile
from its hoop. She spoke deliberately.

"That's a recent terminology. It's called ecology and all of a
sudden people are trying to get on the bandwagon. But that's part
of our beliefs. When we were placed on the earth we were right
with nature. That isn't just something recent. That's our life. As
Indian people we believe in taking care of mother earth because
she means something to us. Our religion, that's what we believe
in, our everyday practice; and politics, that's our action; We carry
on from there. You know, you can't separate anything, you can't
separate ecology, you can't separate religion. That's our way of
life."

I agree with Margret that truth is found in wholeness, the
integration of all endeavors and ways of being. And I believe that
if the imbalances that threaten our society and our planet are ever
to be righted, it will be women who will lead that effort, for we
are trained to value and nurture life, and our own procreative
powers remind us of nature's fecundity and wrath.

The latest insurrection of women that has been going on now
for over ten years, is taking place in the Midwest as surely as
everywhere else in this country. There, as women challenge authority structures and struggle to free themselves from restrictive

and dehumanizing roles, I saw the discomfort that such a restructuring of authority can cause. At the University of Nebraska at Lincoln, I spoke with the head of the Womens Studies department, Moira Ferguson. She told me that her students, many of them young women from the farms and the small towns, go from her classes out into a community in which disparaging attitudes to women and ethnic minorities are the rule. The students, who have begun to challenge such ideas both in the classroom and in the rest of their lives, find themselves at odds with their friends and family. "Quite often," Moira said, "students will come to me during the semester and say how difficult it's becoming for them in their social group."

The other side of this dilemma is experienced by the friends and family of these young women, for they are affected by these changes without having participated in the process that brought them about. At the Willa Cather Pioneer Memorial in Red Cloud, Sue Fintel spoke of the impact of women's new assertiveness on her own family. "My daughter-in-law chose a career over being married to our son," she said, and her bitterness and sorrow, her sympathy with her son, were evident in her voice and eyes. Sue herself, she told me, had kept a home and raised three children while working at a job, "and I thought if I did it, so could she." But, as Ruth Chaplin's niece Jolene pointed out in the South Side Cafe two years ago, women make more choices now in their lives than when Sue Fintel was a young woman.

Still, the hard crust of accepted practice is difficult to break through. Especially in the arena of home and family, changes may come very slowly and with great effort. Farm woman Jane Snavely described how her own and her husband's attitudes toward the roles of wife and husband have altered over the years, but she admits that the liberalization of his views has not led to his helping her in the house. On the farms, she said, among couples where the women work outside in the fields, the men probably help less with housework than do men in the towns. In Concordia, a young professional woman told me that her husband, a lawyer, refuses to share household tasks with her. Although they work equally long hours and are equally committed to their professions, he claims that because he makes more money than she, he should have to do no work at home. Couples like organic farmers Yvonne and Bob Hauck, who have arrived at an equitable sharing of work, are in the minority.

The conflict between the interests of men and women carries over into the world of employment, where it makes perfect sense that women want "men's jobs"—for the wages paid for traditional women's jobs are far below most men's wages. Especially in the small towns and farming areas, where there are no factories or large businesses, the situation is difficult. Here there is very little employment for women other than waitressing, clerking in the stores, and working as aides in the nursing homes. Jean Davis, a Ph.D. candidate at Kansas State and herself an older woman with grown children, is developing a program for rural "displaced homemakers"—women who, because of divorce or the death or illness of a spouse, or other factors, must go out into the world for the first time to earn a living for themselves and their families. She points out that the conventional view of these women as "unskilled" is grossly unfair, for they are actually often highly competent in childrearing, sewing, homemaking, gardening, cooking, and other endeavors they may have been pursuing for years. She hopes to find ways for their skills to be used in paid occupations.

Those women who take jobs formerly filled by men encounter the problem of acceptance by their coworkers, and their experiences differ widely. In Concordia, a young woman told me about her stint as a laborer on a bridge-building project. "I was the only woman working there. I knew practically all the men except for the boss and the foreman. They didn't give me much of a hard time." Jane Snavely said of her job at the Hansen Livestock Auction Barn, "One of my family has worked at the sale barn ever since it was built." I haven't had any problems there about being a woman. Most everybody there knows me and three-fourths of the people sells stuff knows me." The acceptance of these two at construction site and auction barn may result from their relationship to the small rural community in which they live. They were known by the men, were familiar as people and members of the community long before they took the jobs. Yvonne Hauck reported to me a different experience, one that is more typical of the treatment of women in nontraditional jobs. She had held a job building trusses for rafters, where she worked exclusively with men. Her coworkers harassed her mercilessly, going so far as to lie about her to the boss to get her fired. But Yvonne lived in a much larger town (Manhattan, Kansas, is a community of 27,575 people), with the attendant alienation, so that the men on her job saw her not as a person known to them but as an aggressive woman, and thus a threat to their male competence and identity.

I remember sitting with Michele Hauck in the tall grass of the field, while she told me with a fourteen-year-old's bright optimism that she does not expect to encounter the discrimination her mother had to face on her job and in her struggle to be accepted into trade apprenticeship. Yet Yvonne's experiences, the widows penalized by the inheritance tax, Darlene Tate having to prove herself in her job at Northern Natural Gas: these instances of inequality are occurring right now in Michele's world. The changes she believes in are taking place, but they are happening more slowly and with much more agony and effort than she imagines.

In Lincoln, Nebraska, lives a woman who works politically to rectify these injustices. Monica Usasz is a slim, blond, serious woman who was born in Nebraska, grew up on a farm, and has spent only six months of her life outside her home state. Her awareness of issues in the world about her began when her husband became a Conscientious Objector during the Vietnam war. In support of him, she began to counsel young men about alternatives to the draft; that activity brought her into contact with political people, and she began to broaden her views. Now unmarried, a feminist, and firmly a part of the women's community centered around the university in Lincoln, she works as secretary to the Lincoln Commission on the Status of Women. She talks enthusiastically of the Commission's efforts to confront the problems of access to abortion, displaced homemakers, battered women.

Monica also serves as a board member of Nebraskans for Peace, for she sees connections between the oppression of women and the harm being done to the physical world, and she wants to alert her fellow citizens to threats to their environment. Nebraskans for Peace, she says, pinpoints specific issues for action, such as the transporting of radioactive waste in trucks on Route 80 through Lincoln, and the immediate dangers to people who now live near nuclear plants.

One of Monica's major efforts is to awaken and involve more women in political work. She tries to lead women to broaden their concerns from strictly feminist or lesbian issues to the dangers threatening the earth itself; and in so doing she has become well-known and respected in her community as a determined worker for change.

Contamination of earth, air, and water is a serious matter here in this heart of the country; for the intensive use of chemical fertilizers and insecticides is routine in the promotion of high-yield agriculture. Farm women suffer the pressures of the inflated cost of farming, sharing with their husbands the insecurity this situation engenders. To meet economic demands, farmers must wrest from the earth as large a crop as possible, and in this endeavor they resort to the massive use of chemicals. But the women are more and more conscious of the effects of these substances, which they experience in their daily lives. In community after community, small dramas are played out. An old farmer suffers from headaches, for which his doctor can find no cause. Finally the water he drinks is tested and found to contain nitrates. Elsewhere in the county there are rumors of animals aborting, of a young girl going blind. As the farmers and their wives gossip at barn sales and stock auctions, after church, in the cafes, these stories are passed around. Everyone knows the environment is being gravely, perhaps irrevocably, altered.

Yvonne Hauck, on her organic farm near Aurora, shows me photographs of plants affected by the county's spraying of insecticides. Virginia Racette makes a grim joke about nuclear contamination, saying, "If there are any animals left after a while, you're

not sure you'll recognize them." The use of herbicides, insecticides, seed dressings, fungicides, and fumigants, all considered
necessary for the pursuit of modern agriculture, make farming an
increasingly dangerous occupation.

Women are especially sensitive to these threats to health because, throughout the centuries, it has fallen to us to nurture and
protect the young, to care for the sick, the weak, and the elderly.
On the Great Plains, farm women are beginning to demand information on nuclear and chemical dangers; in this they respond to
the chemically induced illnesses in their husbands and other male
relatives, the allergies and birth defects in their children and
grandchildren.

Because of the heavy use of chemicals, modern farming requires more and more technical know-how. "There's this new
fertilizer they're comin' out with, new insecticides," Virginia Racette states. "They're getting to the point where pretty soon the
farmer can't do any of that for himself because it's too dangerous.
Now they have to have a little certificate that says they are eligible
to handle the stuff. They go to school for three days and answer a
little questionnaire and they get a little certificate for five dollars
that says you are now an accomplished insecticide sprayer or
whatever." She ponders the ironies of this, and her voice breaks
out in anger. "I *hate* insecticides. I don't think they're natural. I
met a man at the hospital when my dad was in there that had
worked in a store, and all he had done was move the insecticides
from one shelf to another, or he had helped unpack them. He had
gotten this stuff into his bloodstream and he had to go in to have
a transfusion every so often to replace the blood. He told Shine up
there, he said, 'Stay away from the stuff, it's like playin' with
dynamite.' He said, 'You really don't know the damage you're
doing.' Well, Shine still doesn't even wear a mask when he uses
insecticides!"

There are people living not very far from Virginia and Shine's
farm who are trying to find alternative solutions to the problems
of agriculture, and energy as well. Unfortunately, my visit with
them on their farm outside Salina was very brief, only an hour of

introduction to the many complicated projects they are pursuing. Dana and Wes Jackson devote themselves to a search for better ways to grow crops, heat houses and drive machinery, build shelters and dispose of waste. Dressed in a knitted hat and several layers of heavy wool shirts, Dana took me on a tour of their land. Here I saw wind machines that charge batteries to power electric lights, a compost maker in a barrel, a solar greenhouse. We looked at an igloo-shaped structure built of bundles of old newspapers reinforced with iron bars and chicken wire and covered with concrete. It was constructed as an experiment in housing, Dana tells me, by one of the students who came to study with the Jacksons. Then we stopped to look at the plots of ground seeded with perennial plants, from which the Jacksons hope someday to develop crops to take the place of the annuals traditionally planted by farmers.

Dana was once a high school English teacher, but, since the founding of The Land Institute (the name of this experimental farm and teaching institution), she has applied herself to the myriad tasks involved in its operation. She edits *The Land Report,* a publication sensitive to women's contribution to the environmental struggle.* The day of my visit she was rather harried, having spent all week writing explanatory material about the activities here. She told me that the investigations undertaken on the land are not strictly scientific but involve social, political, economic, and religious considerations as well.

To escape the fierce prairie wind, we went inside the building where the students, who come from many states, gather to hear lectures and plan their projects. I browsed among the conservation publications arranged on racks around the walls, while Dana pointed out the ones touching on some aspects of women's lives. We talked about my encounters with rural women. Later that day when I left The Land Institute, I remember her giving her opinion that there is a "significant difference" in farm women today, as they begin to act in their own behalf and enter into politics.

---

* *The Land Report* is published by The Land Institute, Route #3, Salina, Kansas 67401.

The farm wife is in a particularly contradictory position. While her participation in the labor of the farm is empowering and productive of independence, socially and legally she is viewed as a dependent. In the past she was excluded from membership in farm organizations; thus while her labor alongside her husband was taken for granted, her participation in policy decisions was not allowed. As Frances Hill points out in her writing on women and farm politics, "These paradoxes did not arise from simple male chauvinism among farmers. Rather, the operation of the farm organizations reflected values of the industrializing, urbanizing society in which the farm organizations were established."* Whatever the reason, because women were not included in the decision-making process, the essential and continual labor of women and children on the so-called "family farms" became invisible. It was only by creating their own independent organizations that farm women began to be seen and heard. Now, as these organizations conduct letter-writing campaigns, send lobbyists to state legislatures, and engage in other activities to make their needs known, they create an atmosphere of increased respect for women, and their actions reach out to affect the lives of individual women on the farms. Gathered in the organizations they have formed, farm women build collective power as they become more informed about issues that determine their lives. As individuals, women can no longer be conveniently subsumed under their husband's name or concerns. This movement of farm women in the Midwest is a strong corrective to the disparity between their considerable accomplishments and the social and legal status they have been assigned.

Another kind of opportunity for midwestern women to build strength and think in new ways exists in the "women's communities" found usually in the university towns. These loose networks of feminists are formed by heterosexual and lesbian women who have joined together to work politically. The members of

---

* From "Women and Farm Politics—National Level" *New Land Review* (Summer 1979).

these communities generally agree that changes in one's personal life must go along with activity in the public world; and they strive to equalize their relationships with husbands or other men, to develop noncompetitive, supportive relationships with female lovers and friends, to share responsibility for children and to raise their children to be as free as possible from restrictive sex-role stereotypes. In the public arena, they organize to combat the problems of unequal employment opportunities, of rape and wife battery, access to birth control and abortion, and other issues crucial to women; and they work for ratification of the Equal Rights Amendment. Role models of labor, feminist, and temperance heroines are amply present in the history of the Great Plains states: in their activism the young women of today contact and continue that heritage.

Many of these women believe that there is a women's culture separate from the dominant culture. This they see consisting of the totality of the arts and crafts, the special skills and capacities of women, which have been generally denigrated or denied recognition. Growing up in their families' homes, they were surrounded with the evidence of female relatives' needlework and tailoring, building and inventing and recording on the frontier. By calling attention to and validating these women's activities they honor the lives of their foremothers; in so doing they hope to develop a strong shared identity and build the strength to change the institutions of this society to include an affirmation of female inventiveness and talent. They make the effort to unearth and preserve already existing, often ancient women's culture, and to create new culture themselves in writing, music, crafts, skills, spirituality, and scholarship.

These midwestern communities are linked in an ever-strengthening network with each other and with the larger, more visible women's communities in the major cities of east and west coasts.

Moira Ferguson at the University of Nebraska, in her capacity as head of Women's Studies, has many strong associations with the women's community in Lincoln. Yet she comes originally from Scotland and, although she has spent a number of years in this country, her view of midwesterners has the detachment of an outsider's perspective. Moira said she thought midwesterners were sophisticated in ways that people on either coast are not. "I think they're very sophisticated about how to live and how to survive, and how to use the land they know and love. And their bodies and their hands and feet and their lives are wrapped up with that survival. I think people in the Midwest have a good sense of their relationship to nature, whether that's a Native American influence or not, I don't know. But I think the whole idea of surviving is known in a different way in the Midwest. People on the coast who are involved in politics think about survival in a very much wider sense: the system is corrupt, something has to be done, let's organize, let's get people together, let's address problems, let's show all these different oppressions that people have, and let's unite. That's one form of dealing with things. People in the Midwest are doing what they've always done. They're bringing themselves up in a healthy way, they're having good relationships to the land and to other people. And they will eventually, I think, become part of the revolutionary process."

Moira's students who are changing their lives, the farm women concerned about pollution, the women who work to ensure justice for themselves and their children, the women who are creating a new appreciation of women's culture, are already part of a revolutionary process. Their words and actions indicate their awareness that many elements are involved in the struggle to save our lives, our country, our planet. Perhaps in this merging of concerns midwestern women will approach the Native American model in which spirituality is embodied in daily life, action arising from that source as well as from political awareness. Many of these heartland women who are seeking change in their working lives, their personal lives, their relationship to the environment, would join Margret Mahkuc in saying, "You can't separate anything. This is our life too."

Margret Mahkuc

At the University of Nebraska, Lincoln: *Norma Dugan, Sandy Schank, Moira Ferguson, Jean Potmesil, Hortense Spillers, Teresa Holder*

Quilting

The women in this book I call "heartwomen" not simply because they live in the center of the country. As I traveled about, listening to them and seeing them in their homes, at their workplaces, with their children, their spouses, their friends, their animals, a common quality began to be discernible among them. It seemed to me that they gave themselves to their lives wholly, without holding back—that they lived, one might say, from the heart. I think of Darlene Tate in St. Joseph, with her four daughters, her "man's job," her farm work. I remember her spirit and her cheerfulness, how fully present and engaged in her life she is, in a way that is often not true of dwellers in more metropolitan settings. She and the other women in this book are living full out, laboring for the most part prodigiously, and enjoying the rewards of close involvement in the lives of many people. I was often moved by the generosity of their lives.

The townswomen as well as the farm women led me to an awareness of community. Not simple community. It has its hierarchy, its outcasts, its social intricacies. But I felt how crucially one is connected to the lives around one, by one's work over decades and even generations, by one's accessibility and responsiveness to one's neighbors. This seemed an essentially female way of being: not to stand out against the environment but to integrate with it. The web of lives is bound together by the women, their millions of small actions performed daily and hourly, their presence in or support of most activities.

My investigation of histories showed me, not a uniform experience, the great pioneer dream as it is endlessly fed to us on movie and TV screens, but a complex of realities, distinct cultures existing side by side on the prairie, interacting uneasily and often violently. Both the Native American women and the black women I met brought home to me the brutality of our culture toward people of color. This was as unmistakable in Topeka and Salina as it is on the streets of Miami or New York City.

Among the women who, as Ruth Chaplin would put it, "told me their lives," I found that prideful insistence on autonomy that developed in the early years when survival depended on one's efforts alone. I saw how ideals and the hopes that accompanied them, as well as necessary skills, were passed down through the generations from mother to daughter. Sometimes this preserving and transmitting of culture was accomplished by the making of beautiful objects, as in the work of a seventy-one-year-old woman who lives in a modest frame house on the outskirts of Concordia.

In her crowded yet monastic bedroom, the colors surrounded us, luminous as the reflections of crystals falling about the room. Jessalee Girard, whose hair curled in thin grey wisps about her head, stood with plump arms folded across her breast. Her husband is dead now, she had told me, her children living in other towns. The narrow iron bed, the quilting frame, both spoke of a life stripped of inessentials. Jessalee had draped her many quilts across her bed to show me, creating a wild exuberance of color. When I left her warm, cluttered house, I took with me the "monkeywrench" quilt, her gift to my friend Ann.

That was my last visit in Kansas before heading back toward the West Coast. Often during the long drive that followed, I looked at the quilt on the car seat next to me, thinking how women have always saved and pieced together the castoffs, pioneer women having to use and reuse every scrap of cloth, so that a woman might cut up a feedsack and make trousers of it; then, when they were worn out, a dress for the baby; then rags and headscarves; until finally the remaining pieces she would stitch into the pattern of a quilt. But thrift and the need for warm coverings were not the only motivations for this labor. Some women made quilts as gifts for relatives or friends; some made them to exercise their powers of invention, their talent for design; a woman might create a pattern and sew a quilt as a memorial to family or community or national events. As women in these and so many other ways have always guarded and passed on family history to their children, in a similar manner the midwestern woman artist transmits culture. Each of the artists of the Midwest I met, it seemed, made an integration: Denise Low bringing together her psychic and spiritual with her intellectual capacities, Jo Ann Schmidman combining artistic and political concerns, Barbara Grier pursuing her bibliographic and publishing work along with the full acceptance and living out of a sexual orientation that challenges the deepest premises of heterosexist culture.

As I traveled the miles of dusty country roads to visit the farm and small town women, as I talked with them at home or in the cafes, accompanied them to social functions, met them at work, often I experienced a coming together of elements in my life that had been neatly separated. The wonderment of my early years returned to me, and I re-experienced the love in my family that was never spoken aloud but was expressed in ways so taken for granted that they went unnoticed. I think of the VFW hall dance in Clyde, at which one of the older men led me around the floor in a brisk foxtrot. I found myself following easily, for I had known how to dance that way since I was a little girl. At events like that one, in big shadowy halls, a three-piece band whomping out the tune of "That's My Desire" or "He's Just My Bill," my father had danced first with my older sister and then with me, his movements somehow both lively and dignified, teaching us to follow his strong lead. I moved on the balls of my feet, as he had taught me, grasping his fingers, feeling the pressure of his large, warm hand on my back. We danced in smooth circles around the outside of the hall, and for a few minutes I escaped from my usual condition into a gracefulness that was intoxicating. It is strange to remember him so gratefully, so admiringly, this difficult man. Strange to feel so strongly his caring for me. For years we have communicated mostly with anger, venting our frustration upon each other, unable to manage the strong feelings each has for the other.

In the kitchens where I sat with the farm women, I found intimations of my mother, especially of my times with her in the morning kitchen when I, youngest of three, was left each day after the others went to school. We listened to the radio, my mother and I, she going about her work, I sitting at the table watching her; and we developed a way of being together in easy silence.

Besides my child self, in the heartland I met again the shy, arrogant young woman I had been when I left the Midwest for New York. It happened as I walked one evening in Concordia, coming from the downtown area to circle the courthouse square and stand finally before Marion Ellet's house. Shadow under the trees in her yard made a deep black pool, in which shone one bright spark like a reflected star. Shrouded in darkness, I stood pondering that lighted doorbell and conjured Marion opening the door, coming out onto the porch to greet me. But instead of her the specter who met me under the trees was my self of twenty years ago. Here was that young woman who had believed in literature with an almost mystical fervor, that young writer who was the model of the individualistic artist as it has been handed down to us by generations of men, who only grudgingly acknowledged her kinship with other human beings, and who identified, not with women, not even women writers, but with male literary figures. It was hard at first to be with her there in the darkness, for I had judged her stringently in the intervening years, had put aside her values. But it seemed appropriate to meet her, for this was the Midwest: all that she had rebelled against was here, all of the precious life-stuff that made her was here. Mostly, now, I saw her passion and her belief, and could appreciate them; for I saw that when she was growing up, given the opportunities open to her, she could only have done what she did. I felt compassion for her, realizing that it was time now to take her back inside myself. And I let her enter.

During my journey, especially among women whose age, skin color, ethnic background, or lifestyle were different from mine, I began to experience a new view of my origins. With black women, with women of different European backgrounds, sometimes our communication leapt all barriers, until I identified with them and began to know that they, too, were my people. My encounters with Native American women taught me respect for their separate culture and their history on the same prairie as my own white ancestors. While I felt most personally safe in my own particular subculture, my sense of my foremothers—the women who not only created me physically but provided the emotional-intellectual-spiritual environment in which my mind and spirit developed—was expanded to include the many colors and kinds of people who built the Midwest and live there still.

My sense of time altered too, as I tried to draw a thread from the adventures and homely details set down on the brittle pages of the pioneer women's journals, through the generations to Darlene Tate in her hard hat crawling down into a giant machine. The account in a book of the Potawatomis' life near Green Bay, Wisconsin led me in a tortuous trail to Minnie LeClere, living her last years on the Kansas reservation. The Exodusters' disembarkation from Mississippi river boats in St. Louis gave me my first clues to the lives of Bessie and Bob Caldwell in Salina, Kansas.

The awakening of childhood memories, the discovery of a richer human identification, the sense of generations preceding my own: all this led to a desire that both surprised and disconcerted me. It was the need to return, not just to the Midwest, that gigantic region that encompasses the place of my birth and much else, but to visit the actual city, street, house, where I lived my young life. Feeling this eagerness to return, I asked myself what that journey could mean to me. And I recognized within it the possibility of reclaiming the earliest beginnings of my woman's life. Asking again, I discovered that I had made a split, abandoning my early life to my parents in the particular place in which it had occurred, while I took possession of my adult life and called it my own. But I had not realized then how much that was crucial in my life would be put aside. It had seemed natural to breathe a sigh of relief and say of childhood, of adolescence, "Good riddance." Now I know that my having left did not sever the filaments that stretch back to connect me with the significant people and places of my childhood. This is my place still. It is neither possible nor necessary to accept exile anymore.

Heartwomen have led me to this resolve. Young and old, they remain in my mind, as if they lived next door to me and I saw them every other day. Some visits I especially savor, as I do the time spent with Teresa Mahon, who at eighty-six still lives on the river-bottom farm where the flood struck in 1935, surprising her husband. Her eyes are pale, her white hair neatly waved at her cheeks and forehead. She sat with me at her dining room table and leafed through her album of old brown-toned photographs. I was aware of her age as we talked, of her fragility, and the long life she had lived already. I remember my feelings as I left her farmhouse that day. I drove for a time between fields of milo, then stopped the car to get out and wade through the weeds to the fence, where I pulled off the top of a milo plant—a sheaf of close-packed red-brown grains—and stood holding it, looking back at the shed where Teresa had showed me the old farm wagon. She stood next to the wagon, stroking the slats of its side, old hand on old wood, veined, flawed, worn smooth by time. The shadow of the shed roof fell like an axe splitting her figure, that which was gentlest and most expressive in her dimmed by shadow; colors of blouse, of hair, still brightly alive. I stood crumbling the milo in my palm, looking out across the field swollen with grain ready for harvest.

Now, writing here at my desk, I remember her answering the phone in her house during our visit, telling the caller she could not talk because "I'm as busy as a one-armed man buttoning his sleeve." And I know she's doing fine.

Such encounters remain with me, and let me know that I will return soon to see those people who raised me, who are not a lot younger than Teresa. I will go informed, enriched by the women who move in the pages of this book. They have challenged and enlightened me, and were as gracious as they could be to a prodigal daughter making her halting, circuitous journey home.

Jessalee Girard

Bibliography

Armitage, Sue, Theresa Banfield, and Sarah Jacobus. "Black Women and Their Communities in Colorado." *Frontiers,* vol. II, no. 2, Summer 1977. Special Issue: Women's Oral History.

Barns, Cass G. *The Sod House.* Lincoln: University of Nebraska Press, 1970.

Basso, K. H. "To Give Up on Words." In *Language and Social Context,* edited by Paolo Giglioli. England: Penguin Books Ltd., 1972.

Baum, L. Frank. *The Wizard of Oz.* Chicago: Reilly & Lee Co., 1956.

Bennett, Mildred R. *The World of Willa Cather.* Lincoln and London: University of Nebraska Press, 1961.

Brown, Dee. *Bury My Heart at Wounded Knee.* New York: Holt, Rinehart, 1971.

Chapman, Stephen. "Welfare Tractors." *The New Republic,* March 3, 1979.

Clifton, James A. *The Prairie People.* Lawrence: The Regents Press of Kansas, 1977.

Cooper, Patricia, and Norma Bradley Buferd. *The Quilters.* New York: Doubleday, 1977.

Edmunds, R. David. *The Potawatomis: Keepers of the Fire.* Norman: University of Oklahoma Press, 1978.

Emery, Janet Pease. *It Takes People To Make a Town.* Salina, Kansas: Arrow Printing Co., 1971.

Garson, Barbara. *All the Livelong Day.* New York: Doubleday, 1975.

Goodwyn, Lawrence. *The Populist Moment.* Oxford, London, New York: Oxford University Press, 1978.

Grier, Barbara. *The Lesbian in Literature.* 3rd ed. Tallahassee: Naiad Press, 1981.

Gusfield, Joseph R. *Symbolic Crusade.* Urbana, Chicago, and London: University of Illinois Press, 1963.

Hill, Frances. "Women and Farm Politics—National Level." *New Land Review,* Summer 1979. Published by Center for Rural Affairs, Walthill, Nebraska.

Ise, John. *Sod and Stubble.* Lincoln: University of Nebraska Press, 1936, 1967.

Jett, M. Alice. "Call Us Farm Women, Please!" *Successful Farming,* February 1979.

Land Report, The. Salina, Kansas: The Land Institute.

Landes, Ruth. *The Prairie Potawatomi.* Madison, Milwaukee, and London: The University of Wisconsin Press, 1970.

Landrine, Hope. "Blaming the Victim: Feminist Racism and Feminist Classism." *Off Our Backs,* vol. IX, no. 10, November 1979.

Lewis, Edith. *Willa Cather Living: A Personal Record.* Lincoln and London: University of Nebraska Press, 1953.

Martin, Del, and Phyllis Lyon. *Lesbian/Woman.* San Francisco: Glide Publications, 1972.

Miller, Nyle H., Edgar Langsdorf, and Robert W. Richmond. *Kansas in Newspapers,* Topeka: State Historical Society, 1963.

Newton, Esther, and Shirley Walton. *Womenfriends: A Soap Opera.* New York: Friends Press, 1976.

Olsen, Tillie. *Yonnondio: From the Thirties.* New York: Delta, 1974.

Painter, Nell Irvin. *Exodusters.* New York: Knopf, 1977.

Pauly, David, and Richard Manning. "A Harvest of Ill Will." *Newsweek,* February 19, 1979.

Philips, Susan U. "Some Sources of Cultural Variability in the Regulation of Talk." *Language in Society,* 5, 1976.

————. "Warm Springs 'Indian Time': How the Regulation of Participation Affects the Progression of Events." In *Explorations in the Ethnography of Speaking,* edited by Richard Bauman and Joel Sherzer. London: Cambridge University Press, 1974.

Rich, Everett. *The Heritage of Kansas.* Lawrence: University of Kansas Press, 1960.

Rubin, Lillian Breslow. *Worlds of Pain.* New York: Basic Books, 1976.

Savage, W. Sherman. *Blacks in the West.* Westport, Connecticut and London: Greenwood Press, 1976.

Sergeant, Elizabeth Shepley. *Willa Cather: A Memoir.* Lincoln: University of Nebraska Press, 1963.

Selzer, Richard. *Mortal Lessons.* New York: Simon and Schuster, 1977.

Skjold, Norma Jane. "Nebraska Women and Farm Politics." *New Land Review,* Summer 1979. Published by Center for Rural Affairs, Walthill, Nebraska.

Slote, Bernice, with photographs by Lucia Woods and others. *Willa Cather: A Pictorial Memoir.* Lincoln: University of Nebraska Press, 1973.

Spring, Leverett Wilson. *Kansas, Prelude to the War for the Union.* Boston: Houghton, Mifflin and Company, 1885.

Stratton, Joanna L. *Pioneer Women.* New York: Simon and Schuster, 1981.

Thomas, Sister M. Evangeline, Ph.D. *Footprints on the Frontier.* Westminster, Maryland: The Newman Press, 1948.

Wilder, Laura Ingalls. *Little House on the Prairie.* New York: Harper & Row, Perennial Library edition, 1975.

Zornow, William Frank. *Kansas: A History of the Jayhawk State.* Norman: University of Oklahoma Press, 1957.